ON HEROES,
HERO-WORSHIP, AND
THE HEROIC IN HISTORY

BY

THOMAS CARLYLE

Prophets of Sensibility:

Precursors of Modern Cultural Thought

GENERAL EDITOR

PROFESSOR HAROLD BLOOM
YALE UNIVERSITY

CHELSEA HOUSE
NEW YORK 1983

This edition is an edited reprint of the
1908 Everyman's Library edition by J.M. Dent & Sons Ltd
Copyright © 1983 by Chelsea House Publishers
Printed and bound in the United States of America

ISBN: 0-87754-325-9

PROPHETS OF SENSIBILITY: PRECURSORS OF MODERN CULTURAL THOUGHT

by Harold Bloom
Professor of the Humanities
Yale University

It was one of the peculiarities of literary Modernism, in the Age of Pound, Joyce and Eliot, and of their New Critical followers, to argue that the imaginative literature of the twentieth century had its true origins in seventeenth-century sensibility. In this polemical contention, Eliot could insist that his poetic and critical stance, or more simply his personal culture, had its sources in Lancelot Andrewes and John Donne, rather, say, than in Walter Pater and Matthew Arnold. Assertions of a remote ancestry have the special charm of escaping the immediate squalors of the family romance. We need not smile too ironically at the personal mythologies of an Eliot or a Pound when we reflect upon the even more formidable Sigmund Freud, who in *Beyond the Pleasure Principle* cheerfully proclaims his descent from Empedocles, safely distant at two millennia, while stubbornly denying his palpable precursor, Arthur Schopenhauer.

But the wry humor of these necessary strategems of the spirit cannot be allowed to obscure the truth of intellectual and aesthetic genealogy. Wallace Stevens once remarked that genealogy is the art of correcting other genealogists' mistakes. One broad way of characterizing the Prophets of Sensibility series is to observe that it intends to correct Eliot's persuasive misreading of the family relationship between nineteenth- and twentieth-century thought and literature. A book like Walter Pater's early masterpiece, *The Renaissance,* reverberates endlessly in such characteristic modern creators as Yeats, Eliot, Joyce, Pound, Stevens, Woolf, Hart Crane, and even in a vitalistic heretic like D. H. Lawrence. None of them (except for Yeats) would have granted Pater's authority and fatherhood, yet he haunts them all (and many others) both in cadence and in concept. Pater, like Arnold, Ruskin, Carlyle, Butler, Hazlitt, De Quincey, and Coleridge is simply too close for the comfort of autonomy to assert itself.

Certainly the anxiety of influence is a crucial sorrow in the vexed story of the true heritage of Modernism. But, as an anxiety, it may conceal deeper continuities between Romantic and Victorian forerunners and their belated heirs. Prophecy, an ancient Hebraic mode of literature, became in the nineteenth century a new kind of vitalistic mode, one that erased the always wavering boundaries between criticism and creation. What, after all, is the literary genre of Pater's *The Renaissance?* The prose *Imaginary Conversations* of Landor and the verse monologues of Browning are no more radical as experiments than are these reveries of Walter Pater. Pater blends moral reflection, prose poetry, psychological portraiture, art and literary criticism, cultural history and a curious kind of mythopoeic fiction into an amalgam that defies conventional description, but that has the ultimate purpose of subverting Christian evaluations of the *agon* between the desires of this world and the work of the spirit. As a prophet, Pater restores to art the epiphanies appropriated by orthodox dualisms, whether of religion or of philosophy.

Pater's *The Renaissance* dramatizes the authentic burden of the Prophets of Sensibility. This burden is not so much secularization as it is the problematic transferences and descents of authority from earlier times, when it could be recognized and accepted, to the threshold of our age, where authority can be recognized precisely as what has vanished, and what could not be accepted if somehow it reappeared. Freud, who devised the clinical transference of the model of the taboo, attempted to make of psychoanalysis a modernist *praxis* that would reestablish the images of authority upon a supposedly scientific basis. Ruskin, Carlyle, Pater and the other Victorian prophets assumed, rather, that authority could be established again only upon an aesthetic basis. Had Freud (and Nietzsche) written in English, we would group them now with the Prophets of Sensibility. Science and philosophy, like religion, have yielded to the literary culture, and the pragmatic consequences of that yielding are at the center of Romantic and Victorian prophecy.

Prophecy, in the Hebraic sense, was moral truth-telling of the most violent kind, always following the formula of "The Word of God came to me . . ." The God Word that came to the nineteenth-century prophets mixed perception and sensation into a new kind of sensibility, one that is still with us today. Difficult to describe, this sensibility emphasizes a continuum haunted by intimations of mortality punctuated by brief bursts of radiance–privileged moments in which a peculiar vividness gives the illusion of redeeming life. It may be the stigma of the nineteenth-century Prophets of Sensibility that (except for Pater) they sought to combat this climate of the spirit but oddly fostered it implicitly (even as Pater did so overtly). The increasing internalization of the self depended upon an augmentation of estrangement from the object world, and what was intended as prophetic warning and lament as to this estrangement became instead a subtle suggestion of an inevitable movement in elite sensibility.

Today we have the strange anomaly that Nietzsche, the Continental version of the Prophets of Sensibility, is credited with fathering the future, while the

Prophets are neglected. But time's revenges work themselves out, and these writers will father the future again, even as they prophesied our current sensibility. They could not save or even preserve the post-Christian spirituality they sought to imbue in society, but they fostered in its place a pragmatic triumph of literary culture, beyond religion and beyond speculative philosophy. Psychoanalysis, despite its scientism, is only another form of that literary culture. So, in another way, are the textualist literary criticism and language-oriented "human sciences" that are vivid parts of Structuralist and post-Structuralist formulations. There are true and false prophets of sensibility, even as there were true and false prophets among the ancient Hebrews. The test for prophecy finally is canonization; the books that return from the dead certify themselves as inescapable, and so as a vital part of the truth. We can say of each of us in relation to the books in this Prophets of Sensibility series what Pater said of his hero in *Marius the Epicurean*. The experience of reading them

> . . . gave him a definitely ascertained measure of his moral or intellectual need, of the demand his soul must make upon the powers, whatsoever they might be, which had brought him, as he was, into the world at all. . . .

ON
HEROES, HERO-WORSHIP,

AND

THE HEROIC IN HISTORY

———◆◇◆———

LECTURE I

THE HERO AS DIVINITY.   ODIN.   PAGANISM:

SCANDINAVIAN MYTHOLOGY

[Tuesday, 5th May 1840]

WE have undertaken to discourse here for a little **An** on Great Men, their manner of appearance **illimitable** in our world's business, how they have shaped **topic** themselves in the world's history, what ideas men formed of them, what work they did;—on Heroes, namely, and on their reception and performance; what I call Hero-worship and the Heroic in human affairs.   Too evidently this is a large topic; deserving quite other treatment than we can expect to give it at present.   A large topic; indeed, an illimitable one; wide as Universal History itself. For, as I take it, Universal History, the history of what man has accomplished in this world, is at bottom the History of the Great Men who have worked here.   They were the leaders of men, these great ones; the modellers, patterns, and in a wide

I   A

The marrow of History sense creators, of whatsoever the general mass of men contrived to do or to attain; all things that we see standing accomplished in the world are properly the outer material result, the practical realisation and embodiment, of Thoughts that dwelt in the Great Men sent into the world: the soul of the whole world's history, it may justly be considered, were the history of these. Too clearly it is a topic we shall do no justice to in this place !

One comfort is, that Great Men, taken up in any way, are profitable company. We cannot look, however imperfectly, upon a great man, without gaining something by him. He is the living light-fountain, which it is good and pleasant to be near. The light which enlightens, which has enlightened the darkness of the world; and this not as a kindled lamp only, but rather as a natural luminary shining by the gift of Heaven; a flowing light-fountain, as I say, of native original insight, of manhood and heroic nobleness;—in whose radiance all souls feel that it is well with them. On any terms whatsoever, you will not grudge to wander in such neighbourhood for a while. These Six classes of Heroes, chosen out of widely-distant countries and epochs, and in mere external figure differing altogether, ought, if we look faithfully at them, to illustrate several things for us. Could we see *them* well, we should get some glimpses into the very marrow of the world's history. How happy, could I but, in any measure, in such times as these, make manifest to you the meanings of Heroism; the divine relation (for I may well call it such) which in all times unites a Great Man to other men; and thus, as it were, not exhaust my subject, but so much as break ground on it! At all events, I must make the attempt.

It is well said, in every sense, that a man's religion is the chief fact with regard to him. A man's, or a nation of men's. By religion I do not mean here the church-creed which he professes, the articles of faith which he will sign and, in words or otherwise, assert; not this wholly, in many cases not this at all. We see men of all kinds of professed creeds attain to almost all degrees of worth or worthlessness under each or any of them. This is not what I call religion, this profession and assertion; which is often only a profession and assertion from the outworks of the man, from the mere argumentative region of him, if even so deep as that. But the thing a man does practically believe (and this is often enough *without* asserting it even to himself, much less to others); the thing a man does practically lay to heart, and know for certain, concerning his vital relations to this mysterious Universe, and his duty and destiny there, that is in all cases the primary thing for him, and creatively determines all the rest. That is his *religion ;* or it may be, his mere scepticism and *no-religion :* the manner it is in which he feels himself to be spiritually related to the Unseen World or No-World; and I say, if you tell me what that is, you tell me to a very great extent what the man is, what the kind of things he will do is. Of a man or of a nation we inquire, therefore, first of all, What religion they had? Was it Heathenism,—plurality of gods, mere sensuous representation of this Mystery of Life, and for chief recognised element therein Physical Force? Was it Christianism; faith in

The oldest form of Heroism an Invisible, not as real only, but as the only reality; Time, through every meanest moment of it, resting on Eternity; Pagan empire of Force displaced by a nobler supremacy, that of Holiness? Was it Scepticism, uncertainty and inquiry whether there was an Unseen World, any Mystery of Life except a mad one;—doubt as to all this, or perhaps unbelief and flat denial? Answering of this question is giving us the soul of the history of the man or nation. The thoughts they had were the parents of the actions they did; their feelings were parents of their thoughts: it was the unseen and spiritual in them that determined the outward and actual;— their religion, as I say, was the great fact about them. In these Discourses, limited as we are, it will be good to direct our survey chiefly to that religious phasis of the matter. That once known well, all is known. We have chosen as the first Hero in our series, Odin the central figure of Scandinavian Paganism; an emblem to us of a most extensive province of things. Let us look for a little at the Hero as Divinity, the oldest primary form of Heroism.

Surely it seems a very strange-looking thing this Paganism; almost inconceivable to us in these days. A bewildering, inextricable jungle of delusions, confusions, falsehoods and absurdities, covering the whole field of Life! A thing that fills us with astonishment, almost, if it were possible, with incredulity,—for truly it is not easy to understand that sane men could ever calmly, with their eyes open, believe and live by such a set of doctrines. That men should have worshipped their poor fellowman as a God, and not him only, but stocks and stones, and all manner of animate and inanimate

objects; and fashioned for themselves such a dis- **Pagan-**
tracted chaos of hallucinations by way of Theory **ism not**
of the Universe : all this looks like an incredible **Quackery**
fable.   Nevertheless it is a clear fact that they did
it.   Such hideous inextricable jungle of misworships,
misbeliefs, men, made as we are, did actually hold
by, and live at home in.   This is strange.   Yes,
we may pause in sorrow and silence over the depths
of darkness that are in man ; if we rejoice in the
heights of purer vision he has attained to.   Such
things were and are in man ; in all men ; in us too.

Some speculators have a short way of accounting
for the Pagan religion : mere quackery, priestcraft,
and dupery, say they ; no sane man ever did believe
it,—merely contrived to persuade other men, not
worthy of the name of sane, to believe it !   It will
be often our duty to protest against this sort of
hypothesis about men's doings and history ; and I
here, on the very threshold, protest against it in
reference to Paganism, and to all other *isms* by
which man has ever for a length of time striven
to walk in this world.   They have all had a truth
in them, or men would not have taken them up.
Quackery and dupery do abound ; in religions,
above all in the more advanced decaying stages
of religions, they have fearfully abounded : but
quackery was never the originating influence in
such things ; it was not the health and life of
such things, but their disease, the sure precursor
of their being about to die !   Let us never forget
this.   It seems to me a most mournful hypothesis,
that of quackery giving birth to any faith even in
savage men.   Quackery gives birth to nothing ;
gives death to all things.   We shall not see into
the true heart of anything, or if we look merely

The truth behind error at the quackeries of it; if we do not reject the quackeries altogether; as mere diseases, corruptions, with which our and all men's sole duty is to have done with them, to sweep them out of our thoughts as out of our practice. Man everywhere is the born enemy of lies. I find Grand Lamaism itself to have a kind of truth in it. Read the candid, clear-sighted, rather sceptical Mr Turner's *Account of his Embassy* to that country, and see. They have their belief, these poor Thibet people, that Providence sends down always an Incarnation of Himself into every generation. At bottom some belief in a kind of Pope! At bottom still better, belief that there is a *Greatest* Man; that *he* is discoverable; that, once discovered, we ought to treat him with an obedience which knows no bounds! This is the truth of Grand Lamaism; the 'discoverability' is the only error here. The Thibet priests have methods of their own of discovering what Man is Greatest, fit to be supreme over them. Bad methods: but are they so much worse than our methods,—of understanding him to be always the eldest born of a certain genealogy? Alas, it is a difficult thing to find good methods for !——We shall begin to have a chance of understanding Paganism, when we first admit that to its followers it was, at one time, earnestly true. Let us consider it very certain that men did believe in Paganism; men with open eyes, sound senses, men made altogether like ourselves; that we, had we been there, should have believed in it. Ask now, What Paganism could have been?

Another theory, somewhat more respectable, attributes such things to Allegory. It was a play of poetic minds, say these theorists; a shadowing-

forth, in allegorical fable, in personification and
visual form, of what such poetic minds had known
and felt of this Universe. Which agrees, add
they, with a primary law of human nature, still
everywhere observably at work, though in less
important things, That what a man feels intensely,
he struggles to speak-out of him, to see represented
before him in visual shape, and as if with a kind of
life and historical reality in it. Now doubtless
there is such a law, and it is one of the deepest
in human nature ; neither need we doubt that it
did operate fundamentally in this business. The
hypothesis which ascribes Paganism wholly or
mostly to this agency, I call a little more respectable ; but I cannot yet call it the true hypothesis.
Think, would *we* believe, and take with us as our
life-guidance, an allegory, a poetic sport? Not
sport but earnest is what we should require. It is
a most earnest thing to be alive in this world; to
die is not sport for a man. Man's life never was
a sport to him ; it was a stern reality, altogether a
serious matter to be alive !

I find, therefore, that though these Allegory
theorists are on the way towards truth in this
matter, they have not reached it either. Pagan
Religion is indeed an Allegory, a Symbol of what
men felt and knew about the Universe; and all
Religions are Symbols of that, altering always as
that alters : but it seems to me a radical perversion,
and even *in*version, of the business, to put that forward as the origin and moving cause, when it was
rather the result and termination. To get beautiful
allegories, a perfect poetic symbol, was not the want
of men ; but to know what they were to believe
about this Universe, what course they were to steer

Religion not primarily allegory

in it; what, in this mysterious Life of theirs, they
had to hope and to fear, to do and to forbear
doing.   The *Pilgrim's Progress* is an Allegory,
and a beautiful, just and serious one : but consider
whether Bunyan's Allegory could have *preceded*
the Faith it symbolises!   The Faith had to be
already there, standing believed by everybody;—
of which the Allegory could *then* become a shadow;
and, with all its seriousness, we may say a *sportful*
shadow, a mere play of the Fancy, in comparison
with that awful Fact and scientific certainty which
it poetically strives to emblem.   The Allegory is
the product of the certainty, not the producer of
it; not in Bunyan's, nor in any other case.   For
Paganism, therefore, we have still to inquire,
Whence came that scientific certainty, the parent
of such a bewildered heap of allegories, errors and
confusions?   How was it, what was it?

Surely it were a foolish attempt to pretend 'explaining,' in this place, or in any place, such a
phenomenon as that far-distant distracted cloudy
imbroglio of Paganism,—more like a cloudfield
than a distant continent of firm land and facts!
It is no longer a reality, yet it was one.   We
ought to understand that this seeming cloudfield
was once a reality; that not poetic allegory, least
of all that dupery and deception was the origin of
it.   Men, I say, never did believe idle songs, never
risked their soul's life on allegories; men in all times,
especially in early earnest times, have had an instinct
for detecting quacks, for detesting quacks.   Let us
try if, leaving out both the quack theory and the
allegory one, and listening with affectionate attention
to that far-off confused rumour of the Pagan ages,
we cannot ascertain so much as this at least, That

there was a kind of fact at the heart of them ; that they too were not mendacious and distracted, but in their own poor way true and sane !

You remember that fancy of Plato's, of a man who had grown to maturity in some dark distance, and was brought on a sudden into the upper air to see the sun rise. What would his wonder be, his rapt astonishment at the sight we daily witness with indifference ! With the free open sense of a child, yet with the ripe faculty of a man, his whole heart would be kindled by that sight, he would discern it well to be Godlike, his soul would fall down in worship before it. Now, just such a childlike greatness was in the primitive nations. The first Pagan Thinker among rude men, the first man that began to think, was precisely this child-man of Plato's. Simple, open as a child, yet with the depth and strength of a man. Nature had as yet no name to him ; he had not yet united under a name the infinite variety of sights, sounds, shapes and motions, which we now collectively name Universe, Nature, or the like,—and so with a name dismiss it from us. To the wild deep-hearted man all was yet new, not veiled under names or formulas ; it stood naked, flashing-in on him there, beautiful, awful, unspeakable. Nature was to this man, what to the Thinker and Prophet it forever is, *preter-*natural. This green flowery rock-built earth, the trees, the mountains, rivers, many-sounding seas ; —that great deep sea of azure that swims over-head ; the winds sweeping through it ; the black cloud fashioning itself together, now pouring out fire, now hail and rain ; what *is* it ? Ay, what ? At bottom we do not yet know ; we can never know at all. It is not by our superior insight that

The world a miracle we escape the difficulty; it is by our superior levity, our inattention, our *want* of insight. It is by *not* thinking that we cease to wonder at it. Hardened round us, encasing wholly every notion we form, is a wrappage of traditions, hearsays, mere *words*. We call that fire of the black thundercloud 'electricity,' and lecture learnedly about it, and grind the like of it out of glass and silk: but *what* is it? What made it? Whence comes it? Whither goes it? Science has done much for us; but it is a poor science that would hide from us the great deep sacred infinitude of Nescience, whither we can never penetrate, on which all science swims as a mere superficial film. This world, after all our science and sciences, is still a miracle; wonderful, inscrutable, *magical* and more, to whosoever will *think* of it.

That great mystery of TIME, were there no other: the illimitable, silent, never-resting thing called Time, rolling, rushing on, swift, silent, like an all-embracing ocean-tide, on which we and all the Universe swim like exhalations, like apparitions which *are*, and then *are not*: this is forever very literally a miracle; a thing to strike us dumb,—for we have no word to speak about it. This Universe, ah me—what could the wild man know of it; what can we yet know? That it is a Force, and thousand-fold Complexity of Forces; a Force which is *not* *we*. That is all; it is not we, it is altogether different from *us*. Force, Force, everywhere Force; we ourselves a mysterious Force in the centre of that. 'There is not a leaf rotting on the highway but has Force in it: how else could it rot?' Nay surely, to the Atheistic Thinker, if such a one were possible, it must be a miracle too, this

huge illimitable whirlwind of Force, which envelops
us here ; never-resting whirlwind, high as Immensity,
old as Eternity.   What is it ?   God's creation, the
religious people answer ; it is the Almighty God's !
Atheistic science babbles poorly of it, with scientific
nomenclatures, experiments and what-not, as if it
were a poor dead thing, to be bottled up in Leyden
jars and sold over counters : but the natural sense of
man, in all times, if he will honestly apply his sense,
proclaims it to be a living thing,—ah, an unspeakable, godlike thing ; towards which the best attitude
for us, after never so much science, is awe, devout
prostration and humility of soul ; worship if not in
words, then in silence.

But now I remark farther : What in such a time
as ours it requires a Prophet or Poet to teach us,
namely, the stripping-off of those poor undevout
wrappages, nomenclatures and scientific hearsays,—
this, the ancient earnest soul, as yet unencumbered
with these things, did for itself.   The world, which
is now divine only to the gifted, was then divine
to whosoever would turn his eye upon it.   He stood
bare before it face to face.   'All was Godlike or
God : '—Jean Paul still finds it so ; the giant Jean
Paul, who has power to escape out of hearsays :
but there then were no hearsays.   Canopus shining-
down over the desert, with its blue diamond brightness (that wild blue spirit-like brightness, far brighter
than we ever witness here), would pierce into the
heart of the wild Ishmaelitish man, whom it was
guiding through the solitary waste there.   To his
wild heart, with all feelings in it, with no *speech* for
any feeling, it may seem a little eye, that Canopus,
glancing-out on him from the great deep Eternity ;
revealing the inner Splendour to him.   Cannot we

All things in nature emblems of God understand how these men *worshipped* Canopus; became what we call Sabeans, worshipping the stars? Such is to me the secret of all forms of Paganism. Worship is transcendent wonder; wonder for which there is now no limit or measure; that is worship. To these primeval men, all things and everything they saw exist beside them were an emblem of the Godlike, of some God.

And look what perennial fibre of truth was in that. To us also, through every star, through every blade of grass, is not a God made visible, if we will open our minds and eyes? We do not worship in that way now: but is it not reckoned still a merit, proof of what we call a 'poetic nature,' that we recognise how every object has a divine beauty in it; how every object still verily is 'a window through which we may look into Infinitude itself'? He that can discern the loveliness of things, we call him Poet, Painter, Man of Genius, gifted, lovable. These poor Sabeans did even what he does,—in their own fashion. That they did it, in what fashion soever, was a merit: better than what the entirely stupid man did, what the horse and camel did,— namely, nothing!

But now if all things whatsoever that we look upon are emblems to us of the Highest God, I add that more so than any of them is man such an emblem. You have heard of St. Chrysostom's celebrated saying in reference to the Shekinah, or Ark of Testimony, visible Revelation of God, among the Hebrews: "The true Shekinah is Man!" Yes, it is even so: this is no vain phrase; it is veritably so. The essence of our being, the mystery in us that calls itself "I,"—ah, what words have we for such things?—is a breath of Heaven;

the Highest Being reveals himself in man. This *And in especial, Man* body, these faculties, this life of ours, is it not all as a vesture for that Unnamed ? ' There is but one ' Temple in the Universe,' says the devout Novalis, ' and that is the Body of Man. Nothing is holier ' than that high form. Bending before men is a ' reverence done to this Revelation in the Flesh. ' We touch Heaven when we lay our hand on a ' human body ! ' This sounds much like a mere flourish of rhetoric ; but it is not so. If well meditated, it will turn out to be a scientific fact ; the expression, in such words as can be had, of the actual truth of the thing. *We* are the miracle of miracles,—the great inscrutable mystery of God. We cannot understand it, we know not how to speak of it ; but we may feel and know, if we like, that it is verily so.

Well ; these truths were once more readily felt than now. The young generations of the world, who had in them the freshness of young children, and yet the depth of earnest men, who did not think that they had finished-off all things in Heaven and Earth by merely giving them scientific names, but had to gaze direct at them there, with awe and wonder : they felt better what of divinity is in man and Nature ;—they, without being mad, could *worship* Nature, and man more than anything else in Nature. Worship, that is, as I said above, admire without limit : this, in the full use of their faculties, with all sincerity of heart, they could do. I consider Hero-worship to be the grand modifying element in that ancient system of thought. What I called the perplexed jungle of Paganism sprang, we may say, out of many roots : every admiration, adoration of a star or natural object, was a root or

Religion based on Hero-worship fibre of a root; but Hero-worship is the deepest root of all; the tap-root, from which in a great degree all the rest were nourished and grown.

And now if worship even of a star had some meaning in it, how much more might that of a Hero! Worship of a Hero is transcendent admiration of a Great Man. I say great men are still admirable; I say there is, at bottom, nothing else admirable! No nobler feeling than this of admiration for one higher than himself dwells in the breast of man. It is to this hour, and at all hours, the vivifying influence in man's life. Religion I find stand upon it; not Paganism only, but far higher and truer religions,—all religion hitherto known. Hero-worship, heartfelt prostrate admiration, submission, burning, boundless, for a noblest godlike Form of Man,—is not that the germ of Christianity itself? The greatest of all Heroes is One—whom we do not name here! Let sacred silence meditate that sacred matter; you will find it the ultimate perfection of a principle extant throughout man's whole history on earth.

Or coming into lower, less *un*speakable provinces, is not all Loyalty akin to religious Faith also? Faith is loyalty to some inspired Teacher, some spiritual Hero. And what therefore is loyalty proper, the life-breath of all society, but an effluence of Hero-worship, submissive admiration for the truly great? Society is founded on Hero-worship. All dignities of rank, on which human association rests, are what we may call a *Hero*archy (Government of Heroes),—or a Hierarchy, for it is ' sacred ' enough withal! The Duke means *Dux*, Leader; King is *Kön-ning*, *Kan-ning*, Man that *knows* or *cans*. Society everywhere is some representation, not *in-*

supportably inaccurate, of a graduated Worship of **The Hero** Heroes;—reverence and obedience done to men **and his** really great and wise. Not *in*supportably inaccurate, **critics** I say! They are all as bank-notes, these social dignitaries, all representing gold;—and several of them, alas, always are *forged* notes. We can do with some forged false notes; with a good many even; but not with all, or the most of them forged! No : there have to come revolutions then; cries of Democracy, Liberty, and Equality, and I know not what:—the notes being all false, and no gold to be had for *them*, people take to crying in their despair that there is no gold, that there never was any!—'Gold,' Hero-worship, *is* nevertheless, as it was always and everywhere, and cannot cease till man himself ceases.

I am well aware that in these days Hero-worship, the thing I call Hero-worship, professes to have gone out, and finally ceased. This, for reasons which it will be worth while some time to inquire into, is an age that as it were denies the existence of great men; denies the desirableness of great men. Show our critics a great man, a Luther for example, they begin to what they call 'account' for him; not to worship him, but take the dimensions of him, —and bring him out to be a little kind of man! He was the 'creature of the Time,' they say; the Time called him forth, the Time did everything, he nothing—but what we the little critic could have done too! This seems to me but melancholy work. The Time call forth? Alas, we have known Times *call* loudly enough for their great man; but not find him when they called! He was not there; Providence had not sent him; the Time, *calling* its loudest, had to go down to con-

Great men the lightning to the fuel fusion and wreck because he would not come when called.

For if we will think of it, no Time need have gone to ruin, could it have *found* a man great enough, a man wise and good enough: wisdom to discern truly what the Time wanted, valour to lead it on the right road thither; these are the salvation of any Time. But I liken common languid Times, with their unbelief, distress, perplexity, with their languid doubting characters and embarrassed circumstances, impotently crumbling-down into ever worse distress towards final ruin;—all this I liken to dry dead fuel, waiting for the lightning out of Heaven that shall kindle it. The great man, with his free force direct out of God's own hand, is the lightning. His word is the wise healing word which all can believe in. All blazes round him now, when he has once struck on it, into fire like his own. The dry mouldering sticks are thought to have called him forth. They did want him greatly; but as to calling him forth—!—Those are critics of small vision, I think, who cry: "See, is it not the sticks that made the fire?" No sadder proof can be given by a man of his own littleness than disbelief in great men. There is no sadder symptom of a generation than such general blindness to the spiritual lightning, with faith only in the heap of barren dead fuel. It is the last consummation of unbelief. In all epochs of the world's history, we shall find the Great Man to have been the indispensable saviour of his epoch;—the lightning, without which the fuel never would have burnt. The History of the World, I said already, was the Biography of Great Men.

Such small critics do what they can to promote unbelief and universal spiritual paralysis; but happily they cannot always completely succeed. In all **Voltaire** times it is possible for a man to arise great enough **as hero** to feel that they and their doctrines are chimeras and cobwebs. And what is notable, in no time whatever can they entirely eradicate out of living men's hearts a certain altogether peculiar reverence for Great Men; genuine admiration, loyalty, adoration, however dim and perverted it may be. Hero-worship endures for ever while man endures. Boswell venerates his Johnson, right truly even in the Eighteenth century. The unbelieving French believe in their Voltaire; and burst-out round him into very curious Hero-worship, in that last act of his life when they 'stifle him under roses.' It has always seemed to me extremely curious this of Voltaire. Truly, if Christianity be the highest instance of Hero-worship, then we may find here in Voltaireism one of the lowest! He whose life was that of a kind of Antichrist, does again on this side exhibit a curious contrast. No people ever were so little prone to admire at all as those French of Voltaire. *Persiflage* was the character of their whole mind; adoration had nowhere a place in it. Yet see! The old man of Ferney comes up to Paris; an old, tottering, infirm man of eighty-four years. They feel that he too is a kind of Hero; that he has spent his life in opposing error and injustice, delivering Calases, unmasking hypocrites in high places;—in short that *he* too, though in a strange way, has fought like a valiant man. They feel withal that, if *persiflage* be the great thing, there never was such a *persifleur*. He is the realised ideal of every one of them; the thing they are all wanting to be; of all Frenchmen the most French. *He* is properly their god,—such god as they are fit

B

Hero-worship indestructible

for. Accordingly all persons, from the Queen Antoinette to the Douanier at the Porte St. Denis, do they not worship him? People of quality disguise themselves as tavern-waiters. The Maître de Poste, with a broad oath, orders his Postillion, "*Va bon train*; thou art driving M. de Voltaire." At Paris his carriage is 'the nucleus of a comet, whose train fills whole streets.' The ladies pluck a hair or two from his fur, to keep it as a sacred relic. There was nothing highest, beautifulest, noblest in all France, that did not feel this man to be higher, beautifuler, nobler.

Yes, from Norse Odin to English Samuel Johnson, from the divine Founder of Christianity to the withered Pontiff of Encyclopedism, in all times and places, the Hero has been worshipped. It will ever be so. We all love great men; love, venerate, and bow down submissive before great men: nay can we honestly bow down to anything else? Ah, does not every true man feel that he is himself made higher by doing reverence to what is really above him? No nobler or more blessed feeling dwells in man's heart. And to me it is very cheering to consider that no sceptical logic, or general triviality, insincerity and aridity of any Time and its influences can destroy this noble inborn loyalty and worship that is in man. In times of unbelief, which soon have to become times of revolution, much down-rushing, sorrowful decay and ruin is visible to everybody. For myself in these days, I seem to see in this indestructibility of Hero-worship the everlasting adamant lower than which the confused wreck of revolutionary things cannot fall. The confused wreck of things crumbling and even crashing and tumbling all round us in

these revolutionary ages, will get down so far ; *no* Scan-
farther.   It is an eternal corner-stone, from which dinavian
they can begin to build themselves up again.   That paganism
man, in some sense or other, worships Heroes ;
that we all of us reverence and must ever reverence
Great Men : this is, to me, the living rock amid
all rushings-down whatsoever ;—the one fixed point
in modern revolutionary history, otherwise as if
bottomless and shoreless.

So much of truth, only under an ancient obsolete
vesture, but the spirit of it still true, do I find in the
Paganism of old nations.   Nature is still divine,
the revelation of the workings of God ; the Hero
is still worshipable : this, under poor cramped incipient forms, is what all Pagan religions have
struggled, as they could, to set forth.   I think
Scandinavian Paganism, to us here, is more interesting than any other.   It is, for one thing, the
latest ; it continued in these regions of Europe till
the eleventh century : eight-hundred years ago the
Norwegians were still worshippers of Odin.   It is
interesting also as the creed of our fathers ; the men
whose blood still runs in our veins, whom doubtless
we still resemble in so many ways.   Strange : they
did believe that, while we believe so differently.
Let us look a little at this poor Norse creed, for
many reasons.   We have tolerable means to do
it ; for there is another point of interest in these
Scandinavian mythologies : that they have been
preserved so well.

In that strange island Iceland,—burst-up, the
geologists say, by fire from the bottom of the sea ;
a wild land of barrenness and lava ; swallowed
many months of every year in black tempests, yet

The with a wild gleaming beauty in summer-time;
Eddas towering up there, stern and grim, in the North
Ocean; with its snow jokuls, roaring geysers,
sulphur-pools and horrid volcanic chasms, like the
waste chaotic battle-field of Frost and Fire;—
where of all places we least looked for Literature
or written memorials, the record of these things
was written down. On the seaboard of this wild
land is a rim of grassy country, where cattle can
subsist, and men by means of them and of what
the sea yields; and it seems they were poetic men
these, men who had deep thoughts in them, and
uttered musically their thoughts. Much would be
lost, had Iceland not been burst-up from the sea,
not been discovered by the Northmen! The old
Norse Poets were many of them natives of Iceland.

Sæmund, one of the early Christian Priests there,
who perhaps had a lingering fondness for Paganism,
collected certain of their old Pagan songs, just
about becoming obsolete then,—Poems or Chants
of a mythic, prophetic, mostly all of a religious
character: that is what Norse critics call the *Elder*
or Poetic *Edda*. *Edda*, a word of uncertain
etymology, is thought to signify *Ancestress*. Snorro
Sturleson, an Iceland gentleman, an extremely
notable personage, educated by this Sæmund's
grandson, took in hand next, near a century afterwards, to put together, among several other books
he wrote, a kind of Prose Synopsis of the whole
Mythology; elucidated by new fragments of
traditionary verse. A work constructed really
with great ingenuity, native talent, what one might
call unconscious art; altogether a perspicuous clear
work, pleasant reading still: this is the *Younger* or
Prose *Edda*. By these and the numerous other

Sagas, mostly Icelandic, with the commentaries, **Asgard** Icelandic or not, which go on zealously in the **and** North to this day, it is possible to gain some direct **Jötun-** insight even yet; and see that old Norse system of **heim** Belief, as it were, face to face. Let us forget that it is erroneous Religion; let us look at it as old Thought, and try if we cannot sympathise with it somewhat.

The primary characteristic of this old Northland Mythology I find to be Impersonation of the visible workings of Nature. Earnest simple recognition of the workings of Physical Nature, as a thing wholly miraculous, stupendous and divine. What we now lecture of as Science, they wondered at, and fell down in awe before, as Religion. The dark hostile powers of Nature they figure to them-selves as ' *Jötuns,*' Giants, huge shaggy beings of a demonic character. Frost, Fire, Sea-tempest; these are Jötuns. The friendly powers again, as Summer-heat, the Sun, are Gods. The empire of this Universe is divided between these two; they dwell apart, in perennial internecine feud. The Gods dwell above in Asgard, the Garden of the Asen, or Divinities; Jötunheim, a distant dark chaotic land, is the home of the Jötuns.

Curious all this; and not idle or inane, if we will look at the foundation of it! The power of *Fire,* or *Flame,* for instance, which we designate by some trivial chemical name, thereby hiding from ourselves the essential character of wonder that dwells in it as in all things, is with these old Northmen, Loke, a most swift subtle *Demon,* of the brood of the Jötuns. The savages of the Ladrones Islands too (say some Spanish voyagers) thought Fire, which they never had seen before,

Norse nature-gods was a devil or god, that bit you sharply when you touched it, and that lived upon dry wood. From us too no Chemistry, if it had not Stupidity to help it, would hide that Flame is a wonder. What *is* Flame?—*Frost* the old Norse Seer discerns to be a monstrous hoary Jötun, the Giant *Thrym, Hrym:* or *Rime,* the old word now nearly obsolete here, but still used in Scotland to signify hoar-frost. *Rime* was not then as now a dead chemical thing, but a living Jötun or Devil; the monstrous Jötun *Rime* drove home his Horses at night, sat 'combing their manes,'—which Horses were *Hail-Clouds,* or fleet *Frost-Winds.* His Cows—No, not his, but a kinsman's, the Giant Hymir's Cows are *Icebergs:* this Hymir 'looks at the rocks' with his devil-eye, and they *split* in the glance of it.

Thunder was not then mere Electricity, vitreous or resinous; it was the God Donner (Thunder) or Thor,—God also of beneficent Summer-heat. The thunder was his wrath; the gathering of the black clouds is the drawing down of Thor's angry brows; the fire-bolt bursting out of Heaven is the all-rending Hammer flung from the hand of Thor: he urges his loud chariot over the mountain-tops,— that is the peal: wrathful he 'blows in his red beard,'—that is the rustling storm-blast before the thunder begin. Balder again, the White God, the beautiful, the just and benignant (whom the early Christian Missionaries found to resemble Christ), is the Sun—beautifulest of visible things; wondrous too, and divine still, after all our Astronomies and Almanacs! But perhaps the notablest god we hear tell-of is one of whom Grimm the German Etymologist finds trace: the God *Wünsch,* or Wish. The God *Wish;* who could give us all that we *wished!* Is not this the sincerest yet rudest voice **The god** of the spirit of man? The *rudest* ideal that man **Aegir** ever formed; which still shows itself in the latest forms of our spiritual culture. Higher considerations have to teach us that the God *Wish* is not the true God.

Of the other Gods or Jötuns I will mention only for etymology's sake, that Sea-tempest is the Jötun *Aegir*, a very dangerous Jötun;—and now to this day, on our river Trent, as I learn, the Nottingham bargemen, when the River is in a certain flooded state (a kind of backwater, or eddying swirl it has, very dangerous to them), call it *Eager ;* they cry out, " Have a care, there is the *Eager* coming! " Curious; that word surviving, like the peak of a submerged world! The *oldest* Nottingham bargemen had believed in the God Aegir. Indeed, our English blood too in good part is Danish, Norse; or rather, at bottom, Danish and Norse and Saxon have no distinction, except a superficial one,—as of Heathen and Christian, or the like. But all over our Island we are mingled largely with Danes proper,—from the incessant invasions there were : and this, of course, in a greater proportion along the east coast; and greatest of all, as I find, in the North Country. From the Humber upwards, all over Scotland, the Speech of the common people is still in a singular degree Icelandic ; its Germanism has still a peculiar Norse tinge. They too are ' Normans,' Northmen, —if that be any great beauty !—

Of the chief god, Odin, we shall speak by and by. Mark at present so much; what the essence of Scandinavian and indeed of all Paganism is : a recognition of the forces of Nature as godlike, stupendous,

Norse myths personal Agencies,—as Gods and Demons. Not inconceivable to us. It is the infant Thought of man opening itself, with awe and wonder, on this ever-stupendous Universe. To me there is in the Norse System something very genuine, very great and manlike. A broad simplicity, rusticity, so very different from the light gracefulness of the old Greek Paganism, distinguishes this Scandinavian System. It is Thought; the genuine Thought of deep, rude, earnest minds, fairly opened to the things about them; a face-to-face and heart-to-heart inspection of the things,—the first characteristic of all good Thought in all times. Not graceful lightness, half-sport, as in the Greek Paganism; a certain homely truthfulness aud rustic strength, a great rude sincerity, discloses itself here. It is strange, after our beautiful Apollo statues and clear smiling mythuses, to come down upon the Norse Gods 'brewing ale' to hold their feast with Aegir, the Sea-Jötun; sending out Thor to get the caldron for them in the Jötun country; Thor, after many adventures, clapping the Pot on his head, like a huge hat, and walking off with it,—quite lost in it, the ears of the Pot reaching down to his heels! A kind of vacant hugeness, large awkward gianthood, characterises that Norse System; enormous force, as yet altogether untutored, stalking helpless with large uncertain strides. Consider only their primary mythus of the Creation. The Gods, having got the Giant Ymer slain, a Giant made by 'warm wind,' and much confused work, out of the conflict of Frost and Fire,—determined on constructing a world with him. His blood made the sea; his flesh was the Land, the Rocks his bones; of his eyebrows they formed Asgard their Gods'-dwelling;

his skull was the great blue vault of Immensity, and **The tree** the brains of it became the Clouds. What a Hyper- **Igdrasil** Brobdignagian business! Untamed Thought, great, giantlike, enormous;—to be tamed in due time into the compact greatness, not giant-like, but godlike and stronger than gianthood, of the Shakspeares, the Goethes!—Spiritually as well as bodily these men are our progenitors.

I like, too, that representation they have of the Tree Igdrasil. All Life is figured by them as a Tree. Igdrasil, the Ash-tree of Existence, has its roots deep-down in the kingdoms of Hela or Death; its trunk reaches up heaven-high, spreads its boughs over the whole Universe: it is the Tree of Existence. At the foot of it, in the Death-kingdom, sit three *Nornas*, Fates,—the Past, Present, Future; watering its roots from the Sacred Well. Its 'boughs,' with their buddings and dis-leafings,—events, things suffered, things done, catastrophes,—stretch through all lands and times. Is not every leaf of it a biography, every fibre there an act or word? Its boughs are Histories of Nations. The rustle of it is the noise of Human Existence, onwards from of old. It grows there, the breath of Human Passion rustling through it;— or stormtost, the stormwind howling through it like the voice of all the gods. It is Igdrasil, the Tree of Existence. It is the past, the present, and the future; what was done, what is doing, what will be done; 'the infinite conjugation of the verb *To do*.' Considering how human things circulate, each inex-tricably in communion with all,—how the word I speak to you to-day is borrowed, not from Ulfila the Mœsogoth only, but from all men since the first man began to speak,—I find no

The work similitude so true as this of a Tree.   Beautiful;
of the altogether beautiful and great.   The '*Machine
Poet of the Universe,'—alas, do but think of that in
contrast !

Well, it is strange enough this old Norse view of
Nature ; different enough from what we believe of
Nature.   Whence it specially came, one would not
like to be compelled to say very minutely !   One
thing we may say : It came from the thoughts of
Norse men ;—from the thought, above all, of the
first Norse man who had an original power of thinking.   The First Norse ' man of genius,' as we should
call him !   Innumerable men had passed by, across
this Universe, with a dumb vague wonder, such as
the very animals may feel ; or with a painful, fruit-
lessly inquiring wonder, such as men only feel ;—till
the great Thinker came, the *original* man, the Seer ;
whose shaped spoken Thought awakes the slumber-
ing capability of all into Thought.   It is ever the
way with the Thinker, the spiritual Hero.   What
he says, all men were not far from saying, were
longing to say.   The Thoughts of all start up, as
from painful enchanted sleep, round his Thought ;
answering to it, Yes, even so !   Joyful to men as
the dawning of day from night ; *is* it not, indeed,
the awakening for them from no-being into being,
from death into life ?   We still honour such a man ;
call him Poet, Genius, and so forth : but to these
wild men he was a very magician, a worker of
miraculous unexpected blessing for them ; a Prophet,
a God !—Thought once awakened does not again
slumber ; unfolds itself into a System of Thought ;
grows, in man after man, generation after generation,
  –till its full stature is reached, and *such* System

of Thought can grow no farther, but must give place **Odin**
to another.

For the Norse people, the Man now named
Odin, and Chief Norse God, we fancy, was such a
man. A Teacher, and Captain of soul and of
body; a Hero, of worth *im*measurable; admiration for whom, transcending the known bounds,
became adoration. Has he not the power of articulate Thinking; and many other powers, as yet
miraculous? So, with boundless gratitude, would
the rude Norse heart feel. Has he not solved for
them the sphinx-enigma of this Universe; given
assurance to them of their own destiny there? By
him they know now what they have to do here,
what to look for hereafter. Existence has become
articulate, melodious by him; he first has made Life
alive!—We may call this Odin, the origin of Norse
Mythology: Odin, or whatever name the First Norse
Thinker bore while he was a man among men. His
view of the Universe once promulgated, a like view
starts into being in all minds; grows, keeps ever
growing, while it continues credible there. In all
minds it lay written, but invisibly, as in sympathetic
ink; at his word it starts into visibility in all.
Nay, in every epoch of the world, the great event,
parent of all others, is it not the arrival of a Thinker
in the world!—

One other thing we must not forget; it will
explain, a little, the confusion of these Norse Eddas.
They are not one coherent System of Thought; but
properly the *summation* of several successive systems.
All this of the old Norse Belief which is flung-out
for us, in one level of distance in the Edda, like a
picture painted on the same canvas, does not at all
stand so in the reality. It stands rather at all

Growth of the Edda manner of distances and depths, of successive generations since the Belief first began. All Scandinavian thinkers, since the first of them, contributed to the Scandinavian System of Thought; in ever-new elaboration and addition, it is the combined work of them all. What history it had, how it changed from shape to shape, by one thinker's contribution after another, till it got to the full final shape we see it under in the *Edda*, no man will now ever know: *its* Councils of Trebisond, Councils of Trent, Athanasiuses, Dantes, Luthers, are sunk without echo in the dark night! Only that it had such a history we can all know. Wheresoever a thinker appeared, there in the thing he thought-of was a contribution, accession, a change or revolution made. Alas, the grandest 'revolution' of all, the one made by the man Odin himself, is not this too sunk for us like the rest! Of Odin what history? Strange rather to reflect that he *had* a history! That this Odin, in his wild Norse vesture, with his wild beard and eyes, his rude Norse speech and ways, was a man like us; with our sorrows, joys, with our limbs, features;—intrinsically all one as we: and did such a work! But the work, much of it, has perished; the worker, all to the name. "*Wednes*day," men will say to-morrow; Odin's day! Of Odin there exists no history; no document of it; no guess about it worth repeating.

Snorro indeed, in the quietest manner, almost in a brief business style, writes down, in his *Heims-kringla*, how Odin was a heroic Prince, in the Black-Sea region, with Twelve Peers, and a great people straitened for room. How he led these *Asen* (Asiatics) of his out of Asia; settled them in the North parts of Europe, by warlike conquest;

invented Letters, Poetry and so forth,—and came **Con-**
by and by to be worshipped as Chief God by these **jecture**
Scandinavians, his Twelve Peers made into Twelve
Sons of his own, Gods like himself: Snorro has no
doubt of this.   Saxo Grammaticus, a very curious
Northman of that same century, is still more un-
hesitating; scruples not to find out a historical fact
in every individual mythus, and writes it down as a
terrestrial event in Denmark or elsewhere.   Torfæus,
learned and cautious, some centuries later, assigns by
calculation a *date* for it : Odin, he says, came into
Europe about the Year 70 before Christ.   Of all
which, as grounded on mere uncertainties, found to
be untenable now, I need say nothing.   Far, very
far beyond the Year 70 !   Odin's date, adventures,
whole terrestrial history, figure and environment are
sunk from us forever into unknown thousands of
years.

Nay Grimm, the German Antiquary, goes so far
as to deny that any man Odin ever existed.   He
proves it by etymology.   The word *Wuotan*, which
is the original form of *Odin*, a word spread, as name
of their chief Divinity, over all the Teutonic Nations
everywhere ; this word, which connects itself, according to Grimm, with the Latin *vadere*, with the
English *wade* and suchlike,—means primarily *Movement*, Source of Movement, Power ; and is the fit
name of the highest god, not of any man.   The
word signifies Divinity, he says, among the old
Saxon, German and all Teutonic Nations ; the
adjectives formed from it all signify *divine, supreme,*
or something pertaining to the chief god.   Like
enough !   We must bow to Grimm in matters
etymological.   Let us consider it fixed that *Wuotan*
means *Wading*, force of *Movement*.   And now still,

The man Odin what hinders it from being the name of a Heroic Man and *Mover*, as well as of a god? As for the adjectives, and words formed from it,—did not the Spaniards in their universal admiration for Lope, get into the habit of saying 'a Lope flower,' a 'Lope *dama*,' if the flower or woman were of surpassing beauty? Had this lasted, *Lope* would have grown, in Spain, to be an adjective signifying *godlike* also. Indeed, Adam Smith, in his *Essay on Language*, surmises that all adjectives whatsoever were formed precisely in that way: some very green thing chiefly notable for its greenness, got the appellative name *Green*, and then the next thing remarkable for that quality, a tree for instance, was named the *green* tree,—as we still say 'the *steam* coach,' 'four-horse coach,' or the like. All primary adjectives, according to Smith, were formed in this way; were at first substantives and things. We cannot annihilate a man for etymologies like that! Surely there was a First Teacher and Captain; surely there must have been an Odin, palpable to the sense at one time; no adjective, but a real Hero of flesh and blood! The voice of all tradition, history or echo of history, agrees with all that thought will teach one about it, to assure us of this.

How the man Odin came to be considered a *god*, the chief god?—that surely is a question which nobody would wish to dogmatise upon. I have said, his people knew no *limits* to their admiration of him; they had as yet no scale to measure admiration by. Fancy your own generous heart's-love of some greatest man expanding till it *transcended* all bounds, till it filled and overflowed the whole field of your thought! Or what if this man Odin,— since a great deep soul, with the afflatus and mysterious tide of vision and impulse rushing on him he **The man** knows not whence, is ever an enigma, a kind of **made god** terror and wonder to himself,—should have felt that perhaps *he* was divine; that *he* was some effluence of the ' Wuotan,' ' *Movement*,' Supreme Power and Divinity, of whom to his rapt vision all Nature was the awful Flame-image; that some effluence of *Wuotan* dwelt here in him! He was not necessarily false; he was but mistaken, speaking the truest he knew. A great soul, any sincere soul, knows not *what* he is,—alternates between the highest height and the lowest depth; can, of all things, the least measure—Himself! What others take him for, and what he guesses that he may be; these two items strangely act on one another, help to deter-mine one another. With all men reverently admir-ing him; with his own wild soul full of noble ardours and affections, of whirlwind chaotic darkness and glorious new light; a divine Universe bursting all into godlike beauty round him, and no man to whom the like ever had befallen, what could he think himself to be? "Wuotan?" All men answered, "Wuotan!"—

And then consider what mere Time will do in such cases; how if a man was great while living, he becomes tenfold greater when dead. What an enormous *camera-obscura* magnifier is Tradition! How a thing grows in the human Memory, in the human Imagination, when love, worship and all that lies in the human Heart, is there to encourage it. And in the darkness, in the entire ignorance; with-out date or document, no book, no Arundel-marble; only here and there some dumb monumental cairn. Why, in thirty or forty years, were there no books, any great man would grow *mythic*, the contemporaries who had once seen him, being all dead. And in three-hundred years, and three-thousand years—!—To attempt *theorising* on such matters would profit little : they are matters which refuse to be *theoremed* and diagramed ; which Logic ought to know that she *cannot* speak of. Enough for us to discern, far in the uttermost distance, some gleam as of a small real light shining in the centre of that enormous camera-obscura image ; to discern that the centre of it all was not a madness and nothing, but a sanity and something.

This light, kindled in the great dark vortex of the Norse mind, dark but living, waiting only for light ; this is to me the centre of the whole. How such light will then shine out, and with wondrous thousandfold expansion spread itself, in forms and colours, depends not on *it*, so much as on the National Mind recipient of it. The colours and forms of your light will be those of the *cut-glass* it has to shine through.—Curious to think how, for every man, any the truest fact is modelled by the nature of the man ! I said, The earnest man, speaking to his brother men, must always have stated what seemed to him a *fact*, a real Appearance of Nature. But the way in which such Appearance or fact shaped itself,—what sort of *fact* it became for him,—was and is modified by his own laws of thinking ; deep, subtle, but universal, ever-operating laws. The world of Nature, for every man, is the Phantasy of Himself ; this world is the multiplex 'Image of his own Dream.' Who knows to what unnameable subtleties of spiritual law all these Pagan Fables owe their shape ! The number *Twelve*, divisiblest of all, which could be halved, quartered, parted into three, into six, the most remarkable

number,—this was enough to determine the *Signs of* **Odin's**
the Zodiac, the number of Odin's *Sons*, and innumer- **runes**
able other Twelves.   Any vague rumour of number
had a tendency to settle itself into Twelve.   So
with regard to every other matter.   And quite unconsciously too,—with no notion of building-up
'Allegories'!   But the fresh clear glance of those
First Ages would be prompt in discerning the secret
relations of things, and wholly open to obey these.
Schiller finds in the *Cestus of Venus* an everlasting
æsthetic truth as to the nature of all Beauty;
curious:—but he is careful not to insinuate that the
old Greek Mythists had any notion of lecturing
about the 'Philosophy of Criticism'!——On the
whole we must leave those boundless regions.
Cannot we conceive that Odin was a reality?
Error indeed, error enough : but sheer falsehood,
idle fables, allegory aforethought,—we will not
believe that our Fathers believed in these.

Odin's *Runes* are a significant feature of him.
Runes, and the miracles of 'magic' he worked by
them, make a great feature in tradition.   Runes are
the Scandinavian Alphabet; suppose Odin to have
been the inventor of Letters, as well as 'magic,'
among that people!   It is the greatest invention
man has ever made, this of marking-down the unseen
thought that is in him by written characters.   It is
a kind of second speech, almost as miraculous as
the first.   You remember the astonishment and incredulity of Atahualpa the Peruvian King; how
he made the Spanish Soldier who was guarding
him scratch *Dios* on his thumb-nail, that he might
try the next soldier with it, to ascertain whether
such a miracle was possible.   If Odin brought

Odin a poet Letters among his people, he might work magic enough!

Writing by Runes has some air of being original among the Norsemen: not a Phœnician Alphabet, but a native Scandinavian one. Snorro tells us farther that Odin invented Poetry; the music of human speech, as well as that miraculous runic marking of it. Transport yourselves into the early childhood of nations; the first beautiful morning-light of our Europe, when all yet lay in fresh young radiance as of a great sunrise, and our Europe was first beginning to think, to be! Wonder, hope; infinite radiance of hope and wonder, as of a young child's thoughts, in the hearts of these strong men! Strong sons of Nature; and here was not only a wild Captain and Fighter; discerning with his wild flashing eyes what to do, with his wild lion-heart daring and doing it; but a Poet too, all that we mean by a Poet, Prophet, great devout Thinker and Inventor,—as the truly Great Man ever is. A Hero is a Hero at all points; in the soul and thought of him first of all. This Odin, in his rude semi-articulate way, had a word to speak. A great heart laid open to take in this great Universe, and man's Life here, and utter a great word about it. A Hero, as I say, in his own rude manner; a wise, gifted, noble-hearted man. And now, if we still admire such a man beyond all others, what must these wild Norse souls, first awakened into thinking, have made of him! To them, as yet without names for it, he was noble and noblest; Hero, Prophet, God; *Wuotan*, the greatest of all. Thought is Thought, however it speak or spell itself. Intrinsically, I conjecture, this Odin must have been of the same sort of stuff as the greatest kind of men. A great thought in the wild deep heart of him! The His rough words he articulated, are they not the rudi- shadow mental roots of those English words we still use? over He worked so, in that obscure element. But he history was as a *light* kindled in it; a light of Intellect, rude Nobleness of heart, the only kind of lights we have yet; a Hero, as I say: and he had to shine there, and make his obscure element a little lighter, —as is still the task of us all.

We will fancy him to be the Type Norseman; the finest Teuton whom that race had yet produced. The rude Norse heart burst-up into *boundless* admira- tion round him; into adoration. He is as a root of so many great things; the fruit of him is found growing, from deep thousands of years, over the whole field of Teutonic Life. Our own Wednes- day, as I said, is it not still Odin's Day? Wednes- bury, Wansborough, Wanstead, Wandsworth: Odin grew into England too, these are still leaves from that root! He was the Chief God to all the Teutonic Peoples; their Pattern Norseman;—in such way did *they* admire their Pattern Norseman; that was the fortune he had in the world.

Thus if the man Odin himself have vanished utterly, there is this huge Shadow of him which still projects itself over the whole History of his People. For this Odin once admitted to be God, we can understand well that the whole Scandinavian Scheme of Nature, or dim No-scheme, whatever it might before have been, would now begin to develop itself altogether differently, and grow thenceforth in a new manner. What this Odin saw into, and taught with his runes and his rhymes, the whole Teutonic People laid to heart and carried forward. His way of thought became their way of thought:

Primitive
Hero-
worship

—such, under new conditions, is the history of every great thinker still. In gigantic confused lineaments, like some enormous camera-obscura shadow thrown upwards from the dead deeps of the Past, and covering the whole Northern Heaven, is not that Scandinavian Mythology in some sort the Portraiture of this man Odin? The gigantic image of *his* natural face, legible or not legible there, expanded and confused in that manner! Ah, Thought, I say, is always Thought. No great man lives in vain. The History of the world is but the Biography of great men.

To me there is something very touching in this primeval figure of Heroism; in such artless, helpless, but hearty entire reception of a Hero by his fellow-men. Never so helpless in shape, it is the noblest of feelings, and a feeling in some shape or other perennial as man himself. If I could show in any measure, what I feel deeply for a long time now, That it is the vital element of manhood, the soul of man's history here in our world,—it would be the chief use of this discoursing at present. We do not now call our great men Gods, nor admire *without* limit; ah, no, *with* limit enough! But if we have no great men, or do not admire at all,—that were a still worse case.

This poor Scandinavian Hero-worship, that whole Norse way of looking at the Universe, and adjusting oneself there, has an indestructible merit for us. A rude childlike way of recognising the divineness of Nature, the divineness of Man; most rude, yet heart-felt, robust, giantlike; betokening what a giant of a man this child would grow to!—It was a truth, and is none. Is it not as the half-dumb stifled voice of the long-buried generations of our own Fathers, calling out of the depths of ages to us, in whose veins their blood still runs: "This then, this is what *we* made of the world : this is all the image and notion we could form to ourselves of this great mystery of a Life and Universe. Despise it not. You are raised high above it, to large free scope of vision ; but you too are not yet at the top. No, your notion too, so much enlarged, is but a partial, imperfect one : that matter is a thing no man will ever, in time or out of time, comprehend ; after thousands of years of ever-new expansion, man will find himself but struggling to comprehend again a part of it : the thing is larger than man, not to be comprehended by him ; an Infinite thing ! "

The essence of the Scandinavian, as indeed of all Pagan Mythologies, we found to be recognition of the divineness of Nature ; sincere communion of man with the mysterious invisible Powers visibly seen at work in the world round him. This, I should say, is more sincerely done in the Scandinavian than in any Mythology I know. Sincerity is the great characteristic of it. Superior sincerity (far superior) consoles us for the total want of old Grecian grace. Sincerity, I think, is better than grace. I feel that these old Northmen were looking into Nature with open eye and soul : most earnest, honest ; childlike, and yet manlike ; with a great-hearted simplicity and depth and freshness, in a true, loving, admiring, unfearing way. A right valiant, true old race of men. Such recognition of Nature one finds to be the chief element of Paganism : recognition of Man, and his Moral Duty, though this too is not wanting, comes to be the chief element only in purer forms of religion.

Elements of the Norse faith Here, indeed, is a great distinction and epoch in Human Beliefs; a great landmark in the religious development of Mankind. Man first puts himself in relation with Nature and her Powers, wonders and worships over those; not till a later epoch does he discern that all Power is Moral, that the grand point is the distinction for him of Good and Evil, of *Thou shalt* and *Thou shalt not.*

With regard to all these fabulous delineations in the *Edda,* I will remark, moreover, as indeed was already hinted, that most probably they must have been of much newer date; most probably, even from the first, were comparatively idle for the old Norsemen, and as it were a kind of Poetic sport. Allegory and Poetic Delineation, as I said above, cannot be religious Faith; the Faith itself must first be there, then Allegory enough will gather round it, as the fit body round its soul. The Norse Faith, I can well suppose, like other Faiths, was most active while it lay mainly in the silent state, and had not yet much to say about itself, still less to sing.

Among those shadowy *Edda* matters, amid all that fantastic congeries of assertions, and traditions, in their musical Mythologies, the main practical belief a man could have was probably not much more than this: of the *Valkyrs* and the *Hall of Odin ;* of an inflexible *Destiny ;* and that the one thing needful for a man was *to be brave.* The *Valkyrs* are Choosers of the Slain: a Destiny inexorable, which it is useless trying to bend or soften, has appointed who is to be slain; this was a fundamental point for the Norse believer;—as indeed it is for all earnest men everywhere, for a Mahomet, a Luther, for a Napoleon too. It lies at the basis this for every such man; it is the woof out of which his whole system of thought is woven. **Valour** The *Valkyrs ;* and then that these *Choosers* lead the **is value** brave to a heavenly *Hall of Odin ;* only the base and slavish being thrust elsewhither, into the realms of Hela the Death-goddess: I take this to have been the soul of the whole Norse Belief. They understood in their heart that it was indispensable to be brave ; that Odin would have no favour for them, but despise and thrust them out, if they were not brave. Consider too whether there is not something in this! It is an everlasting duty, valid in our day as in that, the duty of being brave. *Valour* is still *value*. The first duty of a man is still that of subduing *Fear*. We must get rid of Fear ; we cannot act at all till then. A man's acts are slavish, not true but specious: his very thoughts are false, he thinks too as a slave and coward, till he have got Fear under his feet. Odin's creed, if we disentangle the real kernel of it, is true to this hour. A man shall and must be valiant ; he must march forward, and quit himself like a man—trusting imperturbably in the appointment and *choice* of the upper Powers ; and, on the whole, not fear at all. Now and always, the completeness of his victory over Fear will determine how much of a man he is.

It is doubtless very savage that kind of valour of the old Northmen. Snorro tells us they thought it a shame and misery not to die in battle ; and if natural death seemed to be coming on, they would cut wounds in their flesh, that Odin might receive them as warriors slain. Old kings, about to die, had their body laid into a ship ; the ship sent forth, with sails set and slow fire burning it ; that, once out at sea, it might blaze-up in flame, and in such manner bury worthily the old hero, at once in the

Forest-felling kings sky and in the ocean! Wild bloody valour; yet valour of its kind; better, I say, than none. In the old Sea-kings too, what an indomitable rugged energy! Silent, with closed lips, as I fancy them, unconscious that they were specially brave; defying the wild ocean with its monsters, and all men and things;—progenitors of our own Blakes and Nelsons! No Homer sang these Norse Sea-kings; but Agamemnon's was a small audacity, and of small fruit in the world, to some of them;—to Hrolf's of Normandy, for instance! Hrolf, or Rollo Duke of Normandy, the wild Sea-king, has a share in governing England at this hour.

Nor was it altogether nothing, even that wild sea-roving and battling, through so many generations. It needed to be ascertained which was the *strongest* kind of men; who were to be ruler over whom. Among the Northland Sovereigns, too, I find some who got the title *Wood-cutter;* Forest-felling Kings. Much lies in that. I suppose at bottom many of them were forest-fellers as well as fighters, though the Skalds talk mainly of the latter,—misleading certain critics not a little; for no nation of men could ever live by fighting alone; there could not produce enough come out of that! I suppose the right good fighter was oftenest also the right good forest-feller,—the right good improver, discerner, doer and worker in every kind; for true valour, different enough from ferocity, is the basis of all. A more legitimate kind of valour that; showing itself against the untamed Forests and dark brute Powers of Nature, to conquer Nature for us. In the same direction have not we their descendants since carried it far? May such valour last forever with us!

That the man Odin, speaking with a Hero's *The seed* voice and heart, as with an impressiveness out of *and the* Heaven, told his People the infinite importance of *banyan-* Valour, how man thereby became a god; and that *tree* his People, feeling a response to it in their own hearts, believed this message of his, and thought it a message out of Heaven, and him a Divinity for telling it them: this seems to me the primary seed-grain of the Norse Religion, from which all manner of mythologies, symbolic practices, speculations, allegories, songs and sagas would naturally grow. Grow,— how strangely! I called it a small light shining and shaping in the huge vortex of Norse darkness. Yet the darkness itself was *alive;* consider that. It was the eager inarticulate unin-structed Mind of the whole Norse People, longing only to become articulate, to go on articulating ever farther! The living doctrine grows, grows;— like a Banyan-tree; the first *seed* is the essential thing: any branch strikes itself down into the earth, becomes a new root; and so, in endless complexity, we have a whole wood, a whole jungle, one seed the parent of it all. Was not the whole Norse Religion, accordingly, in some sense, what we called 'the enormous shadow of this man's likeness'? Critics trace some affinity in some Norse mythuses, of the Creation and suchlike, with those of the Hindoos. The Cow Adumbla, 'licking the rime from the rocks,' has a kind of Hindoo look. A Hindoo Cow, transported into frosty countries. Probably enough; indeed we may say undoubtedly, these things will have a kindred with the remotest lands, with the earliest times. Thought does not die, but only is changed. The first man that began to think in this Planet of ours, he was the beginner

The
story of
Balder
of all. And then the second man, and the third man:—nay, every true Thinker to this hour is a kind of Odin, teaches men *his* way of thought, spreads a shadow of his own likeness over sections of the History of the World.

Of the distinctive poetic character or merit of this Norse Mythology I have not room to speak; nor does it concern us much. Some wild Prophecies we have, as the *Völuspa* in the *Elder Edda;* of a rapt, earnest, sibylline sort. But they were comparatively an idle adjunct of the matter, men who as it were but toyed with the matter, these later Skalds; and it is *their* songs chiefly that survive. In later centuries, I suppose, they would go on singing, poetically symbolising, as our modern Painters paint, when it was no longer from the innermost heart, or not from the heart at all. This is everywhere to be well kept in mind.

Gray's fragments of Norse Lore, at any rate, will give one no notion of it;—any more than Pope will of Homer. It is no square-built gloomy palace of black ashlar marble, shrouded in awe and horror, as Gray gives it us: no; rough as the North Rocks, as the Iceland deserts, it is; with a heartiness, homeliness, even a tint of good humour and robust mirth in the middle of these fearful things. The strong old Norse heart did not go upon theatrical sublimities; they had not time to tremble. I like much their robust simplicity; their veracity, directness of conception. Thor 'draws down his brows' in a veritable Norse rage; 'grasps his hammer till the *knuckles grow white.*' Beautiful traits of pity too, an honest pity. Balder 'the white God' dies; the beautiful, benignant; he is the Sungod. They try all Nature for a remedy ; but he is dead. Frigga, **Thor** his mother, sends Hermoder to seek or see him : nine days and nine nights he rides through gloomy deep valleys, a labyrinth of gloom ; arrives at the Bridge with its gold roof: the Keeper says, " Yes, Balder did pass here ; but the Kingdom of the Dead is down yonder, far towards the North." Hermoder rides on ; leaps Hell-gate, Hela's gate : does see Balder, and speak with him : Balder cannot be delivered. Inexorable ! Hela will not, for Odin or any God, give him up. The beautiful and gentle has to remain there. His Wife had volunteered to go with him, to die with him. They shall forever remain there. He sends his ring to Odin ; Nanna his wife sends her *thimble* to Frigga, as a remembrance —Ah me !—

For indeed Valour is the fountain of Pity too ;— of Truth, and all that is great and good in man. The robust homely vigour of the Norse heart attaches one much, in these delineations. Is it not a trait of right honest strength, says Uhland, who has written a fine *Essay* on Thor, that the Old Norse heart finds its friend in the Thunder-god ? That it is not frightened away by his thunder ; but finds that Summer-heat, the beautiful noble summer, must and will have thunder withal ! The Norse heart *loves* this Thor and his hammer-bolt ; sports with him. Thor is Summer-heat ; the god of Peaceable Industry as well as Thunder. He is the Peasant's friend ; his true henchman and attendant is Thialfi, *Manual Labour*. Thor himself engages in all manner of rough manual work, scorns no business for its plebeianism ; is ever and anon travelling to the country of the Jötuns, harrying those chaotic Frost-monsters, subduing them, at

Twigs of the world-tree least straitening and damaging them. There is a great broad humour in some of these things.

Thor, as we saw above, goes to Jötun-land, to seek Hymir's Caldron, that the Gods may brew beer. Hymir the huge Giant enters, his grey beard all full of hoar-frost; splits pillars with the very glance of his eye; Thor, after much rough tumult, snatches the Pot, claps it on his head; the 'handles of it reach down to his heels.' The Norse Skald has a kind of loving sport with Thor. This is the Hymir whose cattle, the critics have discovered, are Icebergs. Huge untutored Brobdignag genius,—needing only to be tamed-down; into Shakspeares, Dantes, Goethes! It is all gone now, that old Norse work,—Thor the Thundergod changed into Jack the Giant-killer: but the mind that made it is here yet. How strangely things grow, and die, and do not die! There are twigs of that great world-tree of Norse Belief still curiously traceable. This poor Jack of the Nursery, with his miraculous shoes of swiftness, coat of darkness, sword of sharpness, he is one. *Hynde Etin*, and still more decisively *Red Etin of Ireland*, in the Scottish Ballads, these are both derived from Norseland; *Etin* is evidently a *Jötun*. Nay, Shakspeare's *Hamlet* is a twig too of this same world-tree; there seems no doubt of that. Hamlet, *Amleth*, I find, is really a mythic personage; and his Tragedy, of the poisoned Father, poisoned asleep by drops in his ear, and the rest, is a Norse mythus! Old Saxo, as his wont was, made it a Danish history; Shakspeare, out of Saxo, made it what we see. That is a twig of the world-tree that has *grown*, I think;—by nature or accident that one has grown!

In fact, these old Norse songs have a *truth* in them, an inward perennial truth and greatness,— as, indeed, all must have that can very long preserve itself by tradition alone. It is a greatness not of mere body and gigantic bulk, but a rude greatness of soul. There is a sublime uncomplaining melancholy traceable in these old hearts. A great free glance into the very deeps of thought. They seem to have seen, these brave old Northmen, what Meditation has taught all men in all ages, That this world is after all but a show,— a phenomenon or appearance, no real thing. All deep souls see into that,—the Hindoo Mythologist, the German Philosopher, — the Shakspeare, the earnest Thinker, wherever he may be :

'We are such stuff as Dreams are made of!'

One of Thor's expeditions, to Utgard (the *Outer* Garden, central seat of Jötun-land), is remarkable in this respect. Thialfi was with him, and Loke. After various adventures they entered upon Giant-land ; wandered over plains, wild uncultivated places, among stones and trees. At nightfall they noticed a house; and as the door, which indeed formed one whole side of the house, was open, they entered. It was a simple habitation; one large hall, altogether empty. They stayed there. Suddenly in the dead of the night loud noises alarmed them. Thor grasped his hammer; stood in the door, prepared for fight. His companions within ran hither and thither in their terror, seeking some outlet in that rude hall ; they found a little closet at last, and took refuge there. Neither had Thor any battle : for, lo, in the morning it turned-out that the noise had been

Thor's journey to Utgard only the *snoring* of a certain enormous but peaceable Giant, the Giant Skrymir, who lay peaceably sleeping near by; and this that they took for a house was merely his *Glove*, thrown aside there; the door was the Glove-wrist; the little closet they had fled into was the Thumb! Such a glove; —I remark too that it had not fingers as ours have, but only a thumb, and the rest undivided: a most ancient, rustic glove!

Skrymir now carried their portmanteau all day; Thor, however, had his own suspicions, did not like the ways of Skrymir; determined at night to put an end to him as he slept. Raising his hammer, he struck down into the Giant's face a right thunderbolt blow, of force to rend rocks. The Giant merely awoke; rubbed his cheek, and said, Did a leaf fall? Again Thor struck, so soon as Skrymir again slept; a better blow than before: but the Giant only murmured, Was that a grain of sand? Thor's third stroke was with both his hands (the 'knuckles white' I suppose), and seemed to dint deep into Skrymir's visage; but he merely checked his snore, and remarked, There must be sparrows roosting in this tree, I think; what is that they have dropt?—At the gate of Utgard, a place so high that you had to 'strain your neck bending back to see the top of it,' Skrymir went his ways. Thor and his companions were admitted; invited to take share in the games going on. To Thor, for his part, they handed a drinking-horn; it was a common feat, they told him, to drink this dry at one draught. Long and fiercely, three times over, Thor drank; but made hardly any impression. He was a weak child, they told him; could he lift that Cat he saw there? Small

as the feat seemed, Thor with his whole godlike **Thor's**
strength could not; he bent-up the creature's back, **journey to**
could not raise its feet off the ground, could at the **Utgard**
utmost raise one foot. Why, you are no man, said
the Utgard people; there is an Old Woman that
will wrestle you! Thor, heartily ashamed, seized
this haggard Old Woman; but could not throw her.

And now, on their quitting Utgard, the Chief
Jötun, escorting them politely a little way, said to
Thor: "You are beaten then:—yet be not so
much ashamed; there was deception of appearance
in it. That Horn you tried to drink was the *Sea*:
you did make it ebb; but who could drink that,
the bottomless! The Cat you would have lifted,—
why, that is the *Midgard-snake*, the Great World-
serpent, which, tail in mouth, girds and keeps-up
the whole created world; had you torn that up, the
world must have rushed to ruin! As for the Old
Woman, she was *Time*, Old Age, Duration; with
her what can wrestle? No man nor no god with
her; gods or men, she prevails over all! And
then those three strokes you struck,—look at these
three valleys; your three strokes made these!"
Thor looked at his attendant Jötun: it was Skrymir;—it was, say Norse critics, the old chaotic
rocky *Earth* in person, and that glove-*house* was
some Earth-cavern! But Skrymir had vanished;
Utgard with its skyhigh gates, when Thor grasped
his hammer to smite them, had gone to air; only
the Giant's voice was heard mocking: "Better
come no more to Jötunheim!"—

This is of the allegoric period, as we see, and
half play, not of the prophetic and entirely devout:
but as a mythus is there not real antique Norse gold
in it? More true metal, rough from the Mimer-

The stithy, than in many a famed Greek Mythus *shaped*
Twilight far better! A great broad Brobdignag grin of true
of the humour is in this Skrymir; mirth resting on earnest-
Gods ness and sadness, as the rainbow on black tempest:
only a right valiant heart is capable of that. It is
the grim humour of our own Ben Jonson, rare old
Ben; runs in the blood of us, I fancy; for one
catches tones of it, under a still other shape, out of
the American Backwoods.

That is also a very striking conception, that of the
Ragnarök, Consummation, or *Twilight of the Gods*.
It is in the *Völuspa* Song; seemingly a very old,
prophetic idea. The Gods and Jötuns, the divine
Powers and the chaotic brute ones, after long contest and partial victory by the former, meet at last
in universal world-embracing wrestle and duel;
World-serpent against Thor, strength against
strength; mutually extinctive; and ruin, 'twilight'
sinking into darkness, swallows the created Universe. The old Universe with its Gods is sunk;
but it is not final death: there is to be a new
Heaven and a new Earth; a higher supreme God,
and Justice to reign among men. Curious: this law
of mutation, which also is a law written in man's
inmost thought, had been deciphered by these old
earnest Thinkers in their rude style; and how,
though all dies, and even gods die, yet all death is
but a phœnix fire-death, and new-birth into the
Greater and the Better! It is the fundamental
Law of Being for a creature made of Time, living
in this Place of Hope. All earnest men have seen
into it; may still see into it.

And now, connected with this, let us glance at
the *last* mythus of the appearance of Thor; and end
there. I fancy it to be the latest in date of all

these fables; a sorrowing protest against the advance **Last** of Christianity,—set forth reproachfully by some **appearance of** Conservative Pagan. King Olaf has been harshly **Thor** blamed for his over-zeal in introducing Christianity; surely I should have blamed him far more for an under-zeal in that! He paid dear enough for it; he died by the revolt of his Pagan people, in battle, in the year 1033, at Stickelstad, near that Drontheim, where the chief Cathedral of the North has now stood for many centuries, dedicated gratefully to his memory as *Saint* Olaf. The mythus about Thor is to this effect. King Olaf, the Christian Reform King, is sailing with fit escort along the shore of Norway, from haven to haven; dispensing justice, or doing other royal work: on leaving a certain haven, it is found that a stranger, of grave eyes and aspect, red beard, of stately robust figure, has stept in. The courtiers address him; his answers surprise by their pertinency and depth: at length he is brought to the King. The stranger's conversation here is not less remarkable, as they sail along the beautiful shore; but after some time, he addresses King Olaf thus: " Yes, King Olaf, it is all beautiful, with the sun shining on it there ; green, fruitful, a right fair home for you, and many a sore day had Thor, many a wild fight with the rock Jötuns, before he could make it so. And now you seem minded to put away Thor. King Olaf, have a care ! " said the stranger, drawing-down his brows ;—and when they looked again, he was nowhere to be found.—This is the last appearance of Thor on the stage of this world!

Do we not see well enough how the Fable might arise, without unveracity on the part of any one? It is the way most Gods have come to appear among men: thus, if in Pindar's time 'Neptune was seen once at the Nemean Games,' what was this Neptune too but a 'stranger of noble grave aspect,' *fit* to be 'seen'! There is something pathetic, tragic for me in this last voice of Paganism. Thor is vanished, the whole Norse world has vanished; and will not return ever again. In like fashion to that pass away the highest things. All things that have been in this world, all things that are or will be in it, have to vanish, we have our sad farewell to give them.

That Norse Religion, a rude but earnest, sternly impressive *Consecration of Valour* (so we may define it), sufficed for these old valiant Northmen. Consecration of Valour is not a *bad* thing! We will take it for good, so far as it goes. Neither is there no use in *knowing* something about this old Paganism of our Fathers. Unconsciously, and combined with higher things, it is in *us* yet, that old Faith withal! To know it consciously, brings us into closer and clearer relation with the Past—with our own possessions in the Past. For the whole Past, as I keep repeating, is the possession of the Present; the Past had always something *true*, and is a precious possession. In a different time, in a different place, it is always some other *side* of our common Human Nature that has been developing itself. The actual True is the *sum* of all these; not any one of them by itself constitutes what of Human Nature is hitherto developed. Better to know them all than misknow them. "To which of these Three Religions do you specially adhere?" inquires Meister of his Teacher. "To all the Three!" answers the other: "To all the Three: for they by their union first constitute the True Religion."

LECTURE II

THE HERO AS PROPHET. MAHOMET: ISLAM

[*Friday, 8th May* 1840]

FROM the first rude times of Paganism among The
the Scandinavians in the North, we advance Hero as
to a very different epoch of religion, among a very Prophet
different people: Mahometanism among the Arabs.
A great change; what a change and progress is
indicated here, in the universal condition and
thoughts of men!

The Hero is not now regarded as a God among
his fellowmen; but as one God-inspired, as a prophet.
It is the second phasis of Hero-worship; the first
or oldest, we may say, has passed away without
return; in the history of the world there will not
again be any man, never so great, whom his fellow-
men will take for a god. Nay we might rationally
ask, Did any set of human beings ever really think
the man they *saw* there standing beside them a god,
the maker of this world? Perhaps not: it was
usually some man they remembered, or *had* seen.
But neither can this any more be. The Great Man
is not recognised henceforth as a god any more.

It was a rude gross error, that of counting the
Great Man a god. Yet let us say that it is at all
times difficult to know *what* he is, or how to account
of him and receive him! The most significant
feature in the history of an epoch is the manner it
has of welcoming a Great Man. Ever, to the true
instincts of men, there is something godlike in him.
Whether they shall take him to be a god, to be a

The reception of Great Men

prophet, or what they shall take him to be? that is ever a grand question; by their way of answering that, we shall see, as through a little window, into the very heart of these men's spiritual condition. For at bottom the Great Man, as he comes from the hand of nature, is ever the same kind of thing: Odin, Luther, Johnson, Burns; I hope to make it appear that these are all originally of one stuff; that only by the world's reception of them, and the shapes they assume, are they so immeasurably diverse. The worship of Odin astonishes us—to fall prostrate before the Great Man, into *deliquium* of love and wonder over him, and feel in their hearts that he was a denizen of the skies, a god! This was imperfect enough: but to welcome, for example, a Burns as we did, was that what we can call perfect? The most precious gift that Heaven can give to the Earth; a man of 'genius' as we call it: the Soul of a Man actually sent down from the skies with a God's-message to us—this we waste away as an idle artificial firework, sent to amuse us a little, and sink it into ashes, wreck and ineffectuality: *such* reception of a Great Man I do not call very perfect either! Looking into the heart of the thing, one may perhaps call that of Burns a still uglier phenomenon, betokening still sadder imperfections in mankind's ways, than the Scandinavian method itself! To fall into mere unreasoning *deliquium* of love and admiration, was not good; but such unreasoning, nay irrational supercilious no-love at all is perhaps still worse!—It is a thing forever changing, this of Hero-worship: different in each age, difficult to do well in any age. Indeed, the heart of the whole business of the age, one may say, is to do it well.

We have chosen Mahomet not as the most emi- **Mahomet** nent Prophet, but as the one we are freest to speak **not an** of. He is by no means the truest of Prophets; **impostor** but I do esteem him a true one. Farther, as there is no danger of our becoming, any of us, Mahometans, I mean to say all the good of him I justly can. It is the way to get at his secret: let us try to understand what *he* meant with the world; what the world meant and means with him, will then be a more answerable question. Our current hypotheses about Mahomet, that he was a scheming Impostor, a Falsehood incarnate, that his religion is a mere mass of quackery and fatuity, begins really to be now untenable to any one. The lies, which well-meaning zeal has heaped round this man, are disgraceful to ourselves only. When Pococke inquired of Grotius, Where the proof was of that story of the pigeon, trained to pick peas from Mahomet's ear, and pass for an angel dictating to him? Grotius answered that there was no proof! It is really time to dismiss all that. The word this man spoke has been the life-guidance now of a hundred-and-eighty millions of men these twelve-hundred years. These hundred-and-eighty millions were made by God as well as we. A greater number of God's creatures believe in Mahomet's word at this hour than in any other word whatever. Are we to suppose that it was a miserable piece of spiritual legerdemain, this which so many creatures of the Almighty have lived by and died by? I, for my part, cannot form any such supposition. I will believe most things sooner than that. One would be entirely at a loss what to think of this world at all, if quackery so grew and were sanctioned here.

The Great Man is sincere   Alas, such theories are very lamentable. If we would attain to knowledge of anything in God's true Creation, let us disbelieve them wholly! They are the product of an Age of Scepticism; they indicate the saddest spiritual paralysis, and mere death-life of the souls of men: more godless theory, I think, was never promulgated in this Earth. A false man found a religion? Why, a false man cannot build a brick house! If he do not know and follow *truly* the properties of mortar, burnt clay and what else he works in, it is no house that he makes, but a rubbish-heap. It will not stand for twelve centuries, to lodge a hundred-and-eighty millions; it will fall straight-way. A man must conform himself to Nature's laws, *be* verily in communion with Nature and the truth of things, or Nature will answer him, No, not at all! Speciosities are specious—ah, me!—a Cagliostro, many Cagliostros, prominent world-leaders, do prosper by their quackery, for a day. It is like a forged bank-note; they get it passed out of *their* worthless hands: others, not they, have to smart for it. Nature bursts-up in fire-flames, French Revolutions and suchlike, proclaiming with terrible veracity that forged notes are forged.

But of a Great Man especially, of him I will venture to assert that it is incredible he should have been other than true. It seems to me the primary foundation of him, and of all that can lie in him, this. No Mirabeau, Napoleon, Burns, Cromwell, no man adequate to do anything, but is first of all in right earnest about it; what I call a sincere man. I should say *sincerity*, a deep, great, genuine sincerity, is the first characteristic of all men in any way heroic. Not the sincerity that calls itself sincere; ah, no, that is a very poor matter indeed;—a shallow braggart conscious sincerity; oftenest self-conceit **He sees** mainly.   The Great Man's sincerity is of the kind **the Inner** he cannot speak of, is not conscious of: nay, I **Fact** suppose, he is conscious rather of *in*sincerity; for what man can walk accurately by the law of truth for one day?   No, the Great Man does not boast himself sincere, far from that; perhaps does not ask himself if he is so: I would say rather, his sincerity does not depend on himself; he cannot help being sincere!   The great Fact of Existence is great to him.   Fly as he will, he cannot get out of the awful presence of this Reality.   His mind is so made; he is great by that, first of all.   Fearful and wonderful, real as Life, real as death, is this Universe to him. Though all men should forget its truth, and walk in a vain show, he cannot.   At all moments the Flame-image glares-in upon him; undeniable, there, there! —I wish you to take this as my primary definition of a Great Man.   A little man may have this, it is competent to all men that God has made: but a Great Man cannot be without it.

Such a man is what we call an *original* man: he comes to us at first-hand.   A messenger he, sent from the Infinite Unknown with tidings to us. We may call him Poet, Prophet, God;—in one way or other, we all feel that the words he utters are as no other man's words.   Direct from the Inner Fact of things;—he lives, and has to live, in daily communion with that.   Hearsays cannot hide it from him; he is blind, homeless, miserable, following hearsays; *it* glares-in upon him.   Really his utterances, are they not a kind of 'revelation;'— what we must call such for want of some other name?   It is from the heart of the world that he comes; he is portion of the primal reality of things.

He may
have
faults
enough

God has made many revelations: but this man too, has not God made him, the latest and newest of all? The 'inspiration of the Almighty giveth *him* understanding:' we must listen before all to him.

This Mahomet, then, we will in no wise consider as an Inanity and Theatricality, a poor conscious ambitious schemer; we cannot conceive him so. The rude message he delivered was a real one withal; an earnest confused voice from the unknown Deep. The man's words were not false, nor his workings here below; no Inanity and Simulacrum; a fiery mass of Life cast-up from the great bosom of Nature herself. To *kindle* the world; the world's Maker had ordered it so. Neither can the faults, imperfections, insincerities even, of Mahomet, if such were never so well proved against him, shake this primary fact about him.

On the whole, we make too much of faults; the details of the business hide the real centre of it. Faults? The greatest of faults, I should say, is to be conscious of none. Readers of the Bible above all, one would think, might know better. Who is called there 'the man according to God's own heart'? David, the Hebrew King, had fallen into sins enough; blackest crimes; there was no want of sins. And thereupon the unbelievers sneer and ask, Is this your man according to God's heart? The sneer, I must say, seems to me but a shallow one. What are faults, what are the outward details of a life; if the inner secret of it, the remorse, temptations, true, often-baffled, never-ended struggle of it, be forgotten? 'It is not in man that walketh to direct his steps.' Of all acts, is not, for a man, *repentance* the most divine? The deadliest sin, I say, were that same supercilious **But his** consciousness of no sin;—that is death; the heart **essence** so conscious is divorced from sincerity, humility **is not** and fact; is dead: it is 'pure' as dead dry sand is **there** pure. David's life and history, as written for us in those Psalms of his, I consider to be the truest emblem ever given of a man's moral progress and warfare here below. All earnest souls will ever discern in it the faithful struggle of an earnest human soul towards what is good and best. Struggle often baffled, sore baffled, down as into entire wreck; yet a struggle never ended; ever, with tears, repentance, true unconquerable purpose, begun anew. Poor human nature! Is not a man's walking, in truth, always that: 'a succession of falls'? Man can do no other. In this wild element of a Life, he has to struggle onwards; now fallen, deep-abased; and ever, with tears, repentance, with bleeding heart, he has to rise again, struggle again still onwards. That his struggle *be* a faithful unconquerable one: that is the question of questions. We will put-up with many sad details, if the soul of it were true. Details by themselves will never teach us what it is. I believe we misestimate Mahomet's faults even as faults: but the secret of him will never be got by dwelling there. We will leave all this behind us; and assuring ourselves that he did mean some true thing, ask candidly what it was or might be.

These Arabs Mahomet was born among are certainly a notable people. Their country itself is notable; the fit habitation for such a race. Savage inaccessible rock-mountains, great grim deserts, alternating with beautiful strips of verdure: wherever

The
Arabs water is, there is greenness, beauty; odoriferous
balm-shrubs, date-trees, frankincense-trees.   Consider that wide waste horizon of sand, empty, silent,
like a sand-sea, dividing habitable place from habitable.   You are all alone there, left alone with the
Universe; by day a fierce sun blazing down on it
with intolerable radiance; by night the great deep
Heaven with its stars.   Such a country is fit for a
swift-handed, deep-hearted race of men.   There is
something most agile, active, and yet most meditative, enthusiastic in the Arab character.   The
Persians are called the French of the East; we
will call the Arabs Oriental Italians.   A gifted
noble people; a people of wild strong feelings, and
of iron restraint over these: the characteristic of
noblemindedness, of genius.   The wild Bedouin
welcomes the stranger to his tent, as one having
right to all that is there; were it his worst enemy,
he will slay his foal to treat him, will serve him
with sacred hospitality for three days, will set him
fairly on his way;—and then, by another law as
sacred, kill him if he can.   In words too, as in
action.   They are not a loquacious people, taciturn
rather; but eloquent, gifted when they do speak.
An earnest truthful kind of men.   They are, as
we know, of Jewish kindred: but with that deadly
terrible earnestness of the Jews they seem to com-
bine something graceful, brilliant, which is not
Jewish.   They had 'Poetic contests' among them
before the time of Mahomet.   Sale says, at Ocadh,
in the South of Arabia, there were yearly fairs, and
there, when the merchandising was done, Poets
sang for prizes:—the wild people gathered to hear
that.

One Jewish quality these Arabs manifest; the

outcome of many or of all high qualities; what
we may call religiosity.   From of old they had
been zealous workers, according to their light.
They worshipped the stars, as Sabeans; worshipped many natural objects,—recognised them
as symbols, immediate manifestations, of the Maker
of Nature.   It was wrong; and yet not wholly
wrong.   All God's works are still in a sense
symbols of God.   Do we not, as I urged, still
account it a merit to recognise a certain inexhaust-
ible significance, 'poetic beauty' as we name it,
in all natural objects whatsoever?   A man is a
poet, and honoured, for doing that, and speaking
or singing it,—a kind of diluted worship.   They
had many Prophets, these Arabs; Teachers each
to his tribe, each according to the light he had.
But indeed, have we not from of old the noblest of
proofs, still palpable to every one of us, of what
devoutness and noblemindedness had dwelt in these
rustic thoughtful peoples?   Biblical critics seem
agreed that our own *Book of Job* was written in
that region of the world.   I call that, apart from
all theories about it, one of the grandest things ever
written with pen.   One feels, indeed, as if it were
not Hebrew; such a noble universality, different
from noble patriotism or sectarianism, reigns in it.
A noble Book; all men's Book!   It is our first,
oldest statement of the never-ending Problem,—
man's destiny, and God's ways with him here in
this earth.   And all in such free flowing outlines;
grand in its sincerity, in its simplicity; in its epic
melody, and repose of reconcilement.   There is
the seeing eye, the mildly understanding heart.   So
true everywhere; true eyesight and vision for all
things; material things no less than spiritual; the

The
Caabah

Horse,—'hast thou clothed his neck with *thunder*?'
—he '*laughs* at the shaking of the spear!' Such
living likenesses were never since drawn. Sublime
sorrow, sublime reconciliation: oldest choral melody
as of the heart of mankind;—so soft, and great; as
the summer midnight, as the world with its seas and
stars! There is nothing written, I think, in the
Bible or out of it, of equal literary merit.—

To the idolatrous Arabs one of the most ancient
universal objects of worship was that Black Stone,
still kept in the building called Caabah at Mecca.
Diodorus Siculus mentions this Caabah in a way
not to be mistaken, as the oldest, most honoured
temple in his time; that is, some half-century before our Era. Silvestre de Sacy says there is some
likelihood that the Black Stone is an aerolite. In
that case, some one might *see* it fall out of Heaven!
It stands now beside the Well Zemzem; the
Caabah is built over both. A Well is in all places
a beautiful affecting object, gushing out like life
from the hard earth;—still more so in these hot
dry countries, where it is the first condition of
being. The Well Zemzem has its name from the
bubbling sound of the waters, *zem-zem*; they think
it is the Well which Hagar found with her little
Ishmael in the wilderness: the aerolite and it have
been sacred now, and had a Caabah over them, for
thousands of years. A curious object, that Caabah!
There it stands at this hour, in the black cloth-
covering the Sultan sends it yearly; 'twenty-seven
cubits high;' with circuit, with double circuit of
pillars, with festoon-rows of lamps and quaint orna-
ments: the lamps will be lighted again *this* night,
—to glitter again under the stars. An authentic
fragment of the oldest Past. It is the *Keblah* of

all Moslem: from Delhi all onwards to Morocco, **Mecca** the eyes of innumerable praying men are turned towards *it*, five times, this day and all days: one of the notablest centres in the Habitation of Men.

It had been from the sacredness attached to this Caabah Stone and Hagar's Well, from the pilgrimings of all tribes of Arabs thither, that Mecca took its rise as a Town. A great town once, though much decayed now. It has no natural advantage for a town; stands in a sandy hollow amid bare barren hills, at a distance from the sea; its provisions, its very bread, have to be imported. But so many pilgrims needed lodgings: and then all places of pilgrimage do, from the first, become places of trade. The first day pilgrims meet, merchants have also met: where men see themselves assembled for one object, they find that they can accomplish other objects which depend on meeting together. Mecca became the Fair of all Arabia. And thereby indeed the chief staple and warehouse of whatever Commerce there was between the Indian and Western countries, Syria, Egypt, even Italy. It had at one time a population of 100,000; buyers, forwarders of those Eastern and Western products; importers for their own behoof of provisions and corn. The government was a kind of irregular aristocratic republic, not without a touch of theocracy. Ten Men of a chief tribe, chosen in some rough way, were Governors of Mecca, and Keepers of the Caabah. The Koreish were the chief tribe in Mahomet's time; his own family was of that tribe. The rest of the Nation, fractioned and cut-asunder by deserts, lived under similar rude patriarchal governments by one or several : herdsmen, carriers, traders,

Maho-
met's
birth
generally robbers too; being oftenest at war one with another, or with all: held together by no open bond, if it were not this meeting at the Caabah, where all forms of Arab Idolatry assembled in common adoration;—held mainly by the *inward* indissoluble bond of a common blood and language. In this way had the Arabs lived for long ages, unnoticed by the world: a people of great qualities, unconsciously waiting for the day when they should become notable to all the world. Their Idolatries appear to have been in a tottering state; much was getting into confusion and fermentation among them. Obscure tidings of the most important Event ever transacted in this world, the Life and Death of the Divine Man in Judea, at once the symptom and cause of immeasurable change to all people in the world, had in the course of centuries reached into Arabia too; and could not but, of itself, have produced fermentation there.

It was among this Arab people, so circumstanced, in the year 570 of our Era, that the man Mahomet was born. He was of the family of Hashem, of the Koreish tribe as we said; though poor, connected with the chief persons of his country. Almost at his birth he lost his Father; at the age of six years his Mother too, a woman noted for her beauty, her worth and sense: he fell to the charge of his Grandfather, an old man, a hundred years old. A good old man: Mahomet's Father, Abdallah, had been his youngest favourite son. He saw in Mahomet, with his old life-worn eyes, a century old, the lost Abdallah come back again, all that was left of Abdallah. He loved the little orphan Boy greatly; used to say, They must take

care of that beautiful little Boy, nothing in their His
kindred was more precious than he. At his death, journey to
while the boy was still but two years old, he left Syria
him in charge to Abu Thaleb the eldest of the
Uncles, as to him that now was head of the house.
By this Uncle, a just and rational man as everything
betokens, Mahomet was brought-up in the best
Arab way.

Mahomet, as he grew up, accompanied his Uncle
on trading journeys and suchlike; in his eighteenth
year one finds him a fighter following his Uncle in
war. But perhaps the most significant of all his
journeys is one we find noted as of some years'
earlier date: a journey to the Fairs of Syria. The
young man here first came in contact with a quite
foreign world,—with one foreign element of endless
moment to him: the Christian Religion. I know
not what to make of that 'Sergius, the Nestorian
Monk,' whom Abu Thaleb and he are said to have
lodged with; or how much any monk could have
taught one still so young. Probably enough it is
greatly exaggerated, this of the Nestorian Monk.
Mahomet was only fourteen; had no language but
his own: much in Syria must have been a strange
unintelligible whirlpool to him. But the eyes of
the lad were open; glimpses of many things would
doubtless be taken-in, and lie very enigmatic as yet,
which were to ripen in a strange way into views,
into beliefs and insights one day. These journeys
to Syria were probably the beginning of much to
Mahomet.

One other circumstance we must not forget:
that he had no school-learning; of the thing we
call school-learning none at all. The art of
writing was but just introduced into Arabia; it

seems to be the true opinion that Mahomet never could write! Life in the Desert, with its experiences, was all his education. What of this infinite Universe he, from his dim place, with his own eyes and thoughts, could take in, so much and no more of it was he to know. Curious, if we will reflect on it, this of having no books. Except by what he could see for himself, or hear of by uncertain rumour of speech in the obscure Arabian Desert, he could know nothing. The wisdom that had been before him or at a distance from him in the world, was in a manner as good as not there for him. Of the great brother souls, flame-beacons through so many lands and times, no one directly communicates with this great soul. He is alone there, deep down in the bosom of the Wilderness; has to grow up so,—alone with Nature and his own Thoughts.

But, from an early age, he had been remarked as a thoughtful man. His companions named him ' *Al Amin*, The Faithful.' A man of truth and fidelity; true in what he did, in what he spake and thought. They noted that *he* always meant something. A man rather taciturn in speech; silent when there was nothing to be said; but pertinent, wise, sincere, when he did speak; always throwing light on the matter. This is the only sort of speech *worth* speaking! Through life we find him to have been regarded as an altogether solid, brotherly, genuine man. A serious, sincere character; yet amiable, cordial, companionable, jocose even;—a good laugh in him withal: there are men whose laugh is as untrue as anything about them; who cannot laugh. One hears of Mahomet's beauty: his fine sagacious honest face, brown florid

complexion, beaming black eyes;—I somehow like **Maho-**
too that vein on the brow, which swelled-up black **met's**
when he was in anger: like the '*horse-shoe* vein' **early**
in Scott's *Redgauntlet*. It was a kind of feature **manhood**
in the Hashem family, this black swelling vein in
the brow; Mahomet had it prominent, as would
appear. A spontaneous, passionate, yet just, true-
meaning man! Full of wild faculty, fire and light:
of wild worth, all uncultured; working out his life-
task in the depths of the Desert there.

How he was placed with Kadijah, a rich Widow,
as her Steward, and travelled in her business, again
to the Fairs of Syria; how he managed all, as one
can well understand, with fidelity, adroitness; how
her gratitude, her regard for him grew: the story
of their marriage is altogether a graceful intelligible
one, as told us by the Arab authors. He was
twenty-five; she forty, though still beautiful. He
seems to have lived in a most affectionate, peaceable,
wholesome way with this wedded benefactress;
loving her truly, and her alone. It goes greatly
against the impostor theory, the fact that he lived
in this entirely unexceptionable, entirely quiet and
commonplace way, till the heat of his years was
done. He was forty before he talked of any mission
from Heaven. All his irregularities, real and sup-
posed, date from after his fiftieth year, when the
good Kadijah died. All his 'ambition,' seemingly,
had been, hitherto, to live an honest life; his 'fame,'
the mere good opinion of neighbours that knew him,
had been sufficient hitherto. Not till he was already
getting old, the prurient heat of his life all burnt out,
and *peace* growing to be the chief thing this world
could give him, did he start on the 'career of
ambition;' and, belying all his past character and

Mahomet not an impostor existence, set-up as a wretched empty charlatan to acquire what he could now no longer enjoy! For my share, I have no faith whatever in that.

Ah no: this deep-hearted Son of the Wilderness, with his beaming black eyes and open social deep soul, had other thoughts in him than ambition. A silent great soul; he was one of those who cannot *but* be in earnest; whom Nature herself has appointed to be sincere. While others walk in formulas and hearsays, contented enough to dwell there, this man could not screen himself in formulas; he was alone with his own soul and the reality of things. The great Mystery of Existence, as I said, glared-in upon him, with its terrors, with its splendours; no hearsays could hide that unspeakable fact, "Here am I!" Such *sincerity*, as we named it, has in very truth something of divine. The word of such a man is a Voice direct from Nature's own Heart. Men do and must listen to that as to nothing else;—all else is wind in comparison. From of old, a thousand thoughts, in his pilgrimings and wanderings, had been in this man: What am I? What *is* this unfathomable Thing I live in, which men name Universe? What is Life; what is Death? What am I to believe? What am I to do? The grim rocks of Mount Hara, of Mount Sinai, the stern sandy solitudes answered not. The great Heaven rolling silent overhead, with its blue-glancing stars, answered not. There was no answer. The man's own soul, and what of God's inspiration dwelt there, had to answer!

It is the thing which all men have to ask themselves; which we too have to ask, and answer. This wild man felt it to be of *infinite* moment; all other things of no moment whatever in com-

parison. The jargon of argumentative Greek Sects, **Mahomet**
vague traditions of Jews, the stupid routine of Arab **not an**
Idolatry, there was no answer in these. A Hero, **impostor**
as I repeat, has this first distinction, which indeed
we may call first and last, the Alpha and Omega of
his whole Heroism, That he looks through the
shows of things into *things*. Use and wont, respectable hearsay, respectable formula: all these
are good, or are not good. There is something
behind and beyond all these, which all these must
correspond with, be the image of, or they are—
Idolatries : 'bits of black wood pretending to be
God;' to the earnest soul a mockery and abomination. Idolatries never so gilded, waited on by
heads of the Koreish, will do nothing for this
man. Though all men walk by them, what good
is it? The great Reality stands glaring there upon
him. He there has to answer it, or perish miserably.
Now, even now, or else through all Eternity never!
Answer it; *thou* must find an answer.—Ambition?
What could all Arabia do for this man ; with the
crown of Greek Heraclius, of Persian Chosroes,
and all crowns in the Earth ;—what could they all
do for him? It was not of the Earth he wanted to
hear tell; it was of the Heaven above and of the
Hell beneath. All crowns and sovereignties whatsoever, where would *they* in a few brief years be?
To be Sheik of Mecca or Arabia, and have a bit of
gilt wood put into your hand,—will that be one's
salvation? I decidedly think, not. We will leave
it altogether, this impostor hypothesis, as not credible;
not very tolerable even, worthy chiefly of dismissal
by us.

Mahomet had been wont to retire yearly, during
the month Ramadhan, into solitude and silence ; as

Islam indeed was the Arab custom; a praiseworthy custom, which such a man, above all, would find natural and useful. Communing with his own heart, in the silence of the mountains; himself silent; open to the 'small still voices:' it was a right natural custom! Mahomet was in his fortieth year, when having withdrawn to a cavern in Mount Hara, near Mecca, during this Ramadhan, to pass the month in prayer, and meditation on those great questions, he one day told his wife Kadijah, who with his household was with him or near him this year, That by the unspeakable special favour of Heaven he had now found it all out; was in doubt and darkness no longer, but saw it all. That all these Idols and Formulas were nothing, miserable bits of wood; that there was One God in and over all; and we must leave all Idols, and look to Him. That God is great; and that there is nothing else great! He is the Reality. Wooden Idols are not real; He is real. He made us at first, sustains us yet; we and all things are but the shadow of Him; a transitory garment veiling the Eternal Splendour. '*Allah akbar*, God is great;'—and then also '*Islam*,' That we must *submit* to God. That our whole strength lies in resigned submission to Him, what-soever He do to us. For this world, and for the other! The thing He sends to us, were it death and worse than death, shall be good, shall be best; we resign ourselves to God.—'If this be *Islam*,' says Goethe, 'do we not all live in *Islam?*' Yes, all of us that have any moral life; we all live so. It has ever been held the highest wisdom for a man not merely to submit to Necessity,—Necessity will make him submit,—but to know and believe well that the stern thing which Necessity had ordered was

the wisest, the best, the thing wanted there. To **Sub-**
cease his frantic pretension of scanning this great **mission**
God's-World in his small fraction of a brain; to **to God**
know that it *had* verily, though deep beyond his
soundings, a Just Law, that the soul of it was
Good;—that his part in it was to conform to the
Law of the Whole, and in devout silence follow
that; not questioning it, obeying it as unquestionable.

I say, this is yet the only true morality known.
A man is right and invincible, virtuous and on the
road towards sure conquest, precisely while he joins
himself to the great deep Law of the World, in
spite of all superficial laws, temporary appearances,
profit-and-loss calculations; he is victorious while
he coöperates with that great central Law, not
victorious otherwise:—and surely his first chance
of coöperating with it, or getting into the course of
it, is to know with his whole soul that it *is;* that
it is good, and alone good! This is the soul of
Islam; it is properly the soul of Christianity;—
for Islam is definable as a confused form of Christianity; had Christianity not been, neither had
it been. Christianity also commands us, before all,
to be resigned to God. We are to take no counsel
with flesh-and-blood; give ear to no vain cavils,
vain sorrows and wishes: to know that we know
nothing; that the worst and cruelest to our eyes is
not what it seems; that we have to receive whatsoever befalls us as sent from God above, and say,
It is good and wise, God is great! "Though He
slay me, yet will I trust in Him." Islam means
in its way Denial of Self, Annihilation of Self.
This is yet the highest Wisdom that Heaven has
revealed to our Earth.

Such light had come, as it could, to illuminate

Mahomet the Prophet of God the darkness of this wild Arab soul. A confused dazzling splendour as of life and Heaven, in the great darkness which threatened to be death: he called it revelation and the angel Gabriel;—who of us yet can know what to call it? It is the 'inspiration of the Almighty that giveth us understanding.' To *know ;* to get into the truth of anything, is ever a mystic act,—of which the best Logics can but babble on the surface. 'Is not Belief the true god-announcing Miracle?' says Novalis.—That Mahomet's whole soul, set in flame with this grand Truth vouchsafed him, should feel as if it were important and the only important thing, was very natural. That Providence had unspeakably honoured *him* by revealing it, saving him from death and darkness; that he therefore was bound to make known the same to all creatures: this is what was meant by 'Mahomet is the Prophet of God;' this too is not without its true meaning.—

The good Kadijah, we can fancy, listened to him with wonder, with doubt: at length she answered: Yes, it was *true* this that he said. One can fancy too the boundless gratitude of Mahomet; and how of all the kindnesses she had done him, this of believing the earnest struggling word he now spoke was the greatest. 'It is certain,' says Novalis, 'my Conviction gains infinitely, the moment another soul will believe in it.' It is a boundless favour.— He never forgot this good Kadijah. Long afterwards, Ayesha his young favourite wife, a woman who indeed distinguished herself among the Moslem, by all manner of qualities, through her whole long life; this young brilliant Ayesha was, one day, questioning him: "Now am not I better than Kadijah? She was a widow; old, and had lost

her looks: you love me better than you did her?" **His first**
—"No, by Allah!" answered Mahomet: "No, **converts**
by Allah! She believed in me when none else
would believe. In the whole world I had but one
friend, and she was that!"—Seid, his Slave, also
believed in him; these with his young Cousin Ali,
Abu Thaleb's son, were his first converts.

He spoke of his Doctrine to this man and that;
but the most treated it with ridicule, with indifference; in three years, 1 think, he had gained but
thirteen followers. His progress was slow enough.
His encouragement to go on, was altogether the
usual encouragement that such a man in such a case
meets. After some three years of small success,
he invited forty of his chief kindred to an entertainment; and there stood-up and told them what his
pretension was: that he had this thing to promulgate
abroad to all men; that it was the highest thing,
the one thing: which of them would second him
in that? Amid the doubt and silence of all, young
Ali, as yet a lad of sixteen, impatient of the
silence, started-up, and exclaimed in passionate
fierce language, That he would! The assembly,
among whom was Abu Thaleb, Ali's Father, could
not be unfriendly to Mahomet; yet the sight there,
of one unlettered elderly man, with a lad of sixteen,
deciding on such an enterprise against all mankind,
appeared ridiculous to them; the assembly broke-
up in laughter. Nevertheless it proved not a laughable thing; it was a very serious thing! As for
this young Ali, one cannot but like him. A noble-
minded creature, as he shows himself, now and
always afterwards; full of affection, of fiery daring.
Something chivalrous in him; brave as a lion; yet
with a grace, a truth and affection worthy of

He cannot hold his peace Christian knighthood.   He died by assassination in the Mosque at Bagdad ; a death occasioned by his own generous fairness, confidence in the fairness of others : he said, If the wound proved not unto death, they must pardon the Assassin ; but if it did, then they must slay him straightway, that so they two in the same hour might appear before God, and see which side of that quarrel was the just one !

Mahomet naturally gave offence to the Koreish, Keepers of the Caabah, superintendents of the Idols.   One or two men of influence had joined him : the thing spread slowly, but it was spreading. Naturally, he gave offence to everybody : Who is this that pretends to be wiser than we all ; that rebukes us all, as mere fools and worshippers of wood !   Abu Thaleb the good Uncle spoke with him : Could he not be silent about all that ; believe it all for himself, and not trouble others, anger the chief men, endanger himself and them all, talking of it ?   Mahomet answered : If the Sun stood on his right hand and the Moon on his left, ordering him to hold his peace, he could not obey !   No : there was something in this Truth he had got which was of Nature herself ; equal in rank to Sun, or Moon, or whatsoever thing Nature had made.   It would speak itself there, so long as the Almighty allowed it, in spite of Sun and Moon, and all Koreish and all men and things.   It must do that, and could do no other.   Mahomet answered so ; and, they say, ' burst into tears.'   Burst into tears : he felt that Abu Thaleb was good to him ; that the task he had got was no soft, but a stern and great one.

He went on speaking to who would listen to him ; publishing his Doctrine among the pilgrims as they came to Mecca; gaining adherents in this **The** place and that. Continual contradiction, hatred, **Hegira** open or secret danger attended him. His powerful relations protected Mahomet himself; but by and by, on his own advice, all his adherents had to quit Mecca, and seek refuge in Abyssinia over the sea. The Koreish grew ever angrier; laid plots, and swore oaths among them, to put Mahomet to death with their own hands. Abu Thaleb was dead, the good Kadijah was dead. Mahomet is not solicitous of sympathy from us; but his outlook at this time was one of the dismalest. He had to hide in caverns, escape in disguise; fly hither and thither; homeless, in continual peril of his life. More than once it seemed all-over with him; more than once it turned on a straw, some rider's horse taking fright or the like, whether Mahomet and his Doctrine had not ended there, and not been heard of at all. But it was not to end so.

In the thirteenth year of his mission, finding his enemies all banded against him, forty sworn men, one out of every tribe, waiting to take his life, and no continuance possible at Mecca for him any longer, Mahomet fled to the place then called Yathreb, where he had gained some adherents; the place they now call Medina, or ' *Medinat al Nabi*, the City of the Prophet,' from that circumstance. It lay some 200 miles off, through rocks and deserts; not without great difficulty, in such mood as we may fancy, he escaped thither, and found welcome. The whole East dates its era from this Flight, *Hegira* as they name it: the Year 1 of this Hegira is 622 of our Era, the fifty-third of Mahomet's life. He was now becoming an old man; his friends sinking round him one by one:

Pro-pagation by the sword his path desolate, encompassed with danger: unless he could find hope in his own heart, the outward face of things was but hopeless for him. It is so with all men in the like case. Hitherto Mahomet had professed to publish his Religion by the way of preaching and persuasion alone. But now, driven foully out of his native country, since unjust men had not only given no ear to his earnest Heaven's-message, the deep cry of his heart, but would not even let him live if he kept speaking it,—the wild Son of the Desert resolved to defend himself, like a man and Arab. If the Koreish will have it so, they shall have it. Tidings, felt to be of infinite moment to them and all men, they would not listen to these; would trample them down by sheer violence, steel and murder: well, let steel try it then! Ten years more this Mahomet had: all of fighting, of breathless impetuous toil and struggle; with what result we know.

Much has been said of Mahomet's propagating his Religion by the sword. It is no doubt far nobler what we have to boast of the Christian Religion, that it propagated itself peaceably in the way of preaching and conviction. Yet withal, if we take this for an argument of the truth or false-hood of a religion, there is a radical mistake in it. The sword indeed: but where will you get your sword! Every new opinion, at its starting, is precisely in a *minority of one*. In one man's head alone, there it dwells as yet. One man alone of the whole world believes it; there is one man against all men. That *he* take a sword, and try to propagate with that, will do little for him. You must first get your sword! On the whole, a thing will propagate itself as it can. We do not find, of the Christian Religion either, that it always disdained **Nature as** the sword, when once it had got one.   Charlemagne's **umpire** conversion of the Saxons was not by preaching.   I care little about the sword : I will allow a thing to struggle for itself in this world, with any sword or tongue or implement it has, or can lay hold of.   We will let it preach, and pamphleteer, and fight, and to the uttermost bestir itself, and do, beak and claws, whatsoever is in it; very sure that it will, in the long-run, conquer nothing which does not deserve to be conquered.   What is better than itself, it cannot put away, but only what is worse.   In this great Duel, Nature herself is umpire, and can do no wrong : the thing which is deepest-rooted in Nature, what we call *truest*, that thing and not the other will be found growing at last.

Here however, in reference to much that there is in Mahomet and his success, we are to remember what an umpire Nature is ; what a greatness, composure of depth and tolerance there is in her.   You take wheat to cast into the Earth's bosom : your wheat may be mixed with chaff, chopped straw, barn-sweepings, dust and all imaginable rubbish ; no matter : you cast it into the kind just Earth ; she grows the wheat, — the whole rubbish she silently absorbs, shrouds *it* in, says nothing of the rubbish.   The yellow wheat is growing there ; the good Earth is silent about all the rest,—has silently turned all the rest to some benefit too, and makes no complaint about it !   So everywhere in Nature ! She is true and not a lie ; and yet so great, and just, and motherly in her truth.   She requires of a thing only that it *be* genuine of heart ; she will protect it if so ; will not, if not so.   There is a soul of truth in all the things she ever gave harbour

to.   Alas, is not this the history of all highest
Truth that comes or ever came into the world?
The *body* of them all is imperfection, an element
of light *in* darkness: to us they have to come embodied in mere Logic, in some merely *scientific*
Theorem of the Universe; which *cannot* be complete; which cannot but be found, one day, *in*complete, erroneous, and so die and disappear. The
body of all Truth dies; and yet in all, I say, there
is a soul which never dies; which in new and ever-
nobler embodiment lives immortal as man himself!
It is the way with Nature. The genuine essence
of Truth never dies. That it be genuine, a voice
from the great Deep of Nature, there is the point
at Nature's judgment-seat. What *we* call pure or
impure, is not with her the final question. Not
how much chaff is in you; but whether you have
any wheat. Pure? I might say to many a man:
Yes, you are pure; pure enough; but you are
chaff, — insincere hypothesis, hearsay, formality;
you never were in contact with the great heart of
the Universe at all; you are properly neither pure
nor impure; you *are* nothing, Nature has no
business with you.

Mahomet's Creed we called a kind of Christianity;
and really, if we look at the wild rapt earnestness
with which it was believed and laid to heart, I
should say a better kind than that of those miserable Syrian Sects, with their vain janglings about
Homoiousion and *Homoousion*, the head full of worthless noise, the heart empty and dead! The truth
of it is embedded in portentous error and falsehood;
but the truth of it makes it be believed, not the falsehood: it succeeded by its truth. A bastard kind of
Christianity, but a living kind; with a heart-life in

it : not dead, chopping barren logic merely ! Out of all that rubbish of Arab idolatries, argumentative theologies, traditions, subtleties, rumours and hypotheses of Greeks and Jews, with their idle wire-drawings, this wild man of the Desert, with his wild sincere heart, earnest as death and life, with his great flashing natural eyesight, had seen into the kernel of the matter. Idolatry is nothing : these Wooden Idols of yours, ' ye rub them with oil and wax, and the flies stick on them,'—these are wood, I tell you ! They can do nothing for you ; they are an impotent blasphemous pretence ; a horror and abomination, if ye knew them. God alone is ; God alone has power ; He made us, He can kill us and keep us alive : ' *Allah akbar*, God is great.' Understand that His will is the best for you ; that howsoever sore to flesh-and-blood, you will find it the wisest, best : you are bound to take it so ; in this world and in the next, you have no other thing that you can do ! *[margin: Allah akbar, God is great]*

And now if the wild idolatrous men did believe this, and with their fiery hearts laid hold of it to do it, in what form soever it came to them, I say it was well worthy of being believed. In one form or the other, I say it is still the one thing worthy of being believed by all men. Man does hereby become the high-priest of this Temple of a World. He is in harmony with the Decrees of the Author of this World ; coöperating with them, not vainly withstanding them : I know, to this day, no better definition of Duty than that same. All that is *right* includes itself in this of coöperating with the real Tendency of the World ; you succeed by this (the World's Tendency will succeed), you are good, and in the right course there. *Homoiousion*,

The Koran *Homoousion,* vain logical jangle, then or before or at any time, may jangle itself out, and go whither and how it likes: this is the *thing* it all struggles to mean, if it would mean anything. If it do not succeed in meaning this, it means nothing. Not that Abstractions, logical Propositions, be correctly worded or incorrectly; but that living concrete Sons of Adam do lay this to heart: that is the important point. Islam devoured all these vain jangling Sects; and I think had right to do so. It was a Reality, direct from the great Heart of Nature once more. Arab idolatries, Syrian formulas, whatsoever was not equally real, had to go up in flame, —mere dead *fuel,* in various senses, for this which was *fire.*

It was during these wild warfarings and strugglings, especially after the Flight to Mecca, that Mahomet dictated at intervals his Sacred Book, which they name *Koran,* or *Reading,* 'Thing to be read.' This is the Work he and his disciples made so much of, asking all the world, Is not that a miracle? The Mahometans regard their Koran with a reverence which few Christians pay even to their Bible. It is admitted everywhere as the standard of all law and all practice; the thing to be gone-upon in speculation and life: the message sent direct out of Heaven, which this Earth has to conform to, and walk by; the thing to be read. Their Judges decide by it; all Moslem are bound to study it, seek in it for the light of their life. They have mosques where it is all read daily; thirty relays of priests take it up in succession, get through the whole each day. There, for twelve-hundred years, has the voice of this Book, at all moments, kept sounding through the ears and the hearts of so **The** many men. We hear of Mahometan Doctors that **Koran** had read it seventy-thousand times! **unread-able**

Very curious: if one sought for 'discrepancies of national taste,' here surely were the most eminent instance of that! We also can read the Koran; our Translation of it, by Sale, is known to be a very fair one. I must say, it is as toilsome reading as I ever undertook. A wearisome confused jumble, crude, incondite; endless iterations, long-winded-ness, entanglement; most crude, incondite;—in-supportable stupidity, in short! Nothing but a sense of duty could carry any European through the Koran. We read in it, as we might in the State-Paper Office, unreadable masses of lumber, that perhaps we may get some glimpses of a re-markable man. It is true we have it under dis-advantages: the Arabs see more method in it than we. Mahomet's followers found the Koran lying all in fractions, as it had been written-down at first promulgation; much of it, they say, on shoulder-blades of mutton, flung pellmell into a chest: and they published it, without any discoverable order as to time or otherwise;—merely trying, as would seem, and this not very strictly, to put the longest chapters first. The real beginning of it, in that way, lies almost at the end: for the earliest portions were the shortest. Read in its historical sequence it perhaps would not be so bad. Much of it, too, they say, is rhythmic; a kind of wild chanting song, in the original. This may be a great point; much perhaps has been lost in the Translation here. Yet with every allowance, one feels it difficult to see how any mortal ever could consider this Koran as a Book written in Heaven, too good for the Earth;

But a genuine book as a well-written book, or indeed as a *book* at all; and not a bewildered rhapsody; *written*, so far as writing goes, as badly as almost any book ever was! So much for national discrepancies, and the standard of taste.

Yet I should say, it was not unintelligible how the Arabs might so love it. When once you get this confused coil of a Koran fairly off your hands, and have it behind you at a distance, the essential type of it begins to disclose itself; and in this there is a merit quite other than the literary one. If a book come from the heart, it will contrive to reach other hearts; all art and authorcraft are of small amount to that. One would say the primary character of the Koran is that of its *genuineness*, of its being a *bonâ-fide* book. Prideaux, I know, and others have represented it as a mere bundle of juggleries; chapter after chapter got-up to excuse and varnish the author's successive sins, forward his ambitions and quackeries: but really it is time to dismiss all that. I do not assert Mahomet's continual sincerity: who is continually sincere? But I confess I can make nothing of the critic, in these times, who would accuse him of deceit *prepense;* of conscious deceit generally, or perhaps at all;—still more, of living in a mere element of conscious deceit, and writing this Koran as a forger and juggler would have done! Every candid eye, I think, will read the Koran far otherwise than so. It is the confused ferment of a great rude human soul; rude, untutored, that cannot even read; but fervent, earnest, struggling vehemently to utter itself in words. With a kind of breathless intensity he strives to utter himself; the thoughts crowd on him pellmell: for very multitude of things to say, he can get nothing

said.   The meaning that is in him shapes itself into **Not the**
no form of composition, is stated in no sequence, **work of a**
method, or coherence ;—they are not *shaped* at all, **juggler**
these thoughts of his ; flung-out unshaped, as they
struggle and tumble there, in their chaotic inarticulate state.   We said ' stupid : ' yet natural stupidity
is by no means the character of Mahomet's Book ;
it is natural uncultivation rather.   The man has not
studied speaking ; in the haste and pressure of continual fighting, has not time to mature himself into
fit speech.   The panting breathless haste and vehemence of a man struggling in the thick of battle for
life and salvation ; this is the mood he is in !   A
headlong haste ; for very magnitude of meaning, he
cannot get himself articulated into words.   The successive utterances of a soul in that mood, coloured
by the various vicissitudes of three-and-twenty years ;
now well uttered, now worse : this is the Koran.

For we are to consider Mahomet, through these
three-and-twenty years, as the centre of a world
wholly in conflict.   Battles with the Koreish and
Heathen, quarrels among his own people, back-
slidings of his own wild heart ; all this kept him
in a perpetual whirl, his soul knowing rest no more.
In wakeful nights, as one may fancy, the wild soul
of the man, tossing amid these vortices, would hail
any light of a decision for them as a veritable light
from Heaven ; *any* making-up of his mind, so blessed,
indispensable for him there, would seem the inspiration of a Gabriel.   Forger and juggler ?   No, no !
This great fiery heart, seething, simmering like a
great furnace of thoughts, was not a juggler's.   His
life was a Fact to him ; this God's Universe an
awful Fact and Reality.   He has faults enough.
The man was an uncultured semi-barbarous Son of

Nature, much of the Bedouin still clinging to him:
we must take him for that.   But for a wretched
Simulacrum, a hungry Impostor without eyes or
heart, practising for a mess of pottage such blasphemous swindlery, forgery of celestial documents,
continual high-treason against his Maker and Self,
we will not and cannot take him.

Sincerity, in all senses, seems to me the merit of
the Koran; what had rendered it precious to the
wild Arab men.   It is, after all, the first and last
merit in a book; gives rise to merits of all kinds,—
nay, at bottom, it alone can give rise to merit of
any kind.   Curiously, through these incondite
masses of tradition, vituperation, complaint, ejacu-
lation in the Koran, a vein of true direct insight,
of what we might almost call poetry, is found
straggling.   The body of the Book is made-up
of mere tradition, and as it were vehement enthusiastic extempore preaching.   He returns forever to the old stories of the Prophets as they went
current in the Arab memory: how Prophet after
Prophet, the Prophet Abraham, the Prophet Hud,
the Prophet Moses, Christian and other real and
fabulous Prophets, had come to this Tribe and to
that, warning men of their sin ; and been received
by them even as he Mahomet was,—which is a
great solace to him.   These things he repeats ten,
perhaps twenty times; again and ever again with
wearisome iteration ; has never done repeating them.
A brave Samuel Johnson, in his forlorn garret,
might con-over the Biographies of Authors in that
way !   This is the great staple of the Koran.   But
curiously, through all this, comes ever and anon
some glance as of the real thinker and seer.   He
has actually an eye for the world, this Mahomet:

with a certain directness and rugged vigour, he
brings home still, to our heart, the thing his own
heart has been opened to.   I make but little of
his praises of Allah, which many praise; they are
borrowed I suppose mainly from the Hebrew, at
least they are far surpassed there.   But the eye
that flashes direct into the heart of things, and *sees*
the truth of them ; this is to me a highly interesting object.   Great Nature's own gift; which she
bestows on all; but which only one in the thousand
does not cast sorrowfully away: it is what I call
sincerity of vision ; the test of a sincere heart.

The
world
'a sign
to you'

Mahomet can work no miracles;   he often
answers impatiently: I can work no miracles. I?
'I am a Public Preacher;' appointed to preach
this doctrine to all creatures.   Yet the world, as
we can see, had really from of old been all one
great miracle to him.   Look over the world, says
he; is it not wonderful, the work of Allah;
wholly 'a sign to you,' if your eyes were open !
This Earth, God made it for you : 'appointed
paths in it;' you can live in it, go to and fro on
it.—The clouds in the dry country of Arabia, to
Mahomet they are very wonderful : Great clouds,
he says, born in the deep bosom of the Upper
Immensity, where do they come from !   They hang
there, the great black monsters ; pour-down their rain
deluges 'to revive a dead earth,' and grass springs, and
'tall leafy palm-trees with their date-clusters hang-
'ing round.   Is not that a sign ?'   Your cattle too,
—Allah made them; serviceable dumb creatures ;
they change the grass into milk ; you have your
clothing from them, very strange creatures ; they
come ranking home at evening-time, 'and,' adds
he, 'and are a credit to you!'   Ships also,—he

talks often about ships : Huge moving mountains,
they spread-out their cloth wings, go bounding
through the water there, Heaven's wind driving
them ; anon they lie motionless, God has withdrawn the wind, they lie dead, and cannot stir !
Miracles ? cries he ; what miracle would you
have ? Are not you yourselves there ? God made
you, 'shaped you out of a little clay.' Ye were
small once ; a few years ago ye were not at all.
Ye have beauty, strength, thoughts, 'ye have compassion on one another.' Old age comes-on you,
and gray hairs ; your strength fades into feeble-
ness ; ye sink down, and again are not. 'Ye have
compassion on one another : ' this struck me much :
Allah might have made you having no compassion
on one another,—how had it been then ! This is
a great direct thought, a glance at first-hand into
the very fact of things. Rude vestiges of poetic
genius, of whatsoever is best and truest, are visible in
this man. A strong untutored intellect : eyesight,
heart ; a strong wild man,—might have shaped
himself into Poet, King, Priest, any kind of Hero.

To his eyes it is forever clear that this world
wholly is miraculous. He sees what, as we said once
before, all great thinkers, the rude Scandinavians
themselves, in one way or other, have contrived to
see : That this so solid-looking material world is,
at bottom, in very deed, Nothing ; is a visual and
tactual Manifestation of God's power and presence,
—a shadow hung-out by Him on the bosom of the
void Infinite ; nothing more. The Mountains, he
says, these great rock-mountains, they shall dis-
sipate themselves 'like clouds ; ' melt into the Blue
as clouds do, and not be ! He figures the Earth,
in the Arab fashion, Sale tells us, as an immense

Plain or flat Plate of ground, the mountains are set on that to *steady* it. At the Last Day they shall disappear ' like clouds ; ' the whole Earth shall go spinning, whirl itself off into wreck, and as dust and vapour vanish in the Inane. Allah withdraws his hand from it, and it ceases to be. The universal empire of Allah, presence everywhere of an unspeakable Power, a Splendour, and a Terror not to be named, as the true force, essence and reality, in all things whatsoever, was continually clear to this man. What a modern talks-of by the name, Forces of Nature, Laws of Nature ; and does not figure as a divine thing ; not even as one thing at all, but as a set of things, undivine enough,—saleable, curious, good for propelling steam-ships ! With our Sciences and Cyclopædias, we are apt to forget the *divineness*, in these laboratories of ours. We ought not to forget it ! That once well forgotten, I know not what else were worth remembering. Most sciences, I think, were then a very dead thing ; withered, contentious, empty ;— a thistle in late autumn. The best science, without this, is but as the dead *timber* ; it is not the growing tree and forest,—which gives ever-new timber, among other things ! Man cannot *know* either, unless he can *worship* in some way. His knowledge is a pedantry, and dead thistle, otherwise.

Much has been said and written about the sensuality of Mahomet's Religion ; more than was just. The indulgences, criminal to us, which he permitted, were not of his appointment ; he found them practised, unquestioned from immemorial time in Arabia ; what he did was to curtail them, restrict them, not on one but on many sides. His Religion is not an easy one : with rigorous fasts, lavations,

No knowledge without worship

Religion not based on sensuality strict complex formulas, prayers five times a day, and abstinence from wine, it did not 'succeed by being an easy religion.' As if indeed any religion, or cause holding of religion, could succeed by that! It is a calumny on men to say that they are roused to heroic action by ease, hope of pleasure, recompense,—sugar-plums of any kind, in this world or the next! In the meanest mortal there lies something nobler. The poor swearing soldier, hired to be shot, has his 'honour of a soldier,' different from drill-regulations and the shilling a day. It is not to taste sweet things, but to do noble and true things, and vindicate himself under God's Heaven as a god-made Man, that the poorest son of Adam dimly longs. Show him the way of doing that, the dullest daydrudge kindles into a hero. They wrong man greatly who say he is to be seduced by ease. Difficulty, abnegation, martyrdom, death are the *allurements* that act on the heart of man. Kindle the inner genial life of him, you have a flame that burns-up all lower considerations. Not happiness, but something higher: one sees this even in the frivolous classes, with their 'point of honour' and the like. Not by flattering our appetites; no, by awakening the Heroic that slumbers in every heart, can any Religion gain followers.

Mahomet himself, after all that can be said about him, was not a sensual man. We shall err widely if we consider this man as a common voluptuary, intent mainly on base enjoyments,—nay on enjoyments of any kind. His household was of the frugalest; his common diet barley-bread and water: sometimes for months there was not a fire once lighted on his hearth. They record with just pride that he would mend his own shoes, patch his own

cloak. A poor, hard-toiling, ill-provided man; **Mahomet**
careless of what vulgar men toil for. Not a bad **not a**
man, I should say; something better in him than **sensualist**
hunger of any sort,—or these wild Arab men,
fighting and jostling three-and-twenty years at his
hand, in close contact with him always, would not
have reverenced him so! They were wild men,
bursting ever and anon into quarrel, into all kinds of
fierce sincerity; without right worth and manhood,
no man could have commanded them. They called
him Prophet, you say? Why, he stood there face
to face with them; bare, not enshrined in any
mystery; visibly clouting his own cloak, cobbling
his own shoes; fighting, counselling, ordering in
the midst of them : they must have seen what kind
of a man he *was*, let him be *called* what you like!
No emperor with his tiaras was obeyed as this man
in a cloak of his own clouting. During three-and-
twenty years of rough actual trial. I find something
of a veritable Hero necessary for that, of itself.

His last words are a prayer; broken ejaculations
of a heart struggling-up, in trembling hope, towards
its Maker. We cannot say that his religion made
him *worse* ; it made him better; good, not bad.
Generous things are recorded of him : when he lost
his Daughter, the thing he answers is, in his own
dialect, everyway sincere, and yet equivalent to that
of Christians, 'The Lord giveth, and the Lord
taketh away; blessed be the name of the Lord.'
He answered in like manner of Seid, his emanci-
pated well-beloved Slave, the second of the believers.   Seid had fallen in the War of Tabûc, the
first of Mahomet's fightings with the Greeks.
Mahomet said, It was well; Seid had done his
Master's work, Seid had now gone to his Master :

His
freedom
from cant
it was all well with Seid.   Yet Seid's daughter
found him weeping over the body ;—the old gray-
haired man melting in tears !   " What do I see ? "
said she.—" You see a friend weeping over his
friend."—He went out for the last time into the
mosque, two days before his death ; asked, If he
had injured any man ?   Let his own back bear the
stripes.   If he owed any man ?   A voice answered,
" Yes, me three drachms," borrowed on such an
occasion.   Mahomet ordered them to be paid :
" Better be in shame now," said he, " than at the
Day of Judgment."—You remember Kadijah, and
the " No, by Allah ! "   Traits of that kind show
us the genuine man, the brother of us all, brought
visible through twelve centuries,—the veritable Son
of our common Mother.

Withal I like Mahomet for his total freedom
from cant.   He is a rough self-helping son of the
wilderness ; does not pretend to be what he is not.
There is no ostentatious pride in him ; but neither
does he go much upon humility : he is there as he
can be, in cloak and shoes of his own clouting ;
speaks plainly to all manner of Persian Kings,
Greek Emperors, what it is they are bound to do ;
knows well enough, about himself, ' the respect due
unto thee.'   In a life-and-death war with Bedouins,
cruel things could not fail ; but neither are acts of
mercy, of noble natural pity and generosity wanting.
Mahomet makes no apology for the one, no boast
of the other.   They were each the free dictate of
his heart ; each called-for, there and then.   Not a
mealy-mouthed man !   A candid ferocity, if the
case call for it, is in him ; he does not mince
matters !   The War of Tabûc is a thing he often
speaks of : his men refused, many of them, to march

on that occasion: pleaded the heat of the weather, the harvest, and so forth; he can never forget that. Your harvest? It lasts for a day. What will become of your harvest through all Eternity? Hot weather? Yes, it was hot; 'but Hell will be hotter!' Sometimes a rough sarcasm turns-up: He says to the unbelievers, Ye shall have the just measure of your deeds at that Great Day. They will be weighed-out to you; ye shall not have short weight!—Everywhere he fixes the matter in his eye; he *sees* it: his heart, now and then, is as if struck dumb by the greatness of it. 'Assuredly,' he says: that word, in the Koran, is written-down sometimes as a sentence by itself: 'Assuredly.'

No *Dilettantism* in this Mahomet; it is a business of Reprobation and Salvation with him, of Time and Eternity: he is in deadly earnest about it! Dilettantism, hypothesis, speculation, a kind of amateur-search for Truth, toying and coquetting with Truth: this is the sorest sin. The root of all other imaginable sins. It consists in the heart and soul of the man never having been *open* to Truth;—'living in a vain show.' Such a man not only utters and produces falsehoods, but *is* himself a falsehood. The rational moral principle, spark of the Divinity, is sunk deep in him, in quiet paralysis of life-death. The very falsehoods of Mahomet are truer than the truths of such a man. He is the insincere man: smooth-polished, respectable in some times and places: inoffensive, says nothing harsh to anybody; most *cleanly*,—just as carbonic acid is, which is death and poison.

We will not praise Mahomet's moral precepts as always of the superfinest sort; yet it can be said that there is always a tendency to good in them;

**Maho-
met's
Paradise** that they are the true dictates of a heart aiming towards what is just and true. The sublime forgiveness of Christianity, turning of the other cheek when the one has been smitten, is not here: you *are* to revenge yourself, but it is to be in measure, not overmuch, or beyond justice. On the other hand, Islam, like any great Faith, and insight into the essence of man, is a perfect equaliser of men: the soul of one believer outweighs all earthly kingships; all men, according to Islam too, are equal. Mahomet insists not on the propriety of giving alms, but on the necessity of it; he marks-down by law how much you are to give, and it is at your peril if you neglect. The tenth part of a man's annual income, whatever that may be, is the *property* of the poor, of those that are afflicted and need help. Good all this: the natural voice of humanity, of pity and equity dwelling in the heart of this wild Son of Nature speaks *so*.

Mahomet's Paradise is sensual, his Hell sensual: true; in the one and the other there is enough that shocks all spiritual feeling in us. But we are to recollect that the Arabs already had it so; that Mahomet, in whatever he changed of it, softened and diminished all this. The worst sensualities, too, are the work of doctors, followers of his, not his work. In the Koran there is really very little said about the joys of Paradise; they are intimated rather than insisted on. Nor is it forgotten that the highest joys even there shall be spiritual; the pure Presence of the Highest, this shall infinitely transcend all other joys. He says, 'Your salutation shall be, Peace.' *Salam*, Have Peace!—the thing that all rational souls long for, and seek, vainly here below, as the one blessing. 'Ye shall sit on seats, 'facing one another: all grudges shall be taken **Maho-** away out of your hearts.' All grudges! Ye shall **met's** love one another freely; for each of you, in the eyes **Paradise** of his brothers, there will be Heaven enough!

In reference to this of the sensual Paradise and Mahomet's sensuality, the sorest chapter of all for us, there were many things to be said; which it is not convenient to enter upon here. Two remarks only I shall make, and therewith leave it to your candour. The first is furnished me by Goethe; it is a casual hint of his which seems well worth taking note of. In one of his Delineations, in *Meister's Travels* it is, the hero comes-upon a Society of men with very strange ways, one of which was this: "We require," says the Master, "that each of our people shall restrict himself in one direction," shall go right against his desire in one matter, and *make* himself do the thing he does not wish, "should we allow him the greater latitude on all other sides." There seems to me a great justness in this. Enjoying things which are pleasant; that is not the evil: it is the reducing of our moral self to slavery by them that is. Let a man assert withal that he is king over his habitudes; that he could and would shake them off, on cause shown: this is an excellent law. The Month Ramadhan for the Moslem, much in Mahomet's Religion, much in his own Life, bears in that direction; if not by forethought, or clear purpose of moral improvement on his part, then by a certain healthy manful instinct, which is as good.

But there is another thing to be said about the Mahometan Heaven and Hell. This namely, that, however gross and material they may be, they are an emblem of an everlasting truth, not always so well

The infinite nature of Duty remembered elsewhere. That gross sensual Paradise of his; that horrible flaming Hell; the great enormous Day of Judgment he perpetually insists on: what is all this but a rude shadow, in the rude Bedouin imagination, of that grand spiritual Fact, and Beginning of Facts, which it is ill for us too if we do not all know and feel: the Infinite Nature of Duty? That man's actions here are of *infinite* moment to him, and never die or end at all; that man, with his little life, reaches upwards high as Heaven, downwards low as Hell, and in his threescore years of Time holds an Eternity fearfully and wonderfully hidden: all this had burnt itself, as in flame-characters, into the wild Arab soul. As in flame and lightning, it stands written there; awful, unspeakable, ever present to him. With bursting earnestness, with a fierce savage sincerity, halt, articulating, not able to articulate, he strives to speak it, bodies it forth in that Heaven and that Hell. Bodied forth in what way you will, it is the first of all truths. It is venerable under all embodiments. What is the chief end of man here below? Mahomet has answered this question, in a way that might put some of *us* to shame! He does not, like a Bentham, a Paley, take Right and Wrong, and calculate the profit and loss, ultimate pleasure of the one and of the other; and summing all up by addition and subtraction into a net result, ask you, Whether on the whole the Right does not preponderate considerably? No, it is not *better* to do the one than the other; the one is to the other as life is to death,—as Heaven is to Hell. The one must in nowise be done, the other in nowise left undone. You shall not measure them; they are incommensurable: the one is death

eternal to a man, the other is life eternal. Bentha-
mee Utility, virtue by Profit and Loss; reducing
this God's-world to a dead brute Steam-engine,
the infinite celestial Soul of Man to a kind of
Hay-balance for weighing hay and thistles on,
pleasures and pains on:—If you ask me which
gives, Mahomet or they, the beggarlier and falser
view of Man and his Destinies in this Universe, I
will answer, It is not Mahomet!——

Maho-
metanism
a religion
that is
believed

On the whole, we will repeat that this Religion
of Mahomet's is a kind of Christianity; has a
genuine element of what is spiritually highest looking through it, not to be hidden by all its imperfections. The Scandinavian God *Wish*, the god of all
rude men,—this has been enlarged into a Heaven
by Mahomet; but a Heaven symbolical of sacred
Duty, and to be earned by faith and welldoing, by
valiant action, and a divine patience which is still
more valiant. It is Scandinavian Paganism, and a
truly celestial element superadded to that. Call it
not false; look not at the falsehood of it, look
at the truth of it. For these twelve centuries, it
has been the religion and life-guidance of the fifth
part of the whole kindred of Mankind. Above all
things, it has been a religion heartily *believed*.
These Arabs believe their religion, and try to
live by it! No Christians, since the early ages,
or only perhaps the English Puritans in modern
times, have ever stood by their Faith as the
Moslem do by theirs,—believing it wholly, front-
ing Time with it, and Eternity with it. This
night the watchman on the streets of Cairo when
he cries "Who goes?" will hear from the passenger,
along with his answer, "There is no God but God."
Allah akbar, Islam, sounds through the souls, and

It has made Arabia great whole daily existence, of these dusky millions. Zealous missionaries preach it abroad among Malays, black Papuans, brutal Idolators ;—displacing what is worse, nothing that is better or good.

To the Arab Nation it was as a birth from darkness into light ; Arabia first became alive by means of it. A poor shepherd people, roaming unnoticed in its deserts since the creation of the world : a Hero-Prophet was sent down to them with a word they could believe : see, the unnoticed becomes world-notable, the small has grown world-great ; within one century afterwards, Arabia is at Grenada on this hand, at Delhi on that ;—glancing in valour and splendour and the light of genius, Arabia shines through long ages over a great section of the world. Belief is great, life-giving. The history of a Nation becomes fruitful, soul-elevating, great, so soon as it believes. These Arabs, the man Mahomet, and that one century,—is it not as if a spark had fallen, one spark, on a world of what seemed black unnoticeable sand ; but lo, the sand proves explosive powder, blazes heaven-high from Delhi to Grenada ! I said, the Great Man was always as lightning out of Heaven ; the rest of men waited for him like fuel, and then they too would flame.

LECTURE III

THE HERO AS POET.   DANTE ; SHAKSPEARE.

[*Tuesday,* 12*th May* 1840]

THE Hero as Divinity, the Hero as Prophet, are productions of old ages ; not to be repeated in the new. They presuppose a certain rudeness of

conception, which the progress of mere scientific Varieties
knowledge puts an end to. There needs to be, as it of the
were, a world vacant, or almost vacant of scientific Great
forms, if men in their loving wonder are to fancy Man
their fellow-man either a god or one speaking with
the voice of a god. Divinity and Prophet are past.
We are now to see our Hero in the less ambitious,
but also less questionable, character of Poet; a
character which does not pass. The Poet is a
heroic figure belonging to all ages; whom all ages
possess, when once he is produced, whom the newest age as the oldest may produce ;—and will produce, always when Nature pleases. Let Nature
send a Hero-soul; in no age is it other than
possible that he may be shaped into a Poet.

Hero, Prophet, Poet,—many different names, in
different times and places, do we give to Great
Men; according to varieties we note in them,
according to the sphere in which they have dis-
played themselves! We might give many more
names, on this same principle. I will remark again,
however, as a fact not unimportant to be understood,
that the different *sphere* constitutes the grand origin
of such distinction; that the Hero can be Poet,
Prophet, King, Priest or what you will, according
to the kind of world he finds himself born into. I
confess, I have no notion of a truly great man that
could not be *all* sorts of men. The Poet who
could merely sit on a chair, and compose stanzas,
would never make a stanza worth much. He
could not sing the Heroic warrior, unless he himself were at least a Heroic warrior too. I fancy
there is in him the Politician, the Thinker, Legis-
lator, Philosopher ;—in one or the other degree, he
could have been, he is all these. So too I cannot

understand how a Mirabeau, with that great glowing
heart, with the fire that was in it, with the bursting
tears that were in it, could not have written verses,
tragedies, poems, touched all hearts in that way, had
his course of life and education led him thither-
ward.   The grand fundamental character is that of
Great Man; that the man be great.   Napoleon has
words in him which are like Austerlitz Battles.
Louis Fourteenth's Marshals are a kind of poetical
men withal; the things Turenne says are full of
sagacity and geniality, like sayings of Samuel Johnson.   The great heart, the clear deep-seeing eye:
there it lies; no man whatever, in what province
soever, can prosper at all without these.   Petrarch
and Boccaccio did diplomatic messages, it seems,
quite well: one can easily believe it; they had
done things a little harder than these!   Burns, a
gifted song-writer, might have made a still better
Mirabeau.   Shakspeare,—one knows not what *he*
could not have made, in the supreme degree.

True, there are aptitudes of Nature too.   Nature
does not make all great men, more than all other
men, in the self-same mould.   Varieties of aptitude
doubtless; but infinitely more of circumstance; and
far oftenest it is the *latter* only that are looked to.
But it is as with common men in the learning of
trades.   You take any man, as yet a vague capability of a man, who could be any kind of craftsman; and make him into a smith, a carpenter, a
mason: he is then and thenceforth that and nothing
else.   And if, as Addison complains, you sometimes
see a street-porter staggering under his load on
spindle-shanks, and near at hand a tailor with the
frame of a Samson handling a bit of cloth and
small Whitechapel needle,—it cannot be considered

that aptitude of Nature alone has been consulted **The Divine Idea of the world** here either!—The Great Man also, to what shall he be bound apprentice? Given your Hero, is he to become Conqueror, King, Philosopher, Poet? It is an inexplicably complex controversial-calculation between the world and him! He will read the world and its laws; the world with its laws will be there to be read. What the world, on *this* matter, shall permit and bid is, as we said, the most important fact about the world.—

Poet and Prophet differ greatly in our loose modern notions of them. In some old languages, again, the titles are synonymous; *Vates* means both Prophet and Poet: and indeed at all times, Prophet and Poet, well understood, have much kindred of meaning. Fundamentally indeed they are still the same; in this most important respect especially, That they have penetrated both of them into the sacred mystery of the Universe; what Goethe calls 'the open secret.' "Which is the great secret?" asks one.—"The *open* secret,"—open to all, seen by almost none! That divine mystery, which lies everywhere in all Beings, 'the Divine Idea of the World, that which lies at the bottom of Appearance,' as Fichte styles it; of which all Appearance, from the starry sky to the grass of the field, but especially the Appearance of Man and his work, is but the *vesture*, the embodiment that renders it visible. This divine mystery *is* in all times and in all places; veritably is. In most times and places it is greatly overlooked; and the Universe, definable always in one or the other dialect, as the realised Thought of God, is considered a trivial, inert, commonplace matter,—as if, says the Satirist,

Poet and Prophet it were a dead thing, which some upholsterer had put together! It could do no good, at present, to *speak* much about this; but it is a pity for every one of us if we do not know it, live ever in the knowledge of it. Really a most mournful pity;—a failure to live at all, if we live otherwise!

But now, I say, whoever may forget this divine mystery, the *Vates*, whether Prophet or Poet, has penetrated into it; is a man sent hither to make it more impressively known to us. That always is his message; he is to reveal that to us,—that sacred mystery which he more than others lives ever present with. While others forget it, he knows it;—I might say, he has been driven to know it; without consent asked of *him*, he finds himself living in it, bound to live in it. Once more, here is no Hearsay, but a direct Insight and Belief; this man too could not help being a sincere man! Whosoever may live in the shows of things, it is for him a necessity of nature to live in the very fact of things. A man once more, in earnest with the Universe, though all others were but toying with it. He is a *Vates*, first of all, in virtue of being sincere. So far Poet and Prophet, participators in the 'open secret,' are one.

With respect to their distinction again: The *Vates* Prophet, we might say, has seized that sacred mystery rather on the moral side, as Good and Evil, Duty and Prohibition; the *Vates* Poet on what the Germans call the æsthetic side, as Beautiful, and the like. The one we may call a revealer of what we are to do, the other of what we are to love. But indeed these two provinces run into one another, and cannot be disjoined. The Prophet too has his eye on what we are to love:

how else shall he know what it is we are to do? All men
The highest Voice ever heard on this earth said in some
withal, " Consider the lilies of the field ; they toil sense
not, neither do they spin : yet Solomon in all his poets
glory was not arrayed like one of these." A
glance, that, into the deepest deep of Beauty.
' The lilies of the field,' — dressed finer than
earthly princes, springing-up there in the humble
furrow-field ; a beautiful *eye* looking-out on you,
from the great inner Sea of Beauty ! How could
the rude Earth make these, if her Essence, rugged
as she looks and is, were not inwardly Beauty ? In
this point of view, too, a saying of Goethe's, which
has staggered several, may have meaning: 'The
Beautiful,' he intimates, 'is higher than the Good:
the Beautiful includes in it the Good.' The *true*
Beautiful; which however, I have said somewhere,
' differs from the *false* as Heaven does from Vauxhall ! ' So much for the distinction and identity of
Poet and Prophet.—-

In ancient and also in modern periods we find a
few Poets who are accounted perfect; whom it were
a kind of treason to find fault with. This is noteworthy ; this is right: yet in strictness it is only an
illusion. At bottom, clearly enough, there is no
perfect Poet ! A vein of Poetry exists in the
hearts of all men ; no man is made altogether of
Poetry. We are all poets when we *read* a poem
well. The ' imagination that shudders at the Hell
of Dante,' is not that the same faculty, weaker in
degree, as Dante's own ? No one but Shakspeare
can embody, out of *Saxo Grammaticus*, the story of
Hamlet as Shakspeare did : but every one models
some kind of story out of it ; every one embodies it
better or worse. We need not spend time in de-

Poetry is music fining. Where there is no specific difference, as between round and square, all definition must be more or less arbitrary. A man that has *so* much more of the poetic element developed in him as to have become noticeable, will be called Poet by his neighbours. World-Poets too, those whom we are to take for perfect Poets, are settled by critics in the same way. One who rises *so* far above the general level of Poets will, to such and such critics, seem a Universal Poet; as he ought to do. And yet it is, and must be, an arbitrary distinction. All Poets, all men, have some touches of the Universal; no man is wholly made of that. Most Poets are very soon forgotten: but not the noblest Shakspeare or Homer of them can be remembered *forever*;—a day comes when he too is not!

Nevertheless, you will say, there must be a difference between true Poetry and true Speech not poetical: what is the difference? On this point many things have been written, especially by late German Critics, some of which are not very intelligible at first. They say, for example, that the Poet has an *infinitude* in him; communicates an *Unendlichkeit*, a certain character of 'infinitude,' to whatsoever he delineates. This, though not very precise, yet on so vague a matter is worth remembering: if well meditated, some meaning will gradually be found in it. For my own part, I find considerable meaning in the old vulgar distinction of Poetry being *metrical*, having music in it, being a Song. Truly, if pressed to give a definition, one might say this as soon as anything else: If your delineation be authentically *musical*, musical, not in word only, but in heart and substance, in all the thoughts and utterances of it, in the whole conception of it, then it will be poetical; if not, not.—Musical: how much **Song the** lies in that! A *musical* thought is one spoken by a **central** mind that has penetrated into the inmost heart of the **essence of things** thing; detected the inmost mystery of it, namely the *melody* that lies hidden in it; the inward harmony of coherence which is its soul, whereby it exists, and has a right to be, here in this world. All inmost things, we may say, are melodious; naturally utter themselves in Song. The meaning of Song goes deep. Who is there that, in logical words, can express the effect music has on us? A kind of inarticulate unfathomable speech, which leads us to the edge of the Infinite, and lets us for moments gaze into that!

Nay all speech, even the commonest speech, has something of song in it: not a parish in the world but has its parish-accent;—the rhythm or *tune* to which the people there *sing* what they have to say! Accent is a kind of chanting; all men have accent of their own,—though they only *notice* that of others. Observe too how all passionate language does of itself become musical,—with a finer music than the mere accent; the speech of a man even in zealous anger becomes a chant, a song. All deep things are Song. It seems somehow the very central essence of us, Song; as if all the rest were but wrappages and hulls! The primal element of us; of us, and of all things. The Greeks fabled of Sphere-Harmonies; it was the feeling they had of the inner structure of Nature; that the soul of all her voices and utterances was perfect music. Poetry, therefore, we will call *musical Thought*. The Poet is he who *thinks* in that manner. At bottom, it turns still on power of intellect; it is a man's sincerity and depth of vision that makes him a Poet.

**Estimate
of great
men**
See deep enough, and you see musically; the heart of Nature *being* everywhere music, if you can only reach it.

The *Vates* Poet, with his melodious Apocalypse of Nature, seems to hold a poor rank among us, in comparison with the *Vates* Prophet; his function, and our esteem of him for his function, alike slight. The Hero taken as Divinity; the Hero taken as Prophet; then next the Hero taken only as Poet: does it not look as if our estimate of the Great Man, epoch after epoch, were continually diminishing? We take him first for a god, then for one god-inspired; and now in the next stage of it, his most miraculous word gains from us only the recognition that he is a Poet, beautiful verse-maker, man of genius, or suchlike!—It looks so; but I persuade myself that intrinsically it is not so. If we consider well, it will perhaps appear that in man still there is the *same* altogether peculiar admiration for the Heroic Gift, by what name soever called, that there at any time was.

I should say, if we do not now reckon a Great Man literally divine, it is that our notions of God, of the supreme unattainable Fountain of Splendour, Wisdom and Heroism, are ever rising *higher ;* not altogether that our reverence for these qualities, as manifested in our like, is getting lower. This is worth taking thought of. Sceptical Dilettantism, the curse of these ages, a curse which will not last forever, does indeed in this the highest province of human things, as in all provinces, make sad work; and our reverence for great men, all crippled, blinded, paralytic as it is, comes out in poor plight, hardly recognisable. Men worship the shows of great men; the most disbelieve that there is any

reality of great men to worship. The dreariest, **Shaks-**
fatalest faith; believing which, one would literally **peare and**
despair of human things. Nevertheless look, for **Dante**
example, at Napoleon! A Corsican lieutenant of
artillery; that is the show of *him:* yet is he not
obeyed, *worshipped* after his sort, as all the Tiaraed
and Diademed of the world put together could not
be? High Duchesses, and ostlers of inns, gather
round the Scottish rustic, Burns;—a strange feeling
dwelling in each that they had never heard a man
like this; that, on the whole, this is the man! In
the secret heart of these people it still dimly reveals
itself, though there is no accredited way of uttering
it at present, that this rustic, with his black brows
and flashing sun-eyes, and strange words moving
laughter and tears, is of a dignity far beyond all
others, incommensurable with all others. Do not
we feel it so? But now, were Dilettantism, Scepticism, Triviality, and all that sorrowful brood,
cast-out of us,—as, by God's blessing, they shall
one day be; were faith in the shows of things
entirely swept-out, replaced by clear faith in the
things, so that a man acted on the impulse of that
only, and counted the other non-extant; what a
new livelier feeling towards this Burns were it!

Nay here in these pages, such as they are, have
we not two mere Poets, if not deified, yet we
may say beatified? Shakspeare and Dante are
Saints of Poetry; really, if we will think of it,
canonised, so that it is impiety to meddle with them.
The unguided instinct of the world, working across
all these perverse impediments, has arrived at such
result. Dante and Shakspeare are a peculiar Two.
They dwell apart, in a kind of royal solitude;
none equal, none second to them: in the general

Dante in Giotto's portrait feeling of the world, a certain transcendentalism, a glory as of complete perfection, invests these two. They *are* canonised, though no Pope or Cardinals took hand in doing it! Such, in spite of every perverting influence, in the most unheroic times, is still our indestructible reverence for heroism.—We will look a little at these Two, the Poet Dante and the Poet Shakspeare: what little it is permitted us to say here of the Hero as Poet will most fitly arrange itself in that fashion.

Many volumes have been written by way of commentary on Dante and his Book; yet, on the whole, with no great result. His Biography is, as it were, irrecoverably lost for us. An unimportant, wandering, sorrowstricken man, not much note was taken of him while he lived; and the most of that has vanished, in the long space that now intervenes. It is five centuries since he ceased writing and living here. After all commentaries, the Book itself is mainly what we know of him. The Book;—and one might add that Portrait commonly attributed to Giotto, which, looking on it, you cannot help inclining to think genuine, whoever did it. To me it is a most touching face; perhaps of all faces that I know, the most so. Lonely there, painted as on vacancy, with the simple laurel wound round it; the deathless sorrow and pain, the known victory which is also deathless;—significant of the whole history of Dante! I think it is the mournfulest face that ever was painted from reality; an altogether tragic, heart-affecting face. There is in it, as foundation of it, the softness, tenderness, gentle affection as of a child; but all this is as if congealed into sharp contradiction, into abnegation, isolation, proud hope-

less pain. A soft ethereal soul looking-out so stern, **His**
implacable, grim-trenchant, as from imprisonment **education**
of thick-ribbed ice! Withal it is a silent pain too,
a silent scornful one: the lip is curled in a kind of
godlike disdain of the thing that is eating-out his
heart,—as if it were withal a mean insignificant
thing, as if he whom it had power to torture and
strangle were greater than it. The face of one
wholly in protest, and life - long unsurrendering
battle, against the world. Affection all converted
into indignation: an implacable indignation; slow,
equable, silent, like that of a god! The eye too,
it looks-out as in a kind of *surprise*, a kind of inquiry,
Why the world was of such a sort? This is Dante:
so he looks, this 'voice of ten silent centuries,' and
sings us 'his mystic unfathomable song.'

The little that we know of Dante's Life corre-
sponds well enough with this Portrait and this Book.
He was born at Florence, in the upper class of
society, in the year 1265. His education was the
best then going; much school-divinity, Aristotelean
logic, some Latin classics,—no inconsiderable insight
into certain provinces of things: and Dante, with
his earnest intelligent nature, we need not doubt,
learned better than most all that was learnable.
He has a clear cultivated understanding, and of
great subtlety; the best fruit of education he had
contrived to realise from these scholastics. He
knows accurately and well what lies close to him;
but, in such a time, without printed books or free
intercourse, he could not know well what was
distant: the small clear light, most luminous for
what is near, breaks itself into singular *chiaroscuro*
striking on what is far off. This was Dante's
learning from the schools. In life, he had gone

His early life through the usual destinies; been twice out campaigning as a soldier for the Florentine State, been on embassy; had in his thirty-fifth year, by natural gradation of talent and service, become one of the Chief Magistrates of Florence. He had met in boyhood a certain Beatrice Portinari, a beautiful little girl of his own age and rank, and grown-up thenceforth in partial sight of her, in some distant intercourse with her. All readers know his graceful affecting account of this; and then of their being parted; of her being wedded to another, and of her death soon after. She makes a great figure in Dante's Poem; seems to have made a great figure in his life. Of all beings it might seem as if she, held apart from him, far apart at last in the dim Eternity, were the only one he had ever with his whole strength of affection loved. She died: Dante himself was wedded; but it seems not happily, far from happily. I fancy, the rigorous earnest man, with his keen excitabilities, was not altogether easy to make happy.

We will not complain of Dante's miseries: had all gone right with him as he wished it, he might have been Prior, Podestà, or whatsoever they call it, of Florence, well accepted among neighbours,—and the world had wanted one of the most notable words ever spoken or sung. Florence would have had another prosperous Lord Mayor; and the ten dumb centuries continued voiceless, and the ten other listening centuries (for there will be ten of them and more) had no *Divina Commedia* to hear! We will complain of nothing. A nobler destiny was appointed for this Dante; and he, struggling like a man led towards death and crucifixion, could not help fulfilling it. Give *him* the choice of his happiness! He knew not, more than we do, what was **His exile** really happy, what was really miserable.

In Dante's Priorship, the Guelf - Ghibelline, Bianchi-Neri, or some other confused disturbance rose to such a height, that Dante, whose party had seemed the stronger, was with his friends cast unexpectedly forth into banishment; doomed thenceforth to a life of woe and wandering. His property was all confiscated and more; he had the fiercest feeling that it was entirely unjust, nefarious in the sight of God and man. He tried what was in him to get reinstated; tried even by warlike surprisal, with arms in his hand: but it would not do; bad only had become worse. There is a record, I believe, still extant in the Florence Archives, dooming this Dante, wheresoever caught, to be burnt alive. Burnt alive; so it stands, they say: a very curious civic document. Another curious document, some considerable number of years later, is a Letter of Dante's to the Florentine Magistrates, written in answer to a milder proposal of theirs, that he should return on condition of apologising and paying a fine. He answers, with fixed stern pride: "If I cannot return without calling myself guilty, I will never return, *nunquam revertar.*"

For Dante there was now no home in this world. He wandered from patron to patron, from place to place; proving in his own bitter words, 'How hard is the path, *Come è duro calle.*' The wretched are not cheerful company. Dante, poor and banished, with his proud earnest nature, with his moody humours, was not a man to conciliate men. Petrarch reports of him that being at Can della Scala's court, and blamed one day for his gloom and taciturnity, he answered in no courtier-like way. Della

His Scala stood among his courtiers, with mimes and
brood-buffoons (*nebulones ac histriones*) making him heartily
ings on
the other merry; when turning to Dante, he said: "Is it not
world strange, now, that this poor fool should make himself so entertaining; while you, a wise man, sit
there day after day, and have nothing to amuse us
with at all?" Dante answered bitterly: "No,
not strange; your Highness is to recollect the Proverb, *Like to Like;* "—given the amuser, the amusee
must also be given! Such a man, with his proud
silent ways, with his sarcasms and sorrows, was not
made to succeed at court. By degrees, it came to
be evident to him that he had no longer any resting-
place, or hope of benefit, in this earth. The earthly
world had cast him forth, to wander, wander; no
living heart to love him now; for his sore miseries
there was no solace here.

The deeper naturally would the Eternal World
impress itself on him; that awful reality over which,
after all, this Time-world, with its Florences and
banishments, only flutters as an unreal shadow.
Florence thou shalt never see: but Hell and Purgatory and Heaven thou shalt surely see! What
is Florence, Can della Scala, and the World and
Life altogether? ETERNITY: thither, of a truth,
not elsewhither, art thou and all things bound!
The great soul of Dante, homeless on earth, made
its home more and more in that awful other world.
Naturally his thoughts brooded on that, as on the
one fact important for him. Bodied or bodiless, it
is the one fact important for all men:—but to Dante,
in that age, it was bodied in fixed certainty of scientific shape; he no more doubted of that *Malebolge*
Pool, that it all lay there with its gloomy circles,
with its *alti guai*, and that he himself should see it,

than we doubt that we should see Constantinople if **His book** we went thither. Dante's heart, long filled with this, brooding over it in speechless thought and awe, bursts forth at length into 'mystic unfathomable song;' and this his *Divine Comedy*, the most remarkable of all modern Books, is the result.

It must have been a great solacement to Dante, and was, as we can see, a proud thought for him at times, That he, here in exile, could do this work; that no Florence, nor no man or men, could hinder him from doing it, or even much help him in doing it. He knew too, partly, that it was great; the greatest a man could do. 'If thou follow thy star, *Se tu segui tua stella*,'—so could the Hero, in his forsakenness, in his extreme need, still say to himself: "Follow thou thy star, thou shalt not fail of a glorious haven!" The labour of writing, we find, and indeed could know otherwise, was great and painful for him; he says, This Book, 'which has made me lean for many years.' Ah yes, it was won, all of it, with pain and sore toil,—not in sport, but in grim earnest. His Book, as indeed most good Books are, has been written, in many senses, with his heart's blood. It is his whole history, this Book. He died after finishing it; not yet very old, at the age of fifty-six;—broken-hearted rather, as is said. He lies buried in his death-city Ravenna: *Hic claudor Dantes patriis extorris ab oris.* The Florentines begged back his body, in a century after; the Ravenna people would not give it. "Here am I Dante laid, shut-out from my native shores."

I said, Dante's Poem was a Song: it is Tieck who calls it 'a mystic unfathomable Song;' and such is literally the character of it. Coleridge remarks very pertinently somewhere, that wherever

True and false song you find a sentence musically worded, of true rhythm and melody in the words, there is something deep and good in the meaning too. For body and soul, word and idea, go strangely together here as everywhere. Song: we said before, it was the Heroic of Speech! All *old* Poems, Homer's and the rest, are authentically Songs. I would say, in strictness, that all right Poems are; that whatsoever is not *sung* is properly no Poem, but a piece of Prose cramped into jingling lines,—to the great injury of the grammar, to the great grief of the reader, for most part! What we want to get at is the *thought* the man had, if he had any: why should he twist it into jingle, if he *could* speak it out plainly? It is only when the heart of him is rapt into true passion of melody, and the very tones of him, according to Coleridge's remark, become musical by the greatness, depth and music of his thoughts, that we can give him right to rhyme and sing; that we call him a Poet, and listen to him as the Heroic of Speakers,—whose speech *is* Song. Pretenders to this are many; and to an earnest reader, I doubt, it is for most part a very melancholy, not to say an insupportable business, that of reading rhyme! Rhyme that had no inward necessity to be rhymed; —it ought to have told us plainly, without any jingle, what it was aiming at. I would advise all men who *can* speak their thought, not to sing it; to understand that, in a serious time, among serious men, there is no vocation in them for singing it. Precisely as we love the true song, and are charmed by it as by something divine, so shall we hate the false song, and account it a mere wooden noise, a thing hollow, superfluous, altogether an insincere and offensive thing.

I give Dante my highest praise when I say of his
Divine Comedy that it is, in all senses, genuinely a
Song.   In the very sound of it there is a *canto
fermo;* it proceeds as by a chant.   The language,
his simple *terza rima,* doubtless helped him in this.
One reads along naturally with a sort of *lilt.*   But
I add, that it could not be otherwise; for the
essence and material of the work are themselves
rhythmic.   Its depth, and rapt passion and sincerity,
makes its musical;—go *deep* enough, there is music
everywhere.   A true inward symmetry, what one
calls an architectural harmony, reigns in it, propor-
tionates it all: architectural; which also partakes
of the character of music.   The three kingdoms,
Inferno, Purgatorio, Paradiso, look-out on one another like compartments of a great edifice; a great
supernatural world-cathedral, piled-up there, stern,
solemn, awful; Dante's World of Souls!   It is,
at bottom, the *sincerest* of all Poems; sincerity, here
too, we find to be the measure of worth.   It came
deep out of the author's heart of hearts; and it goes
deep, and through long generations, into ours.
The people of Verona, when they saw him on the
streets, used to say, "*Eccovi l' uom ch' è stato all'
Inferno,* See, there is the man that was in Hell!"
Ah yes, he had been in Hell;—in Hell enough, in
long severe sorrow and struggle; as the like of him
is pretty sure to have been.   Commedias that come-
out *divine* are not accomplished otherwise.   Thought,
true labour of any kind, highest virtue itself, is it
not the daughter of Pain?   Born as out of the
black whirlwind;—true *effort,* in fact, as of a cap-
tive struggling to free himself: that is Thought.   In
all ways we are 'to become perfect through *suffering.*'—But, as I say, no work known to me is so

*'The man
that was
in Hell'*

Dante's elaborated as this of Dante's. It has all been as if
intensity molten, in the hottest furnace of his soul. It had
made him 'lean' for many years. Not the general
whole only; every compartment of it is worked-
out, with intense earnestness, into truth, into clear
visuality. Each answers to the other; each fits in
its place, like a marble stone accurately hewn and
polished. It is the soul of Dante, and in this the
soul of the middle ages, rendered forever rhyth-
mically visible there. No light task; a right intense
one: but a task which is *done*.

Perhaps one would say, *intensity*, with the much
that depends on it, is the prevailing character of
Dante's genius. Dante does not come before us as
a large catholic mind; rather as a narrow and even
sectarian mind: it is partly the fruit of his age and
position, but partly too of his own nature. His
greatness has, in all senses, concentered itself into
fiery emphasis and depth. He is world-great not
because he is world-wide, but because he is world-
deep. Through all objects he pierces as it were
down into the heart of Being. I know nothing so
intense as Dante. Consider, for example, to begin
with the outermost development of his intensity,
consider how he paints. He has a great power of
vision; seizes the very type of a thing; presents
that and nothing more. You remember that first
view he gets of the Hall of Dite: *red* pinnacle,
redhot cone of iron glowing through the dim immensity of gloom;—so vivid, so distinct, visible at
once and forever! It is as an emblem of the whole
genius of Dante. There is a brevity, an abrupt
precision in him: Tacitus is not briefer, more
condensed; and then in Dante it seems a natural
condensation, spontaneous to the man. One smiting

word; and then there is silence, nothing more said. His
His silence is more eloquent than words. It is power of
strange with what a sharp decisive grace he snatches painting
the true likeness of a matter: cuts into the matter
as with a pen of fire. Plutus, the blustering giant,
collapses at Virgil's rebuke; it is ' as the sails sink,
the mast being suddenly broken.' Or that poor
Brunetto Latini, with the *cotto aspetto*, 'face *baked*,'
parched brown and lean; and the ' fiery snow,' that
falls on them there, a ' fiery snow without wind,'
slow, deliberate, never-ending! Or the lids of
those Tombs; square sarcophaguses, in that silent
dim-burning Hall, each with its Soul in torment;
the lids laid open there; they are to be shut at the
Day of Judgment, through Eternity. And how
Farinata rises; and how Cavalcante falls—at hearing of his Son, and the past tense '*fue*'! The
very movements in Dante have something brief;
swift, decisive, almost military. It is of the inmost
essence of his genius this sort of painting. The
fiery, swift Italian nature of the man, so silent,
passionate, with its quick abrupt movements, its
silent ' pale rages,' speaks itself in these things.

For though this of painting is one of the outermost developments of a man, it comes like all else
from the essential faculty of him; it is physiognomical of the whole man. Find a man whose words
paint you a likeness, you have found a man worth
something; mark his manner of doing it, as very
characteristic of him. In the first place, he could
not have discerned the object at all, or seen the
vital type of it, unless he had, what we may call,
sympathised with it,—had sympathy in him to
bestow on objects. He must have been *sincere*
about it too; sincere and sympathetic: a man with-

His sincerity out worth cannot give you the likeness of any object; he dwells in vague outwardness, fallacy and trivial hearsay, about all objects. And indeed may we not say that intellect altogether expresses itself in this power of discerning what an object is? Whatsoever of faculty a man's mind may have will come out here. Is it even of business, a matter to be done? The gifted man is he who *sees* the essential point, and leaves all the rest aside as surplusage: it is his faculty too, the man of business's faculty, that he discern the true *likeness*, not the false superficial one, of the thing he has got to work in. And how much of *morality* is in the kind of insight we get of anything; ' the eye ' seeing in all things what it brought with it the ' faculty of seeing ' ! To the mean eye all things are trivial, as certainly as to the jaundiced they are yellow. Raphael, the Painters tell us, is the best of all Portrait-painters withal. No most gifted eye can exhaust the significance of any object. In the commonest human face there lies more than Raphael will take-away with him.

Dante's painting is not graphic only, brief, true, and of a vividness as of fire in dark night; taken on the wider scale, it is everyway noble, and the outcome of a great soul. Francesca and her Lover, what qualities in that! A thing woven as out of rainbows, on a ground of eternal black. A small flute-voice of infinite wail speaks there, into our very heart of hearts. A touch of womanhood in it too; *della bella persona, che mi fu tolta;* and how, even in the Pit of woe, it is a solace that *he* will never part from her! Saddest tragedy in these *alti guai.* And the racking winds, in that *aer bruno,* whirl them away again, to wail forever!—Strange

to think : Dante was the friend of this poor Fran- **His**
cesca's father ; Francesca herself may have sat **tender-**
upon the Poet's knee, as a bright innocent little **ness**
child.   Infinite pity, yet also infinite rigour of
law : it is so Nature is made ; it is so Dante discerned that she was made.   What a paltry notion
is that of his *Divine Comedy's* being a poor splenetic
impotent terrestrial libel ; putting those into Hell
whom he could not be avenged-upon on earth !   I
suppose if ever pity, tender as a mother's, was in
the heart of any man, it was in Dante's.   But a
man who does not know rigour cannot pity either.
His very pity will be cowardly, egoistic,—senti-
mentality, or little better.   I know not in the
world an affection equal to that of Dante.   It is a
tenderness, a trembling, longing, pitying love : like
the wail of Æolean harps, soft, soft ; like a child's
young heart ;—and then that stern, sore-saddened
heart !   These longings of his towards his Beatrice ;
their meeting together in the *Paradiso* ; his gazing
in her pure transfigured eyes, her that had been
purified by death so long, separated from him so
far :—one likens it to the song of angels ; it is
among the purest utterances of affection, perhaps
the very purest, that ever came out of a human
soul.

For the *intense* Dante is intense in all things ; he
has got into the essence of all.   His intellectual
insight as painter, on occasion too as reasoner, is
but the result of all other sorts of intensity.
Morally great, above all, we must call him ; it is
the beginning of all.   His scorn, his grief are as
transcendent as his love ;—as indeed, what are they
but the *inverse* or *converse* of his love ?   '*A Dio
spiacenti ed a' nemici sui*, Hateful to God and to the

The Purga-torio enemies of God:' lofty scorn, unappeasable silent reprobation and aversion; '*Non ragionam di lor*, We will not speak of *them*, look only and pass.' Or think of this; 'They have not the *hope* to die, *Non han speranza di morte*.' One day, it had risen sternly benign on the scathed heart of Dante, that he, wretched, never-resting, worn as he was, would full surely *die*; 'that Destiny itself could not doom him not to die.' Such words are in this man. For rigour, earnestness and depth, he is not to be paralleled in the modern world; to seek his parallel we must go into the Hebrew Bible, and live with the antique Prophets there.

I do not agree with much modern criticism, in greatly preferring the *Inferno* to the two other parts of the Divine *Commedia*. Such preference belongs, I imagine, to our general Byronism of taste, and is like to be a transient feeling. The *Purgatorio* and *Paradiso*, especially the former, one would almost say, is even more excellent than it. It is a noble thing that *Purgatorio*, 'Mountain of Purification'; an emblem of the noblest conception of that age. If Sin is so fatal, and Hell is and must be so rigorous, awful, yet in Repentance too is man purified; Repentance is the grand Christian act. It is beautiful how Dante works it out. The *tremolar dell' onde* that 'trembling' of the ocean-waves, under the first pure gleam of morning, dawning afar on the wandering Two, is as the type of an altered mood. Hope has now dawned; never-dying Hope, if in company still with heavy sorrow. The obscure sojourn of dæmons and reprobate is underfoot; a soft breathing of penitence mounts higher and higher, to the Throne of Mercy itself. "Pray for me," the denizens of that Mount of

Pain all say to him. "Tell my Giovanna to pray for me," my daughter Giovanna; "I think her mother loves me no more!" They toil painfully up by that winding steep, 'bent-down like corbels of a building,' some of them,—crushed-together so 'for the sin of pride'; yet nevertheless in years, in ages and æons, they shall have reached the top, which is Heaven's gate, and by Mercy shall have been admitted in. The joy too of all, when one has prevailed; the whole Mountain shakes with joy, and a psalm of praise rises, when one soul has perfected repentance and got its sin and misery left behind! I call all this a noble embodiment of a true noble thought.

But indeed the Three compartments mutually support one another, are indispensable to one another. The *Paradiso*, a kind of inarticulate music to me, is the redeeming side of the *Inferno*; the *Inferno* without it were untrue. All three make-up the true Unseen World, as figured in the Christianity of the Middle Ages; a thing forever memorable, forever true in the essence of it, to all men. It was perhaps delineated in no human soul with such depth of veracity as in this of Dante's; a man *sent* to sing it, to keep it long memorable. Very notable with what brief simplicity he passes out of the every-day reality, into the Invisible one; and in the second or third stanza, we find ourselves in the World of Spirits; and dwell there, as among things palpable, indubitable! To Dante they *were* so; the real world, as it is called, and its facts, was but the threshold to an infinitely higher Fact of a World. At bottom, the one was as *preter-*natural as the other. Has not each man a soul? He will not only be a spirit, but is one. To the

A symbol, not an allegory earnest Dante it is all one visible Fact ; he believes it, sees it ; is the Poet of it in virtue of that. Sincerity, I say again, is the saving merit, now as always.

Dante's Hell, Purgatory, Paradise, are a symbol withal, an emblematic representation of his Belief about this Universe :—some Critic in a future age, like those Scandinavian ones the other day, who has ceased altogether to think as Dante did, may find this too all an 'Allegory,' perhaps an idle Allegory ! It is a sublime embodiment, or sublimest, of the soul of Christianity. It expresses, as in huge worldwide architectural emblems, how the Christian Dante felt Good and Evil to be the two polar elements of this Creation, on which it all turns ; that these two differ not by *preferability* of one to the other, but by incompatibility absolute and infinite ; that the one is excellent and high as light and Heaven, the other hideous, black as Gehenna and the Pit of Hell ! Everlasting Justice, yet with Penitence, with everlasting Pity, —all Christianism, as Dante and the Middle Ages had it, is emblemed here. Emblemed : and yet, as I urged the other day, with what entire truth of purpose ; how unconscious of any embleming ! Hell, Purgatory, Paradise : these things were not fashioned as emblems ; was there, in our Modern European Mind, any thought at all of their being emblems ? Were they not indubitable awful facts ; the whole heart of man taking them for practically true, all Nature everywhere confirming them ? So is it always in these things. Men do not believe an Allegory. The future Critic, whatever his new thought may be, who considers this of Dante to have been all got-up as an Allegory, will commit one sore mistake!—Paganism we recognised as a *The voice of ten centuries* veracious expression of the earnest awe-struck feeling of man towards the Universe; veracious, true once, and still not without worth for us. But mark here the difference of Paganism and Christianism; one great difference. Paganism emblemed chiefly the Operations of Nature; the destinies, efforts, combinations, vicissitudes of things and men in this world; Christianism emblemed the Law of Human Duty, the Moral Law of Man. One was for the sensuous nature: a rude helpless utterance of the *first* Thought of men,—the chief recognised virtue, Courage, Superiority to Fear. The other was not for the sensuous nature, but for the moral. What a progress is here, if in that one respect only!—

And so in this Dante, as we said, had ten silent centuries, in a very strange way, found a voice. The *Divina Commedia* is of Dante's writing; yet in truth *it* belongs to ten Christian centuries, only the finishing of it is Dante's. So always. The craftsman there, the smith with that metal of his, with these tools, with these cunning methods,—how little of all he does is properly *his* work! All past inventive men work there with him;—as indeed with all of us, in all things. Dante is the spokesman of the Middle Ages; the Thought they lived by stands here in everlasting music. These sublime ideas of his, terrible and beautiful, are the fruit of the Christian Meditation of all the good men who had gone before him. Precious they; but also is not he precious? Much, had not he spoken, would have been dumb; not dead, yet living voiceless.

A song that will endure On the whole, is it not an utterance, this Mystic Song, at once of one of the greatest human souls, and of the highest thing that Europe had hitherto realised for itself? Christianism, as Dante sings it, is another than Paganism in the rude Norse mind; another than 'Bastard Christianism' half-articulately spoken in the Arab Desert seven-hundred years before!—The noblest *idea* made *real* hitherto among men, is sung, and emblemed-forth abidingly, by one of the noblest men. In the one sense and in the other, are we not right glad to possess it? As I calculate, it may last yet for long thousands of years. For the thing that is uttered from the inmost parts of a man's soul, differs altogether from what is uttered by the outer part. The outer is of the day, under the empire of mode; the outer passes away, in swift endless changes; the inmost is the same yesterday, today and forever. True souls, in all generations of the world, who look on this Dante, will find a brotherhood in him; the deep sincerity of his thoughts, his woes and hopes, will speak likewise to their sincerity; they will feel that this Dante too was a brother. Napoleon in Saint-Helena is charmed with the genial veracity of old Homer. The oldest Hebrew Prophet, under a vesture the most diverse from ours, does yet, because he speaks from the heart of man, speak to all men's hearts. It is the one sole secret of continuing long memorable. Dante, for depth of sincerity, is like an antique Prophet too; his words, like theirs, come from his very heart. One need not wonder if it were predicted that his Poem might be the most enduring thing our Europe has yet made; for nothing so endures as a truly spoken word. All cathedrals, pontificalities, brass and

stone, and outer arrangement never so lasting, are **Dante**
brief in comparison to an unfathomable heart-song **and**
like this: one feels as if it might survive, still of **Mahomet**
importance to men, when these had all sunk into
new irrecognisable combinations, and had ceased
individually to be. Europe has made much; great
cities, great empires, encyclopædias, creeds, bodies
of opinion and practice: but it has made little of
the class of Dante's Thought. Homer yet *is*,
veritably present face to face with every open soul
of us; and Greece, where is *it?* Desolate for
thousands of years; away, vanished; a bewildered
heap of stones and rubbish, the life and existence
of it all gone. Like a dream; like the dust of
King Agamemnon! Greece was; Greece, except
in the *words* it spoke, is not.

The uses of this Dante? We will not say much
about his 'uses.' A human soul who has once got
into that primal element of *Song*, and sung-forth
fitly somewhat therefrom, has worked in the *depths*
of our existence; feeding through long times the
life-*roots* of all excellent human things whatsoever,
—in a way that 'utilities' will not succeed well in
calculating! We will not estimate the Sun by the
quantity of gas-light it saves us; Dante shall be
invaluable, or of no value. One remark I may
make: the contrast in this respect between the
Hero-Poet and the Hero-Prophet. In a hundred
years, Mahomet, as we saw, had his Arabians at
Grenada and at Delhi; Dante's Italians seem to
be yet very much where they were. Shall we say,
then, Dante's effect on the world was small in
comparison? Not so: his arena is far more re-
stricted: but also it is far nobler, clearer;—perhaps
not less but more important. Mahomet speaks to

The real great masses of men, in the coarse dialect adapted to
fruit of it such; a dialect filled with inconsistencies, crudities,
follies: on the great masses alone can he act, and
there with good and with evil strangely blended.
Dante speaks to the noble, the pure and great, in
all times and places. Neither does he grow obsolete,
as the other does. Dante burns as a pure star, fixed
there in the firmament, at which the great and
the high of all ages kindle themselves: he is the
possession of all the chosen of the world for un-
counted time. Dante, one calculates, may long
survive Mahomet. In this way the balance may be
made straight again.

But, at any rate, it is not by what is called their
effect on the world by what *we* can judge of their
effect there, that a man and his work are measured.
Effect? Influence? Utility? Let a man *do* his
work; the fruit of it is the care of Another than
he. It will grow its own fruit; and whether embodied in Caliph Thrones and Arabian Conquests,
so that it 'fills all Morning and Evening Newspapers,'
and all Histories, which are a kind of distilled
Newspapers; or not embodied so at all;—what
matters that? That is not the real fruit of it!
The Arabian Caliph, in so far only as he did
something, was something. If the great Cause of
Man, and Man's work in God's Earth, got no
furtherance from the Arabian Caliph, then no
matter how many scimetars he drew, how many
gold piasters pocketed, and what uproar and blaring
he made in this world—*he* was but a loud-sounding
inanity and futility; at bottom, he *was* not at all.
Let us honour the great empire of *Silence*, once
more! The boundless treasury which we do *not*
jingle in our pockets, or count up and present before

men ! It is perhaps, of all things, the usefulest for **Shak-**
each of us to do, in these loud times.——— **speare**
and
Dante

As Dante, the Italian man, was sent into our
world to embody musically the Religion of the
Middle Ages, the Religion of our Modern Europe,
its Inner Life; so Shakspeare, we may say,
embodies for us the Outer Life of our Europe as
developed then, its chivalries, courtesies, humours,
ambitions, what practical way of thinking, acting,
looking at the world, men then had. As in Homer
we may still construe Old Greece ; so in Shakspeare
and Dante, after thousands of years, what our modern
Europe was, in Faith and in Practice, will still be
legible. Dante has given us the Faith or soul;
Shakspeare, in a not less noble way, has given us
the Practice or body. This latter also we were to
have : a man was sent for it, the man Shakspeare.
Just when that chivalry way of life had reached its
last finish, and was on the point of breaking down
into slow or swift dissolution, as we now see it
everywhere, this other sovereign Poet, with his
seeing eye, with his perennial singing voice, was
sent to take note of it, to give long-enduring
record of it. Two fit men : Dante, deep, fierce
as the central fire of the world ; Shakspeare, wide,
placid, far-seeing, as the Sun, the upper light of
the world. Italy produced the one world-voice ;
we English had the honour of producing the
other.

Curious enough how, as it were by mere accident,
this man came to us. I think always, so great,
quiet, complete and self-sufficing is this Shakspeare,
had the Warwickshire Squire not prosecuted him
for deer-stealing, we had perhaps never heard of

The Tree him as a Poet! The woods and skies, the rustic
Igdrasil Life of Man in Stratford there, had been enough
for this man! But indeed that strange outbudding
of our whole English Existence, which we call the
Elizabethan Era, did not it too come as of its own
accord? The 'Tree Igdrasil' buds and withers by
its own laws,—too deep for our scanning. Yet it
does bud and wither, and every bough and leaf of
it is there, by fixed eternal laws; not a Sir Thomas
Lucy but comes at the hour fit for him. Curious,
I say, and not sufficiently considered: how everything does coöperate with all; not a leaf rotting on
the highway but is indissoluble portion of solar and
stellar systems; no thought, word or act of man
but has sprung withal out of all men, and works
sooner or later, recognisably or irrecognisably, on
all men! It is all a Tree: circulation of sap and
influences, mutual communication of every minutest
leaf with the lowest talon of a root, with every
other greatest and minutest portion of the whole.
The Tree Igdrasil, that has its roots down in the
Kingdoms of Hela and Death, and whose boughs
overspread the highest Heaven!—

In some sense it may be said that this glorious
Elizabethan Era with its Shakspeare, as the outcome and flowerage of all which had preceded it,
is itself attributable to the Catholicism of the Middle
Ages. The Christian Faith, which was the theme
of Dante's Song, had produced this Practical Life
which Shakspeare was to sing. For Religion then,
as it now and always is, was the soul of Practice;
the primary vital fact in men's life. And remark
here, as rather curious, that Middle-Age Catholicism
was abolished, so far as Acts of Parliament could
abolish it, before Shakspeare, the noblest product of

it, made his appearance. He did make his appear- **Shak-**
ance nevertheless. Nature at her own time, with **speare the**
Catholicism or what else might be necessary, sent **chief of**
him forth ; taking small thought of Acts of Parlia- **all poets**
ment. King-Henrys, Queen-Elizabeths go their
way ; and Nature too goes hers. Acts of Parliament, on the whole, are small, notwithstanding the
noise they make. What Act of Parliament, debate
at St Stephen's, on the hustings or elsewhere, was
it that brought this Shakspeare into being? No
dining at Freemasons' Tavern, opening subscription-
lists, selling of shares, and infinite other jangling and
true or false endeavouring ! This Elizabethan Era,
and all its nobleness and blessedness, came without
proclamation, preparation of ours. Priceless Shakspeare was the free gift of Nature ; given altogether
silently ;—received altogether silently, as if it had
been a thing of little account. And yet, very
literally, it is a priceless thing. One should look
at that side of matters too.

Of this Shakspeare of ours, perhaps the opinion
one sometimes hears a little idolatrously expressed
is, in fact, the right one ; I think the best judgment
not of this country only, but of Europe at large, is
slowly pointing to the conclusion, That Shakspeare
is the chief of all Poets hitherto ; the greatest
intellect who, in our recorded world, has left record
of himself in the way of Literature. On the whole,
I know not such a power of vision, such a faculty
of thought, if we take all the characters of it, in
any other man. Such a calmness of depth ; placid
joyous strength ; all things imaged in that great
soul of his so true and clear, as in a tranquil unfathomable sea ! It has been said, that in the
constructing of Shakspeare's Dramas there is, apart

His method from all other 'faculties' as they are called, an understanding manifested, equal to that in Bacon's *Novum Organum*. That is true; and it is not a truth that strikes every one. It would become more apparent if we tried, any of us for himself, how, out of Shakspeare's dramatic materials, *we* could fashion such a result! The built house seems all so fit,—everyway as it should be, as if it came there by its own law and the nature of things,—we forget the rude disorderly quarry it was shaped from. The very perfection of the house, as if Nature herself had made it, hides the builder's merit. Perfect, more perfect than any other man, we may call Shakspeare in this: he discerns, knows as by instinct, what condition he works under, what his materials are, what his own force and its relation to them is. It is not a transitory glance of insight that will suffice; it is deliberate illumination of the whole matter; it is a calmly *seeing* eye; a great intellect, in short. How a man, of some wide thing that he has witnessed, will construct a narrative, what kind of picture and delineation he will give of it,—is the best measure you could get of what intellect is in the man. Which circumstance is vital and shall stand prominent; which unessential, fit to be suppressed; where is the true *beginning*, the true sequence and ending? To find out this, you task the whole force of insight that is in the man. He must *understand* the thing; according to the depth of his understanding, will the fitness of his answer be. You will try him so. Does like join itself to like; does the spirit of method stir in that confusion, so that its embroilment becomes order? Can the man say, *Fiat lux*, Let there be light; and out of chaos make a world? Precisely as there is *light* in himself, will he accomplish this.

Or indeed we may say again, it is in what I called Portrait-painting, delineating of men and things, especially of men, that Shakspeare is great. All the greatness of the man comes out decisively here. It is unexampled, I think, that calm creative perspicacity of Shakspeare. The thing he looks at reveals not this or that face of it, but its inmost heart, and generic secret: it dissolves itself as in light before him, so that he discerns the perfect structure of it. Creative, we said: poetic creation, what is this too but *seeing* the thing sufficiently? The *word* that will describe the thing, follows of itself from such clear intense sight of the thing. And is not Shakspeare's *morality*, his valour, candour, tolerance, truthfulness; his whole victorious strength and greatness, which can triumph over such obstructions, visible there too? Great as the world! No *twisted*, poor convex-concave mirror, reflecting all objects with its own convexities and concavities; a perfectly *level* mirror;—that is to say withal, if we will understand it, a man justly related to all things and men, a good man. It is truly a lordly spectacle how this great soul takes-in all kinds of men and objects, a Falstaff, an Othello, a Juliet, a Coriolanus; sets them all forth to us in their round completeness; loving, just, the equal brother of all. *Novum Organum*, and all the intellect you will find in Bacon, is of a quite secondary order; earthly, material, poor in comparison with this. Among modern men, one finds, in strictness, almost nothing of the same rank. Goethe alone, since the days of Shakspeare, reminds me of it. Of him too you say that he *saw* the object; you may say what he him-

self says of Shakspeare : 'His characters are like
'watches with dial-plates of transparent crystal;
'they show you the hour like others, and the inward
'mechanism also is all visible.'

The seeing eye ! It is this that discloses the
inner harmony of things ; what Nature meant, what
musical idea Nature has wrapped-up in these often
rough embodiments. Something she did mean.
To the seeing eye that something were discernible.
Are they base, miserable things ? You can laugh
over them, you can weep over them ; you can in
some way or other genially relate yourself to them ;
—you can, at lowest, hold your peace about them,
turn away your own and others' face from them, till
the hour come for practically exterminating and
extinguishing them ! At bottom, it is the Poet's
first gift, as it is all men's, that he have intellect
enough. He will be a Poet if he have : a Poet in
word ; or failing that, perhaps still better, a Poet in
act. Whether he write at all ; and if so, whether
in prose or in verse, will depend on accidents : who
knows on what extremely trivial accidents,—perhaps
on his having had a singing-master, on his being
taught to sing in his boyhood ! But the faculty
which enables him to discern the inner heart of
things, and the harmony that dwells there (for
whatsoever exists has a harmony in the heart of it,
or it would not hold together and exist), is not the
result of habits or accidents, but the gift of Nature
herself ; the primary outfit for a Heroic Man in
what sort soever. To the Poet, as to every other,
we say first of all, *See*. If you cannot do that, it
is of no use to keep stringing rhymes together, jingling sensibilities against each other, and *name* yourself a Poet ; there is no hope for you. If you can,

there is, in prose or verse, in action or speculation, **Man's**
all manner of hope. The crabbed old Schoolmaster **nature**
used to ask, when they brought him a new pupil, **indivis-**
" But are ye sure he's *not a dunce?* " Why, **ible**
really one might ask the same thing, in regard to
every man proposed for whatsoever function; and
consider it as the one inquiry needful: Are ye
sure he's not a dunce? There is, in this world, no
other entirely fatal person.

For, in fact, I say the degree of vision that
dwells in a man is a correct measure of the man.
If called to define Shakspeare's faculty, I should
say superiority of Intellect, and think I had included
all under that. What indeed are faculties? We
talk of faculties as if they were distinct, things
separable; as if a man had intellect, imagination,
fancy, &c., as he has hands, feet and arms. That
is a capital error. Then again, we hear of a man's
' intellectual nature,' and of his ' moral nature,' as
if these again were divisible, and existed apart.
Necessities of language do perhaps prescribe such
forms of utterance; we must speak, I am aware, in
that way, if we are to speak at all. But words
ought not to harden into things for us. It seems to
me, our apprehension of this matter is, for the most
part, radically falsified thereby. We ought to know
withal, and to keep for ever in mind, that these
divisions are at bottom but *names ;* that man's
spiritual nature, the vital Force which dwells in
him, is essentially one and indivisible; that what we
call imagination, fancy, understanding, and so forth,
are but different figures of the same Power of
Insight, all indissolubly connected with each other,
physiognomically related; that if we knew one of
them, we might know all of them. Morality itself,

I

Vulpine morality what we call the moral quality of a man, what is this but another *side* of the one vital Force whereby he is and works? All that a man does is physiognomical of him. You may see how a man would fight, by the way in which he sings; his courage, or want of courage, is visible in the word he utters, in the opinion he has formed, no less than in the stroke he strikes. He is *one*; and preaches the same Self abroad in all these ways.

Without hands a man might have feet, and could still walk: but, consider it,—without morality, intellect were impossible for him; a thoroughly immoral *man* could not know anything at all! To know a thing, what we can call knowing, a man must first *love* the thing, sympathise with it: that is, be *virtuously* related to it. If he have not the justice to put down his own selfishness at every turn, the courage to stand by the dangerous-true at every turn, how shall he know? His virtues, all of them, will lie recorded in his knowledge. Nature, with her truth, remains to the bad, to the selfish and the pusillanimous forever a sealed book: what such can know of Nature is mean, superficial, small; for the uses of the day merely.—But does not the very Fox know something of Nature? Exactly so: it knows where the geese lodge! The human Reynard, very frequent everywhere in the world, what more does he know but this and the like of this? Nay, it should be considered, too, that if the Fox had not a certain vulpine *morality*, he could not even know where the geese were, or get at the geese! If he spent his time in splenetic atrabiliar reflections on his own misery, his ill usage by Nature, Fortune and other Foxes, and so forth; and had not courage, promptitude, practicality, and other suitable vulpine gifts and **The** graces, he would catch no geese. We may say **greatest** of the Fox too, that his morality and insight are **Art un-** of the same dimensions; different faces of the same **conscious** internal unity of vulpine life!—These things are worth stating; for the contrary of them acts with manifold very baleful perversion, in this time: what limitations, modifications they require, your own candour will supply.

If I say, therefore, that Shakspeare is the greatest of Intellects, I have said all concerning him. But there is more in Shakspeare's intellect than we have yet seen. It is what I call an unconscious intellect; there is more virtue in it than he himself is aware of. Novalis beautifully remarks of him, that those Dramas of his are Products of Nature too, deep as Nature herself. I find a great truth in this saying. Shakspeare's Art is not Artifice; the noblest worth of it is not there by plan or precontrivance. It grows-up from the deeps of Nature, through this noble sincere soul, who is a voice of Nature. The latest generations of men will find new meanings in Shakspeare, new elucidations of their own human being; 'new harmonies with the infinite structure of the 'Universe; concurrences with later ideas, affinities 'with the higher powers and senses of man.' This well deserves meditating. It is Nature's highest reward to a true simple great soul, that he get thus to be *a part of herself*. Such a man's works, whatsoever he with utmost conscious exertion and forethought shall accomplish, grow up withal *un*consciously, from the unknown deeps in him;—as the oak-tree grows from the Earth's bosom, as the mountains and waters shape themselves; with a symmetry grounded on Nature's own laws, con-

Shak-
speare's
love of
laughter
formable to all Truth whatsoever. How much in Shakspeare lies hid; his sorrows, his silent struggles known to himself; much that was not known at all, not speakable at all; like *roots*, like sap and forces working underground! Speech is great; but Silence is greater.

Withal the joyful tranquillity of this man is notable. I will not blame Dante for his misery: it is as battle without victory; but true battle,— the first, indispensable thing. Yet I call Shakspeare greater than Dante, in that he fought truly, and did conquer. Doubt it not, he had his own sorrows: those *Sonnets* of his will even testify expressly in what deep waters he had waded, and swum struggling for his life;—as what man like him ever failed to have to do? It seems to me a heedless notion, our common one, that he sat like a bird on the bough; and sang forth, free and offhand, never knowing the troubles of other men. Not so; with no man is it so. How could a man travel forward from rustic deer-poaching to such tragedy-writing, and not fall-in with sorrows by the way? Or, still better, how could a man delineate a Hamlet, a Coriolanus, a Macbeth, so many suffering heroic hearts, if his own heroic heart had never suffered?—And now, in contrast with all this, observe his mirthfulness, his genuine overflowing love of laughter! You would say, in no point does he *exaggerate* but only in laughter. Fiery objurgations, words that pierce and burn, are to be found in Shakspeare; yet he is always in measure here; never what Johnson would remark as a specially 'good hater.' But his laughter seems to pour from him in floods; he heaps all manner of ridiculous nicknames on the butt he is bantering, tumbles and tosses him in all sorts of horse-play;

you would say, with his whole heart laughs. And His then, if not always the finest, it is always a genial 'national laughter. Not at mere weakness, at misery or epic' poverty; never. No man who *can* laugh, what we call laughing, will laugh at these things. It is some poor character only *desiring* to laugh, and have the credit of wit, that does so. Laughter means sympathy; good laughter is not ' the crackling of 'thorns under the pot.' Even at stupidity and pretension this Shakspeare does not laugh otherwise than genially. Dogberry and Verges tickle our very hearts; and we dismiss them covered with explosions of laughter: but we like the poor fellows only the better for our laughing; and hope they will get on well there, and continue Presidents of the City-watch. Such laughter, like sunshine on the deep sea, is very beautiful to me.

We have no room to speak of Shakspeare's individual works; though perhaps there is much still waiting to be said on that head. Had we, for instance, all his plays reviewed as *Hamlet,* in *Wilhelm Meister,* is! A thing which might, one day, be done. August Wilhelm Schlegel has a remark on his Historical Plays, *Henry Fifth* and the others, which is worth remembering. He calls them a kind of National Epic. Marlborough, you recollect, said, he knew no English History but what he had learned from Shakspeare. There are really, if we look to it, few as memorable Histories. The great salient points are admirably seized; all rounds itself off, into a kind of rhythmic coherence; it is, as Schlegel says, *epic ;*—as indeed all delineation by a great thinker will be. There are right beautiful things in those Pieces, which indeed

Cramp-
ing
circum-
stance

together form one beautiful thing. That battle of Agincourt strikes me as one of the most perfect things, in its sort, we anywhere have of Shakspeare's. The description of the two hosts: the worn-out, jaded English; the dread hour, big with destiny, when the battle shall begin; and then that deathless valour:. "Ye good yeomen, whose limbs were made in England!" There is a noble Patriotism in it, —far other than the 'indifference' you sometimes hear ascribed to Shakspeare. A true English heart breathes, calm and strong, through the whole business; not boisterous, protrusive; all the better for that. There is a sound in it like the ring of steel. This man too had a right stroke in him, had it come to that!

But I will say, of Shakspeare's works generally, that we have no full impress of him there; even as full as we have of many men. His works are so many windows, through which we see a glimpse of the world that was in him. All his works seem, comparatively speaking, cursory, imperfect, written under cramping circumstances; giving only here and there a note of the full utterance of the man. Passages there are that come upon you like splendour out of Heaven; bursts of radiance, illuminating the very heart of the thing: you say, "That is *true*, spoken once and forever; wheresoever and whensoever there is an open human soul, that will be recognised as true!" Such bursts, however, make us feel that the surrounding matter is not radiant; that it is, in part, temporary, conventional. Alas, Shakspeare had to write for the Globe Play-house: his great soul had to crush itself, as it could, into that and no other mould. It was with him, then, as it is with us all. No man works save under

conditions. The sculptor cannot set his own free **Shak-**
Thought before us; but his Thought as he could **speare not**
translate it into the stone that was given, with the **a sceptic**
tools that were given. *Disjecta membra* are all that
we find of any Poet, or of any man.

Whoever looks intelligently at this Shakspeare
may recognise that he too was a *Prophet*, in his
way; of an insight analogous to the Prophetic,
though he took it up in another strain. Nature
seemed to this man also divine; *un*speakable, deep
as Tophet, high as Heaven: 'We are such stuff
as Dreams are made of!' That scroll in West-
minster Abbey, which few read with understanding,
is of the depth of any seer. But the man sang;
did not preach, except musically. We called Dante
the melodious Priest of Middle-Age Catholicism.
May we not call Shakspeare the still more melodious
Priest of a *true* Catholicism, the 'Universal Church'
of the Future and of all times? No narrow super-
stition, harsh asceticism, intolerance, fanatical fierceness or perversion: a Revelation, so far as it goes,
that such a thousandfold hidden beauty and divineness dwells in all Nature; which let all men worship
as they can! We may say without offence, that
there rises a kind of universal Psalm out of this
Shakspeare too; not unfit to make itself heard
among the still more sacred Psalms. Not in dis-
harmony with these, if we understood them, but in
harmony!—I cannot call this Shakspeare a 'Sceptic,'
as some do; his indifference to the creeds and
theological quarrels of his time misleading them.
No: neither unpatriotic, though he says little about
his Patriotism; nor sceptic, though he says little
about his Faith. Such 'indifference' was the fruit

Shakspeare a Priest of Mankind of his greatness withal: his whole heart was in his own grand sphere of worship (we may call it such): these other controversies, vitally important to other men, were not vital to him.

But call it worship, call it what you will, is it not a right glorious thing, and set of things, this that Shakspeare has brought us? For myself, I feel that there is actually a kind of sacredness in the fact of such a man being sent into this Earth. Is he not an eye to us all; a blessed heaven-sent Bringer of Light?—And, at bottom, was it not perhaps far better that this Shakspeare, everyway an unconscious man, was *conscious* of no Heavenly message? He did not feel, like Mahomet, because he saw into those internal Splendours, that he specially was the 'Prophet of God:' and was he not greater than Mahomet in that? Greater; and also, if we compute strictly, as we did in Dante's case, more successful. It was intrinsically an error that notion of Mahomet's, of his supreme Prophethood: and has come down to us inextricably involved in error to this day; dragging along with it such a coil of fables, impurities, intolerances, as makes it a questionable step for me here and now to say, as I have done, that Mahomet was a true Speaker at all, and not rather an ambitious charlatan, perversity and simulacrum; no Speaker, but a Babbler! Even in Arabia, as I compute, Mahomet will have exhausted himself and become obsolete, while this Shakspeare, this Dante may still be young;—while this Shakspeare may still pretend to be a Priest of Mankind, of Arabia as of other places, for unlimited periods to come!

Compared with any speaker or singer one knows, even with Æschylus or Homer, why should he not,

for veracity and universality, last like them? He
is *sincere* as they; reaches deep down like them, to
the universal and perennial.   But as for Mahomet,
I think it had been better for him *not* to be so conscious!   Alas, poor Mahomet; all that he was *conscious* of was a mere error; a futility and triviality,
—as indeed such ever is.   The truly great in him
too was the unconscious: that he was a wild Arab
lion of the desert, and did speak-out with that great
thunder-voice of his, not by words which he *thought*
to be great, but by actions, by feelings, by a history
which *were* great!   His Koran has become a stupid
piece of prolix absurdity; we do not believe, like
him, that God wrote that!   The Great Man here
too, as always, is a Force of Nature: whatsoever
is truly great in him springs-up from the *in*articulate
deeps.

Well: this is our poor Warwickshire Peasant,
who rose to be Manager of a Playhouse, so that he
could live without begging; whom the Earl of
Southampton cast some kind glances on; whom Sir
Thomas Lucy, many thanks to him, was for sending
to the Treadmill!   We did not account him a god,
like Odin, while he dwelt with us;—on which point
there were much to be said.   But I will say rather,
or repeat: In spite of the sad state Hero-worship
now lies in, consider what this Shakspeare has
actually become among us.   Which Englishman we
ever made, in this land of ours, which million of
Englishmen, would we not give-up rather than the
Stratford Peasant?   There is no regiment of highest
Dignitaries that we would sell him for.   He is the
grandest thing we have yet done.   For our honour
among foreign nations, as an ornament to our English

*Not to
be ex-
changed
for an
Empire*

Shak-
speare
a centre
for the
English
race Household, what item is there that we would not surrender rather than him? Consider now, if they asked us, Will you give-up your Indian Empire or your Shakspeare, you English; never have had any Indian Empire, or never have had any Shakspeare? Really it were a grave question. Official persons would answer doubtless in official language; but we, for our part too, should not we be forced to answer: Indian Empire, or no Indian Empire; we cannot do without Shakspeare! Indian Empire will go, at any rate, some day; but this Shakspeare does not go, he lasts forever with us; we cannot give-up our Shakspeare!

Nay, apart from spiritualities; and considering him merely as a real, marketable, tangibly-useful possession. England, before long, this Island of ours, will hold but a small fraction of the English: in America, in New Holland, east and west to the very Antipodes, there will be a Saxondom covering great spaces of the Globe. And now, what is it that can keep all these together into virtually one Nation, so that they do not fall-out and fight, but live at peace, in brotherlike intercourse, helping one another? This is justly regarded as the greatest practical problem, the thing all manner of sovereignties and governments are here to accomplish: what is it that will accomplish this? Acts of Parliament, administrative prime-ministers cannot. America is parted from us, so far as Parliament could part it. Call it not fantastic, for there is much reality in it: Here, I say, is an English King, whom no time or chance, Parliament or combination of Parliaments, can dethrone! This King Shakspeare, does not he shine, in crowned sovereignty, over us all, as the noblest, gentlest, yet strongest of

rallying-signs; *in*destructible; really more valuable **As Dante**
in that point of view than any other means or **is for the**
appliance whatsoever?   We can fancy him as radiant **Italians**
aloft over all the Nations of Englishmen, a thousand
years hence.   From Paramatta, from New York,
wheresoever, under what sort of Parish-Constable
soever, English men and women are, they will say
to one another: "Yes, this Shakspeare is ours; we
produced him, we speak and think by him; we are
of one blood and kind with him."   The most
common-sense politician, too, if he pleases, may
think of that.

Yes, truly, it is a great thing for a Nation that
it get an articulate voice; that it produce a man
who will speak-forth melodiously what the heart of
it means!   Italy, for example, poor Italy lies dismembered, scattered asunder, not appearing in any
protocol or treaty as a unity at all; yet the noble
Italy is actually *one*:   Italy produced its Dante;
Italy can speak!   The Czar of all the Russias, he
is strong, with so many bayonets, Cossacks and
cannons; and does a great feat in keeping such a
tract of Earth politically together; but he cannot
yet speak.   Something great in him, but it is a
dumb greatness.   He has had no voice of genius,
to be heard of all men and times.   He must learn
to speak.   He is a great dumb monster hitherto.
His cannons and Cossacks will all have rusted into
nonentity, while that Dante's voice is still audible.
The Nation that has a Dante is bound together
as no dumb Russia can be.—We must here end
what we had to say of the *Hero-Poet*.

LECTURE IV

THE HERO AS PRIEST.   LUTHER ; REFORMATION :
KNOX ; PURITANISM.

[Friday, 15th May 1840]

The ideal of the Priest OUR present discourse is to be of the Great Man as Priest. We have repeatedly endeavoured to explain that all sorts of Heroes are intrinsically of the same material ; that given a great soul, open to the Divine Significance of Life, then there is given a man fit to speak of this, to sing of this, to fight and work for this, in a great, victorious, enduring manner ; there is given a Hero, —the outward shape of whom will depend on the time and the environment he finds himself in. The priest too, as I understand it, is a kind of Prophet ; in him too there is required to be a light of inspiration, as we must name it. He presides over the worship of the people ; is the Uniter of them with the Unseen Holy. He is the spiritual Captain of the people ; as the Prophet is their spiritual King with many captains : he guides them heavenward, by wise guidance through this Earth and its work. The ideal of him is, that he too be what we can call a voice from the unseen Heaven ; interpreting, even as the Prophet did, and in a more familiar manner unfolding the same to men. The unseen Heaven,—the ' open secret of the Universe,'— which so few have an eye for ! He is the Prophet shorn of his more awful splendour ; burning with mild equable radiance, as the enlightener of daily life. This, I say, is the ideal of a Priest.

So in old times; so in these, and in all times. One
knows very well that, in reducing ideals to practice,
great latitude of tolerance is needful; very great.
But a Priest who is not this at all, who does not
any longer aim or try to be this, is a character—of
whom we had rather not speak in this place.

Luther and Knox were by express vocation
Priests, and did faithfully perform that function
in its common sense. Yet it will suit us better
here to consider them chiefly in their historical
character, rather as Reformers than Priests. There
have been other Priests perhaps equally notable, in
calmer times, for doing faithfully the office of a
Leader of Worship; bringing down, by faithful
heroism in that kind, a light from Heaven into
the daily life of their people; leading them forward, as under God's guidance, in the way wherein they were to go. But when this same *way* was
a rough one, of battle, confusion and danger, the
spiritual Captain, who led through that, becomes,
especially to us who live under the fruit of his
leading, more notable than any other. He is the
warfaring and battling Priest; who led his people,
not to quiet faithful labour as in smooth times, but
to faithful valorous conflict, in times all violent,
dismembered: a more perilous service, and a more
memorable one, be it higher or not. These two
men we will account our best Priests, inasmuch
as they were our best Reformers. Nay I may
ask, Is not every true Reformer, by the nature
of him, a *Priest* first of all? He appeals to
Heaven's invisible justice against Earth's visible
force; knows that it, the invisible, is strong and
alone strong. He is a believer in the divine truth
of things; a *seer*, seeing through the shows of

The place things; a worshipper, in one way or the other,
of the of the divine truth of things; a Priest, that is.
Reformer If he be not first a Priest, he will never be good
in History for much as a Reformer.

Thus, then, as we have seen Great Men, in various situations, building up Religions, heroic Forms of human Existence in this world, Theories of Life worthy to be sung by a Dante, Practices of Life by a Shakspeare,—we are now to see the reverse process; which also is necessary, which also may be carried on in the Heroic manner. Curious how this should be necessary : yet necessary it is. The mild shining of the Poet's light has to give place to the fierce lightning of the Reformer : unfortunately the Reformer too is a personage that cannot fail in History! The Poet indeed, with his mildness, what is he but the product and ultimate adjustment of Reform, or Prophecy with its fierceness? No wild Saint Dominics and Thebaïd Eremites, there had been no melodious Dante; rough Practical Endeavour, Scandinavian and other, from Odin to Walter Raleigh, from Ulfila to Cranmer, enabled Shakspeare to speak. Nay the finished Poet, I remark sometimes, is a symptom that his epoch itself has reached perfection and is finished ; that before long there will be a new epoch, new Reformers needed.

Doubtless it were finer, could we go along always in the way of *music ;* be tamed and taught by our Poets, as the rude creatures were by their Orpheus of old. Or failing this rhythmic *musical* way, how good were it could we get so much as into the *equable* way; I mean, if *peaceable* Priests, reforming from day to day, would always suffice us! But it is not so; even this latter has not yet been realised.

Alas, the battling Reformer too is, from time to time, a needful and inevitable phenomenon. Obstructions are never wanting: the very things that were once indispensable furtherances become obstructions; and need to be shaken off, and left behind us,—a business often of enormous difficulty. It is notable enough, surely, how a Theorem or spiritual Representation, so we may call it, which once took in the whole Universe, and was completely satisfactory in all parts of it to the highly-discursive acute intellect of Dante, one of the greatest in the world, — had in the course of another century become dubitable to common intellects; become deniable; and is now, to every one of us, flatly incredible, obsolete as Odin's Theorem! To Dante, human Existence, and God's ways with men, were all well represented by those *Malebolges*, *Purgatorios*; to Luther not well. How was this? Why could not Dante's Catholicism continue; but Luther's Protestantism must needs follow? Alas, nothing will *continue*.

'Progress of the Species'

I do not make much of ' Progress of the Species,' as handled in these times of ours; nor do I think you would care to hear much about it. The talk on that subject is too often of the most extravagant, confused sort. Yet I may say, the fact itself seems certain enough; nay we can trace out the inevitable necessity of it in the nature of things. Every man, as I have stated somewhere, is not only a learner but a doer: he learns with the mind given him what has been; but with the same mind he discovers farther, he invents and devises somewhat of his own. Absolutely without originality there is no man. No man whatever believes, or can believe, exactly what his grandfather believed: he enlarges somewhat, by

Material for revolution fresh discovery, his view of the Universe, and consequently his Theorem of the Universe,—which is an *infinite* Universe, and can never be embraced wholly or finally by any view or Theorem, in any conceivable enlargement : he enlarges somewhat, I say ; finds somewhat that was credible to his grandfather incredible to him, false to him, inconsistent with some new thing he has discovered or observed. It is the history of every man ; and in the history of Mankind we see it summed-up into great historical amounts,—revolutions, new epochs. Dante's Mountain of Purgatory does *not* stand 'in the ocean of the other Hemisphere,' when Columbus has once sailed thither ! Men find no such thing extant in the other Hemisphere. It is not there. It must cease to be believed to be there. So with all beliefs whatsoever in this world,—all Systems of Belief, and Systems of Practice that spring from these.

If we add now the melancholy fact, that when Belief waxes uncertain, Practice too becomes unsound, and errors, injustices and miseries everywhere more and more prevail, we shall see material enough for revolution. At all turns, a man who will *do* faithfully, needs to believe firmly. If he have to ask at every turn the world's suffrage ; if he cannot dispense with the world's suffrage, and make his own suffrage serve, he is a poor eye-servant ; the work committed to him will be *mis*-done. Every such man is a daily contributor to the inevitable downfall. Whatsoever work he does, dishonestly, with an eye to the outward look of it, is a new offence, parent of new misery to somebody or other. Offences accumulate till they become insupportable ; and are then violently burst through, cleared off as by explosion. Dante's sublime Catholicism, incredible now in theory, and defaced still worse by **No** faithless, doubting and dishonest practice, has to be **honest** torn asunder by a Luther ; Shakspeare's noble **belief** **wholly** feudalism, as beautiful as it once looked and was, **false** has to end in a French Revolution. The accumulation of offences is, as we say, too literally *exploded*, blasted asunder volcanically ; and there are long troublous periods before matters come to a settlement again.

Surely it were mournful enough to look only at this face of the matter, and find in all human opinions and arrangements merely the fact that they were uncertain, temporary, subject to the law of death ! At bottom, it is not so : all death, here too we find, is but of the body, not of the essence or soul ; all destruction, by violent revolution or howsoever it be, is but new creation on a wider scale. Odinism was *Valour ;* Christianism was *Humility*, a nobler kind of Valour. No thought that ever dwelt honestly as true in the heart of man but *was* an honest insight into God's truth on man's part, and *has* an essential truth in it which endures through all changes, an everlasting possession for us all. And, on the other hand, what a melancholy notion is that, which has to represent all men, in all countries and times except our own, as having spent their life in blind condemnable error, mere lost Pagans, Scandinavians, Mahometans, only that we might have the true ultimate knowledge ! All generations of men were lost and wrong, only that this present little section of a generation might be saved and right. They all marched forward there, all generations since the beginning of the world, like the Russian soldiers into the ditch of Schweidnitz Fort, only to fill-up the ditch with their dead bodies,

All under one Captain that we might march-over and take the place! It is an incredible hypothesis.

Such incredible hypothesis we have seen maintained with fierce emphasis; and this or the other poor individual man, with his sect of individual men, marching as over the dead bodies of all men, towards sure victory: but when he too, with his hypothesis and ultimate infallible credo, sank into the ditch, and became a dead body, what was to be said?—Withal, it is an important fact in the nature of man, that he tends to reckon his own insight as final, and goes upon it as such. He will always do it, I suppose, in one or the other way; but it must be in some wider, wiser way than this. Are not all true men that live, or that ever lived, soldiers of the same army, enlisted, under Heaven's captaincy, to do battle against the same enemy, the Empire of Darkness and Wrong? Why should we misknow one another, fight not against the enemy but against ourselves, from mere difference of uniform? All uniforms shall be good, so they hold in them true valiant men. All fashions of arms, the Arab turban and swift scimetar, Thor's strong hammer smiting down *Jötuns*, shall be welcome. Luther's battle-voice, Dante's march-melody, all genuine things are with us, not against us. We are all under one Captain, soldiers of the same host.—Let us now look a little at this Luther's fighting; what kind of battle it was, and how he comported himself in it. Luther too was of our spiritual Heroes; a Prophet to his country and time.

As introductory to the whole, a remark about Idolatry will perhaps be in place here. One of Mahomet's characteristics, which indeed belongs to all Prophets, is unlimited implacable zeal against

Idolatry. It is the grand theme of Prophets: **Idolatry**
Idolatry, the worshipping of dead Idols as the
Divinity, is a thing they cannot away-with, but
have to denounce continually, and brand with
inexpiable reprobation; it is the chief of all the
sins they see done under the sun. This is worth
noting. We will not enter here into the theological
question about Idolatry. Idol is *Eidolon*, a thing
seen, a symbol. It is not God, but a Symbol of
God; and perhaps one may question whether any
the most benighted mortal ever took it for more
than a Symbol. I fancy, he did not think that
the poor image his own hands had made *was* God;
but that God was emblemed by it, that God was
in it some way or another. And now in this sense,
one may ask, Is not all worship whatsoever a
worship by Symbols, by *eidola*, or things seen?
Whether *seen*, rendered visible as an image or
picture to the bodily eye; or visible only to the
inward eye, to the imagination, to the intellect:
this makes a superficial, but no substantial difference.
It is still a Thing Seen, significant of Godhead;
an Idol. The most rigorous Puritan has his Confession of Faith, and intellectual Representation of
Divine things, and worships thereby; thereby is
worship first made possible for him. All creeds,
liturgies, religious forms, conceptions that fitly invest
religious feelings, are in this sense *eidola*, things seen.
All worship whatsoever must proceed by Symbols,
by Idols:—we may say, all Idolatry is comparative,
and the worst Idolatry is only *more* idolatrous.

Where, then, lies the evil of it? some fatal evil
must lie in it, or earnest prophetic men would not
on all hands so reprobate it. Why is Idolatry so
hateful to Prophets? It seems to me as if, in the

Idolatry become insincere worship of those poor wooden symbols, the thing that had chiefly provoked the Prophet, and filled his inmost soul with indignation and aversion, was not exactly what suggested itself to his own thought, and came out of him in words to others, as the thing. The rudest heathen that worshipped Canopus, or the Caabah Black-Stone, he, as we saw, was superior to the horse that worshipped nothing at all! Nay there was a kind of lasting merit in that poor act of his; analogous to what is still meritorious in Poets: recognition of a certain endless *divine* beauty and significance in stars and all natural objects whatsoever. Why should the Prophet so mercilessly condemn him? The poorest mortal worshipping his Fetish, while his heart is full of it, may be an object of pity, of contempt and avoidance, if you will; but cannot surely be an object of hatred. Let his heart *be* honestly full of it, the whole space of his dark narrow mind illuminated thereby; in one word, let him entirely *believe* in his Fetish,—it will then be, I should say, if not well with him, yet as well as it can readily be made to be, and you will leave him alone, unmolested there.

But here enters the fatal circumstance of Idolatry, that, in the era of the Prophets, no man's mind *is* any longer honestly filled with his Idol or Symbol. Before the Prophet can arise who, seeing through it, knows it to be mere wood, many men must have begun dimly to doubt that it was little more. Condemnable Idolatry is *insincere* Idolatry. Doubt has eaten-out the heart of it: a human soul is seen clinging spasmodically to an Ark of the Covenant, which it half-feels now to have become a Phantasm. This is one of the balefulest sights. Souls are no longer *filled* with their Fetish; but only pretend to be filled, and would fain make themselves feel that they are filled. "You do not believe," said Coleridge; "you only believe that you believe." It is the final scene in all kinds of Worship and Symbolism; the sure symptom that death is now nigh. It is equivalent to what we call Formulism, and Worship of Formulas, in these days of ours. No more immoral act can be done by a human creature; for it is the beginning of all immorality, or rather it is the impossibility henceforth of any morality whatsoever: the innermost moral soul is paralysed thereby, cast into fatal magnetic sleep! Men are no longer *sincere* men. I do not wonder that the earnest man denounces this, brands it, prosecutes it with unextinguishable aversion. He and it, all good and it, are at death-feud. Blamable Idolatry is *Cant*, and even what one may call Sincere-Cant. Sincere-Cant: that is worth thinking of! Every sort of Worship ends with this phasis.

Luther a breaker of Idols

I find Luther to have been a Breaker of Idols, no less than any other Prophet. The wooden gods of the Koreish, made of timber and bees-wax, were not more hateful to Mahomet than Tetzel's Pardons of Sin, made of sheepskin and ink, were to Luther. It is the property of every Hero, in every time, in every place and situation, that he come back to reality; that he stand upon things, and not shows of things. According as he loves, and venerates, articulately or with deep speechless thought, the awful realities of things, so will the hollow shows of things, however regular, decorous, accredited by Koreishes or Conclaves, be intolerable and detestable to him. Protestantism too is the work of a Prophet: the prophet-work of that sixteenth century.

Protest-
antism
means
revolt
The first stroke of honest demolition to an ancient thing grown false and idolatrous; preparatory afar off to a new thing, which shall be true, and authentically divine!——

At first view it might seem as if Protestantism were entirely destructive to this that we call Hero-worship, and represent as the basis of all possible good, religious or social, for mankind. One often hears it said that Protestantism introduced a new era, radically different from any the world had ever seen before: the era of 'private judgment,' as they call it. By this revolt against the Pope, every man became his own Pope; and learnt, among other things, that he must never trust any Pope, or spiritual Hero-captain, any more! Whereby, is not spiritual union, all hierarchy and subordination among men, henceforth an impossibility? So we hear it said.——Now I need not deny that Protestantism was a revolt against spiritual sovereignties, Popes and much else. Nay I will grant that English Puritanism, revolt against earthly sovereignties, was the second act of it; that the enormous French Revolution itself was the third act, whereby all sovereignties earthly and spiritual were, as might seem, abolished or made sure of abolition. Protestantism is the grand root from which our whole subsequent European History branches out. For the spiritual will always body itself forth in the temporal history of men; the spiritual is the beginning of the temporal. And now, sure enough, the cry is everywhere for Liberty and Equality, Independence and so forth: instead of *Kings*, Ballot-boxes and Electoral suffrages; it seems made out that any Hero-sovereign, or loyal obedience of men to a man, in things temporal or things spiritual, has passed away forever from the 'Private world. I should despair of the world altogether, judg-if so. One of my deepest convictions is, that it is ment' not so. Without sovereigns, true sovereigns, temporal and spiritual, I see nothing possible but an anarchy: the hatefulest of things. But I find Protestantism, whatever anarchic democracy it have produced, to be the beginning of new genuine sovereignty and order. I find it to be a revolt against *false* sovereigns; the painful but indispensable first preparative for *true* sovereigns getting place among us! This is worth explaining a little.

Let us remark, therefore, in the first place, that this of 'private judgment' is, at bottom, not a new thing in the world, but only new at that epoch of the world. There is nothing generically new or peculiar in the Reformation; it was a return to Truth and Reality in opposition to Falsehood and Semblance, as all kinds of Improvement and genuine Teaching are and have been. Liberty of private judgment, if we will consider it, must at all times have existed in the world. Dante had not put-out his eyes, or tied shackles on himself; he was at home in that Catholicism of his, a free-seeing soul in it, if many a poor Hogstraten, Tetzel and Dr Eck had now become slaves in it. Liberty of judg-ment? No iron chain, or outward force of any kind, could ever compel the soul of a man to believe or to disbelieve: it is his own indefeasible light, that judgment of his; he will reign, and believe there, by the grace of God alone! The sorriest sophistical Bellarmine, preaching sightless faith and passive obedience, must first, by some kind of *conviction*, have abdicated his right to be convinced. His 'private judgment' indicated that,

Belief versus Hearsay as the advisablest step *he* could take. The right of private judgment will subsist, in full force, wherever true men subsist. A true man *believes* with his whole judgment, with all the illumination and discernment that is in him, and has always so believed. A false man, only struggling to 'believe that he believes,' will naturally manage it in some other way. Protestantism said to this latter, Woe! and to the former, Well done! At bottom, it was no new saying; it was a return to all old sayings that ever had been said. Be genuine, be sincere: that was, once more, the meaning of it. Mahomet believed with his whole mind; Odin with his whole mind,—he, and all *true* Followers of Odinism. They, by their private judgment, had 'judged'—*so*.

And now, I venture to assert, that the exercise of private judgment, faithfully gone about, does by no means necessarily end in selfish independence, isolation; but rather ends necessarily in the opposite of that. It is not honest inquiry that makes anarchy; but it is error, insincerity, half-belief and untruth that make it. A man protesting against error is on the way towards uniting himself with all men that believe in truth. There is no communion possible among men who believe only in hearsays. The heart of each is lying dead; has no power of sympathy even with *things*,—or he would believe *them* and not hearsays. No sympathy even with things; how much less with his fellow-men! He cannot unite with men; he is an anarchic man. Only in a world of sincere men is unity possible;— and there, in the longrun, it is as good as *certain*.

For observe one thing, a thing too often left out of view, or rather altogether lost sight of, in this controversy : That it *is* not necessary a man should himself have *discovered* the truth he is to believe in, and never so *sincerely* to believe in. A Great Man, we said, was always sincere, as the first condition of him. But a man need not be great in order to be sincere; that is not the necessity of Nature and all Time, but only of certain corrupt unfortunate epochs of Time. A man can believe, and make his own, in the most genuine way, what he has received from another ;—and with boundless gratitude to that other ! The merit of *originality* is not novelty; it is sincerity. The believing man is the original man; whatsoever he believes, he believes it for himself, not for another. Every son of Adam can become a sincere man, an original man, in this sense ; no mortal is doomed to be an insincere man. Whole ages, what we call ages of Faith, are original; all men in them, or the most of men in them, sincere. These are the great and fruitful ages : every worker, in all spheres, is a worker not on semblance but on substance; every work issues in a result : the general sum of such work is great ; for all of it, as genuine, tends towards one goal ; all of it is *additive*, none of it subtractive. There is true union, true kingship, loyalty, all true and blessed things, so far as the poor Earth can produce blessedness for men.

[margin note:] **Origin- ality means sincerity**

Hero-worship ? Ah me, that a man be self-sub- sistent, original, true, or what we call it, is surely the farthest in the world from indisposing him to reverence and believe other men's truth ! It only disposes, necessitates and invincibly compels him to *dis*believe other men's dead formulas, hearsays and untruths. A man embraces truth with his eyes open, and because his eyes are open : does he need

Luther's message to shut them before he can love his Teacher of truth? He alone can love, with a right gratitude and genuine loyalty of soul, the Hero-Teacher who has delivered him out of darkness into light. Is not such a one a true Hero and Serpent-queller; worthy of all reverence! The black monster, Falsehood, our one enemy in this world, lies prostrate by his valour; it was he that conquered the world for us!—See, accordingly, was not Luther himself reverenced as a true Pope, or Spiritual Father, *being* verily such? Napoleon, from amid boundless revolt of Sansculottism, became a King. Hero-worship never dies, nor can die. Loyalty and Sovereignty are everlasting in the world:—and there is this in them, that they are grounded not on garnitures and semblances, but on realities and sincerities. Not by shutting your eyes, your 'private judgment;' no, but by opening them, and by having something to see! Luther's message was deposition and abolition to all false Popes and Potentates, but life and strength, though afar off, to new genuine ones.

All this of Liberty and Equality, Electoral suffrages, Independence and so forth, we will take, therefore, to be a temporary phenomenon, by no means a final one. Though likely to last a long time, with sad enough embroilments for us all, we must welcome it, as the penalty of sins that are past, the pledge of inestimable benefits that are coming. In all ways, it behoved men to quit simulacra and return to fact; cost what it might, that did behove to be done. With spurious Popes, and Believers having no private judgment,—quacks pretending to command over dupes,—what can you do? Misery and mischief only. You cannot make an association out of insincere men; you cannot build an edifice

except by plummet and level,—at *right*-angles to **His birth**
one another! In all this wild revolutionary work,
from Protestantism downwards, I see the blessedest
result preparing itself: not abolition of Hero-
worship, but rather what I would call a whole
World of Heroes. If Hero mean *sincere man*, why
may not every one of us be a Hero? A world all
sincere, a believing world: the like has been; the
like will again be,—cannot help being. That were
the right sort of Worshippers for Heroes: never
could the truly Better be so reverenced as where all
were True and Good!—But we must hasten to
Luther and his Life.

Luther's birthplace was Eisleben in Saxony; he
came into the world there on the 10th of November
1483. It was an accident that gave this honour to
Eisleben. His parents, poor mine-labourers in a
village of that region, named Mohra, had gone to
the Eisleben Winter-Fair: in the tumult of this
scene the Frau Luther was taken with travail, found
refuge in some poor house there, and the boy she
bore was named MARTIN LUTHER. Strange enough
to reflect upon it. This poor Frau Luther, she
had gone with her husband to make her small mer-
chandisings; perhaps to sell the lock of yarn she
had been spinning, to buy the small winter-necessaries
for her narrow hut or household; in the whole
world, that day, there was not a more entirely un-
important-looking pair of people than this Miner
and his Wife. And yet what were all Emperors,
Popes and Potentates, in comparison? There was
born here, once more, a Mighty Man; whose
light was to flame as the beacon over long centuries
and epochs of the world; the whole world and its

His rigorous bringing-up history was waiting for this man. It is strange, it is great. It leads us back to another Birth-hour, in a still meaner environment, Eighteen Hundred years ago,—of which it is fit that we *say* nothing, that we think only in silence; for what words are there! The Age of Miracles past? The Age of Miracles is forever here!—

I find it altogether suitable to Luther's function in this Earth, and doubtless wisely ordered to that end by the Providence presiding over him and us and all things, that he was born poor, and brought-up poor, one of the poorest of men. He had to beg, as the school-children in those times did; singing for alms and bread, from door to door. Hardship, rigorous Necessity was the poor boy's companion; no man nor no thing would put-on a false face to flatter Martin Luther. Among things, not among the shows of things, had he to grow. A boy of rude figure, yet with weak health, with his large greedy soul, full of all faculty and sensibility, he suffered greatly. But it was his task to get acquainted with *realities*, and keep acquainted with them, at whatever cost: his task was to bring the whole world back to reality, for it had dwelt too long with semblance! A youth nursed-up in wintry whirlwinds, in desolate darkness and difficulty, that he may step-forth at last from his stormy Scandinavia, strong as a true man, as a god: a Christian Odin,— a right Thor once more, with his thunder-hammer, to smite asunder ugly enough *Jötuns* and Giant-monsters!

Perhaps the turning incident of his life, we may fancy, was that death of his friend Alexis, by lightning, at the gate of Erfurt. Luther had struggled-up through boyhood, better and worse;

displaying, in spite of all hindrances, the largest He becomes a monk intellect, eager to learn: his father judging doubt- less that he might promote himself in the world, set him upon the study of Law. This was the path to rise; Luther, with little will in it either way, had consented: he was now nineteen years of age. Alexis and he had been to see the old Luther people at Mansfeldt; were got back again near Erfurt, when a thunderstorm came on; the bolt struck Alexis, he fell dead at Luther's feet. What is this Life of ours?—gone in a moment, burnt-up like a scroll, into the blank Eternity! What are all earthly preferments, Chancellorships, Kingships? They lie shrunk together—there! The Earth has opened on them; in a moment they are not, and Eternity is. Luther, struck to the heart, determined to devote himself to God and God's service alone. In spite of all dissuasions from his father and others, he became a Monk in the Augustine Convent at Erfurt.

This was probably the first light-point in the history of Luther, his purer will now first decisively uttering itself; but, for the present, it was still as one light-point in an element all of darkness. He says he was a pious monk, *ich bin ein frommer Mönch gewesen;* faithfully, painfully struggling to work-out the truth of this high act of his; but it was to little purpose. His misery had not lessened; had rather, as it were, increased into infinitude. The drudgeries he had to do, as novice in his Convent, all sorts of slave-work, were not his grievance: the deep earnest soul of the man had fallen into all manner of black scruples, dubitations; he believed himself likely to die soon, and far worse than die. One hears with a new interest for poor

His con-
version
Luther that, at this time, he lived in terror of the unspeakable misery; fancied that he was doomed to eternal reprobation. Was it not the humble sincere nature of the man? What was he, that he should be raised to Heaven! He that had known only misery, and mean slavery: the news was too blessed to be credible. It could not become clear to him how, by fasts, vigils, formalities and mass-work, a man's soul could be saved. He fell into the blackest wretchedness; had to wander staggering as on the verge of bottomless Despair.

It must have been a most blessed discovery, that of an old Latin Bible which he found in the Erfurt Library about this time. He had never seen the Book before. It taught him another lesson than that of fasts and vigils. A brother monk too, of pious experience, was helpful. Luther learned now that a man was saved not by singing masses, but by the infinite grace of God: a more credible hypo-thesis. He gradually got himself founded, as on the rock. No wonder he should venerate the Bible, which had brought this blessed help to him. He prized it as the Word of the Highest must be prized by such a man. He determined to hold by that; as through life and to death he firmly did.

This, then, is his deliverance from darkness, his final triumph over darkness, what we call his con-version; for himself the most important of all epochs. That he should now grow daily in peace and clearness; that, unfolding now the great talents and virtues implanted in him, he should rise to im-portance in his Convent, in his country, and be found more and more useful in all honest business of life, is a natural result. He was sent on missions by his Augustine Order, as a man of talent and fidelity fit to do their business well: the Elector of Saxony, Friedrich, named the Wise, a truly wise and just prince, had cast his eye on him as a valuable person; made him Professor in his new University of Wittenberg, Preacher too at Wittenberg; in both which capacities, as in all duties he did, this Luther, in the peaceable sphere of common life, was gaining more and more esteem with all good men.

It was in his twenty-seventh year that he first saw Rome; being sent thither, as I said, on mission from his Convent. Pope Julius the Second, and what was going-on at Rome, must have filled the mind of Luther with amazement. He had come as to the Sacred City, throne of God's Highpriest on Earth; and he found it—what we know! Many thoughts it must have given the man; many which we have no record of, which perhaps he did not himself know how to utter. This Rome, this scene of false priests, clothed not in the beauty of holiness, but in far other vesture, is *false :* but what is it to Luther? A mean man he, how shall he reform a world? That was far from his thoughts. A humble, solitary man, why should he at all meddle with the world? It was the task of quite higher men than he. His business was to guide his own footsteps wisely through the world. Let him do his own obscure duty in it well; the rest, horrible and dismal as it looks, is in God's hand, not in his.

It is curious to reflect what might have been the issue, had Roman Popery happened to pass this Luther by; to go on in its great wasteful orbit, and not come athwart his little path, and force him to assault it! Conceivable enough that, in this case, he might have held his peace about the abuses of Rome; left Providence, and God on high, to deal with them! A modest quiet man; not prompt he to attack irreverently persons in authority. His clear task, as I say, was to do his own duty; to walk wisely in this world of confused wickedness, and save his own soul alive. But the Roman Highpriesthood did come athwart him: afar off at Wittenberg he, Luther, could not get lived in honesty for it; he remonstrated, resisted, came to extremity; was struck-at, struck again, and so it came to wager of battle between them! This is worth attending to in Luther's history. Perhaps no man of so humble, peaceable a disposition ever filled the world with contention. We cannot but see that he would have loved privacy, quiet diligence in the shade; that it was against his will he ever became a notoriety. Notoriety: what would that do for him? The goal of his march through this world was the Infinite Heaven; an indubitable goal for him: in a few years, he should either have attained that, or lost it forever! We will say nothing at all, I think, of that sorrowfulest of theories, of its being some mean shopkeeper grudge, of the Augustine Monk against the Dominican, that first kindled the wrath of Luther, and produced the Protestant Reformation. We will say to the people who maintain it, if indeed any such exist now: Get first into the sphere of thought by which it is so much as possible to judge of Luther, or of any man like Luther, otherwise than distractedly; we may then begin arguing with you.

The Monk Tetzel, sent out carelessly in the way of trade, by Leo Tenth,—who merely wanted to raise a little money, and for the rest seems to have **Argu-** been a Pagan rather than a Christian, so far as he **ment** was anything,—arrived at Wittenberg, and drove **by fire** his scandalous trade there. Luther's flock bought Indulgences : in the confessional of his Church, people pleaded to him that they had already got their sins pardoned. Luther, if he would not be found wanting at his own post, a false sluggard and coward at the very centre of the little space of ground that was his own and no other man's, had to step-forth against Indulgences, and declare aloud that *they* were a futility and sorrowful mockery, that no man's sins could be pardoned by *them*. It was the beginning of the whole Reformation. We know how it went ; forward from this first public challenge of Tetzel, on the last day of October 1517, through remonstrance and argument ;— spreading ever wider, rising ever higher ; till it became unquenchable, and enveloped all the world. Luther's heart's-desire was to have this grief and other griefs amended ; his thought was still far other than that of introducing separation in the Church, or revolting against the Pope, Father of Christendom.—The elegant Pagan Pope cared little about this Monk and his doctrines ; wished, how- ever, to have done with the noise of him : in a space of some three years, having tried various softer methods, he thought good to end it by *fire*. He dooms the Monk's writings to be burnt by the hangman, and his body to be sent bound to Rome, —probably for a similar purpose. It was the way they had ended with Huss, with Jerome, the century before. A short argument, fire. Poor Huss : he came to that Constance Council, with all imaginable promises and safe-conducts ; an

Luther burns the Bull earnest, not rebellious kind of man: they laid him instantly in a stone dungeon 'three-feet wide, six-feet high, seven-feet long;' *burnt* the true voice of him out of this world; choked it in smoke and fire. That was *not* well done!

I, for one, pardon Luther for now altogether revolting against the Pope. The elegant Pagan, by this fire-decree of his, had kindled into noble just wrath the bravest heart then living in this world. The bravest, if also one of the humblest, peaceablest; it was now kindled. These words of mine, words of truth and soberness, aiming faithfully, as human inability would allow, to promote God's truth on Earth, and save men's souls, you, God's vicegerent on earth, answer them by the hangman and fire? You will burn me and them, for answer to the God's-message they strove to bring you? *You* are not God's vicegerent; you are another's than his, I think! I take your Bull, as an emparchmented Lie, and burn *it*. You will do what you see good next: this is what I do.—It was on the 10th of December 1520, three years after the beginning of the business, that Luther, 'with a great concourse of people,' took this indignant step of burning the Pope's fire-decree 'at the Elster-Gate of Wittenberg.' Wittenberg looked on 'with shoutings;' the whole world was looking on. The Pope should not have provoked that 'shout'! It was the shout of the awakening of nations. The quiet German heart, modest, patient of much, had at length got more than it could bear. Formulism, Pagan Popeism, and other Falsehood and corrupt Semblance had ruled long enough: and here once more was a man found who durst tell all men that God's-world stood not on semblances but on realities; that Life was a truth, and not a lie!

At bottom, as was said above, we are to consider Luther as a Prophet Idol-breaker; a bringer-back of men to reality. It is the function of great men and teachers. Mahomet said, These idols of yours are wood; you put wax and oil on them, the flies stick on them: they are not God, I tell you, they are black wood! Luther said to the Pope, This thing of yours that you call a Pardon of Sins, it is a bit of rag-paper with ink. It *is* nothing else; it, and so much like it, is nothing else. God alone can pardon sins. Popeship, spiritual Fatherhood of God's Church, is that a vain semblance, of cloth and parchment? It is an awful fact. God's Church is not a semblance, Heaven and Hell are not semblances. I stand on this, since you drive me to it. Standing on this, I a poor German monk am stronger than you all. I stand solitary, friendless, but on God's Truth; you with your tiaras, triple-hats, with your treasuries and armories, thunders spiritual and temporal, stand on the Devil's Lie, and are not so strong!——

The Diet of Worms, Luther's appearance there on the 17th of April 1521, may be considered as the greatest scene in Modern European History; the point, indeed, from which the whole subsequent history of civilisation takes its rise. After multiplied negotiations, disputations, it had come to this. The young Emperor Charles Fifth, with all the Princes of Germany, Papal nuncios, dignitaries spiritual and temporal, are assembled there: Luther is to appear and answer for himself, whether he will recant or not. The world's pomp and power sits there on this hand: on that, stands-up for

Luther
will not
recant God's Truth, one man, the poor miner Hans
Luther's Son.   Friends had reminded him of
Huss, advised him not to go; he would not be
advised.   A large company of friends rode-out to
meet him, with still more earnest warnings; he
answered, "Were there as many Devils in Worms
as there are roof-tiles, I would on."   The people,
on the morrow, as he went to the Hall of the
Diet, crowded the windows and housetops, some
of them calling out to him, in solemn words, not to
recant: "Whosoever denieth me before men!"
they cried to him,—as in a kind of solemn petition
and adjuration.   Was it not in reality our petition
too, the petition of the whole world, lying in dark
bondage of soul, paralysed under a black spectral
Nightmare and triple-hatted Chimera, calling itself
Father in God, and what not: "Free us; it rests
with thee; desert us not!"

Luther did not desert us.   His speech, of two
hours, distinguished itself by its respectful, wise and
honest tone; submissive to whatsoever could law-
fully claim submission, not submissive to any more
than that.   His writings, he said, were partly his
own, partly derived from the Word of God.   As
to what was his own, human infirmity entered into
it; unguarded anger, blindness, many things doubtless which it were a blessing for him could he
abolish altogether.   But as to what stood on sound
truth and the Word of God, he could not recant
it.   How could he?   "Confute me," he con-
cluded, "by proofs of Scripture, or else by plain
just arguments: I cannot recant otherwise.   For
it is neither safe nor prudent to do ought against
conscience.   Here stand I; I can do no other:
God assist me!"—It is, as we say, the greatest

moment in the Modern History of Men. English **The Re-**
Puritanism, England and its Parliaments, Americas, **formation**
and vast work these two centuries; French Re- **inevitable**
volution, Europe and its work everywhere at present: the germ of it all lay there: had Luther
in that moment done other, it had all been otherwise! The European World was asking him:
Am I to sink ever lower into falsehood, stagnant
putrescence, loathsome accursed death; or, with
whatever paroxysm, to cast the falsehoods out of
me, and be cured and live?—

Great wars, contentions and disunion followed
out of this Reformation; which last down to our
day, and are yet far from ended. Great talk and
crimination has been made about these. They are
lamentable, undeniable; but after all what has
Luther or his cause to do with them? It seems
strange reasoning to charge the Reformation with
all this. When Hercules turned the purifying
river into King Augeas's stables, I have no doubt
the confusion that resulted was considerable all
around: but I think it was not Hercules's blame;
it was some other's blame! The Reformation
might bring what results it liked when it came,
but the Reformation simply could not help coming.
To all Popes and Popes' advocates, expostulating,
lamenting and accusing, the answer of the world
is: Once for all, your Popehood has become
untrue. No matter how good it was, how good
you say it is, we cannot believe it; the light of
our whole mind, given us to walk-by from Heaven
above, finds it henceforth a thing unbelievable.
We will not believe it, we will not try to believe
it,—we dare not! The thing is *untrue;* we were

'**No** traitors against the Giver of all Truth, if we durst
Popery' pretend to think it true. Away with it; let whatsoever likes come in the place of it: with *it* we
can have no farther trade!—Luther and his
Protestantism is not responsible for wars; the false
Simulacra that forced him to protest, they are
responsible. Luther did what every man that God
has made has not only the right, but lies under the
sacred duty, to do: answered a Falsehood when it
questioned him, Dost thou believe me?—No!—
At what cost soever, without counting of costs, this
thing behoved to be done. Union, organisation
spiritual and material, a far nobler than any Popedom
or Feudalism in their truest days, I never doubt, is
coming for the world; sure to come. But on Fact
alone, not on Semblance and Simulacrum, will it be
able either to come, or to stand when come.
With union grounded on falsehood, and ordering
us to speak and act lies, we will not have anything
to do. Peace? A brutal lethargy is peaceable,
the noisome grave is peaceable. We hope for a
living peace, not a dead one!

And yet, in prizing justly the indispensable
blessings of the New, let us not be unjust to the
Old. The Old *was* true, if it no longer is. In
Dante's days it needed no sophistry, self-blinding,
or other dishonesty, to get itself reckoned true.
It was good then; nay there is in the soul of it a
deathless good. The cry of 'No Popery' is
foolish enough in these days. The speculation
that Popery is on the increase, building new chapels
and so forth, may pass for one of the idlest ever
started. Very curious: to count-up a few Popish
chapels, listen to a few Protestant logic-choppings,
—to much dull-droning, drowsy inanity that still

calls itself Protestant, and say: See, Protestantism **Trans-**
is *dead ;* Popeism is more alive than it, will be alive **fusion of**
after it!—Drowsy inanities, not a few, that call **the Old**
themselves Protestant are dead ; but *Protestantism* **New**
has not died yet, that I hear of! Protestantism,
if we will look, has in these days produced its
Goethe, its Napoleon ; German Literature and
the French Revolution ; rather considerable signs
of life! Nay, at bottom, what else is alive *but*
Protestantism? The life of most else that one
meets is a galvanic one merely,—not a pleasant,
not a lasting sort of life!

Popery can build new chapels ; welcome to do
so, to all lengths. Popery cannot come back, any
more than Paganism can,—*which* also still lingers
in some countries. But, indeed, it is with these
things, as with the ebbing of the sea : you look at
the waves oscillating hither, thither on the beach ;
for *minutes* you cannot tell how it is going ; look in
half an hour where it is,—look in half a century
where your Popehood is! Alas, would there were
no greater danger to our Europe than the poor old
Pope's revival! Thor may as soon try to revive.
—And withal this oscillation has a meaning. The
poor old Popehood will not die away entirely, as
Thor has done, for some time yet; nor ought it.
We may say, the Old never dies till this happen,
Till all the soul of good that was in it have got
itself transfused into the practical New. While a
good work remains capable of being done by the
Romish form ; or, what is inclusive of all, while a
pious life remains capable of being led by it, just so
long, if we consider, will this or the other human
soul adopt it, go about as a living witness of it. So
long it will obtrude itself on the eye of us who

Luther's kingly faculty reject it, till we in our practice too have appropriated whatsoever of truth was in it. Then, but also not till then, it will have no charm more for any man. It lasts here for a purpose. Let it last as long as it can.—

Of Luther I will add now, in reference to all these wars and bloodshed, the noticeable fact that none of them began so long as he continued living. The controversy did not get to fighting so long as he was there. To me it is proof of his greatness in all senses, this fact. How seldom do we find a man that has stirred-up some vast commotion, who does not himself perish, swept-away in it! Such is the usual course of revolutionists. Luther continued, in a good degree, sovereign of this greatest revolution; all Protestants, of what rank or function soever, looking much to him for guidance: and he held it peaceable, continued firm at the centre of it. A man to do this must have a kingly faculty: he must have the gift to discern at all turns where the true heart of the matter lies, and to plant himself courageously on that, as a strong true man, that other true men may rally round him there. He will not continue leader of men otherwise. Luther's clear deep force of judgment, his force of all sorts, of *silence*, of tolerance and moderation, among others, are very notable in these circumstances.

Tolerance, I say; a very genuine kind of tolerance: he distinguishes what is essential, and what is not; the unessential may go very much as it will. A complaint comes to him that such and such a Reformed Preacher, 'will not preach without a cassock.' Well, answers Luther, what harm will a cassock do the man? 'Let him have a cassock 'to preach in; let him have three cassocks if he find **His** 'benefit in them!' His conduct in the matter of **valour** Karlstadt's wild image-breaking; of the Anabaptists; of the Peasants' War, shows a noble strength, very different from spasmodic violence. With sure prompt insight he discriminates what is what: a strong just man, he speaks-forth what is the wise course, and all men follow him in that. Luther's Written Works give similar testimony of him. The dialect of these speculations is now grown obsolete for us; but one still reads them with a singular attraction. And indeed the mere grammatical diction is still legible enough; Luther's merit in literary history is of the greatest; his dialect became the language of all writing. They are not well written, these Four-and-twenty Quartos of his; written hastily, with quite other than literary objects. But in no Books have I found a more robust, genuine, I will say noble faculty of a man than in these. A rugged honesty, homeliness, simplicity; a rugged sterling sense and strength. He flashes-out illumination from him; his smiting idiomatic phrases seem to cleave into the very secret of the matter. Good humour too, nay tender affection, nobleness, and depth: this man could have been a Poet too! He had to *work* an Epic Poem, not write one. I call him a great Thinker; as indeed his greatness of heart already betokens that.

Richter says of Luther's words, 'his words are half-battles.' They may be called so. The essential quality of him was, that he could fight and conquer; that he was a right piece of human Valour. No more valiant man, no mortal heart to be called *braver*, that one has record of, ever

The black spot at Wartburg — lived in that Teutonic Kindred, whose character is valour. His defiance of the 'Devils' in Worms was not a mere boast, as the like might be if now spoken. It was a faith of Luther's that there were Devils, spiritual denizens of the Pit, continually besetting men. Many times, in his writings, this turns-up; and a most small sneer has been grounded on it by some. In the room of the Wartburg where he sat translating the Bible, they still show you a black spot on the wall; the strange memorial of one of these conflicts. Luther sat translating one of the Psalms; he was worn-down with long labour, with sickness, abstinence from food: there rose before him some hideous indefinable Image, which he took for the Evil One, to forbid his work: Luther started-up, with fiend-defiance; flung his inkstand at the spectre, and it disappeared! The spot still remains there; a curious monument of several things. Any apothecary's apprentice can now tell us what we are to think of this apparition, in a scientific sense: but the man's heart that dare rise defiant, face to face, against Hell itself, can give no higher proof of fearlessness. The thing he will quail before exists not on this Earth or under it.—Fearless enough! 'The 'Devil is aware,' writes he on one occasion, 'that 'this does not proceed out of fear in me. I have 'seen and defied innumerable Devils. Duke 'George,' of Leipzig, a great enemy of his, 'Duke 'George is not equal to one Devil,'—far short of a Devil! 'If I had business at Leipzig, I would 'ride into Leipzig, though it rained Duke-Georges 'for nine days running.' What a reservoir of Dukes to ride into!—

At the same time, they err greatly who imagine

that this man's courage was ferocity, mere coarse **Luther's** disobedient obstinacy and savagery, as many do. **tender-** Far from that. There may be an absence of fear **ness** which arises from the absence of thought or affection, from the presence of hatred and stupid fury. We do not value the courage of the tiger highly! With Luther it was far otherwise; no accusation could be more unjust than this of mere ferocious violence brought against him. A most gentle heart withal, full of pity and love, as indeed the truly valiant heart ever is. The tiger before a *stronger* foe—flies: the tiger is not what we call valiant, only fierce and cruel. I know few things more touching than those soft breathings of affection, soft as a child's or a mother's, in this great wild heart of Luther. So honest, unadulterated with any cant; homely, rude in their utterance; pure as water welling from the rock. What, in fact, was all that downpressed mood of despair and reprobation, which we saw in his youth, but the outcome of pre-eminent thoughtful gentleness, affections too keen and fine? It is the course such men as the poor Poet Cowper fall into. Luther to a slight observer might have seemed a timid, weak man; modesty, affectionate shrinking tenderness the chief distinction of him. It is a noble valour which is roused in a heart like this, once stirred-up into defiance, all kindled into a heavenly blaze.

In Luther's *Table-Talk*, a posthumous Book of anecdotes and sayings collected by his friends, the most interesting now of all the Books proceeding from him, we have many beautiful unconscious displays of the man, and what sort of nature he had. His behaviour at the deathbed of his little Daughter, so still, so great and loving, is among the most

His
Table-
Talk

affecting things. He is resigned that his little Magdalene should die, yet longs inexpressibly that she might live;—follows, in awestruck thought, the flight of her little soul through those unknown realms. Awe-struck; most heartfelt, we can see; and sincere,—for after all dogmatic creeds and articles, he feels what nothing it is that we know, or can know: His little Magdalene shall be with God, as God wills; for Luther too that is all; *Islam* is all.

Once, he looks-out from his solitary Patmos, the Castle of Coburg, in the middle of the night: The great vault of Immensity, long flights of clouds sailing through it,—dumb, gaunt, huge:—who supports all that? "None ever saw the pillars of it; yet it is supported." God supports it. We must know that God is great, that God is good; and trust, where we cannot see.—Returning home from Leipzig once, he is struck by the beauty of the harvest-fields: How it stands, that golden yellow corn, on its fair taper stem, its golden head bent, all rich and waving there,—the meek Earth, at God's kind bidding, has produced it once again; the bread of man!—In the garden at Wittenburg one evening at sunset, a little bird has perched for the night: That little bird, says Luther, above it are the stars and deep Heaven of worlds; yet it has folded its little wings; gone trustfully to rest there as in its home: the Maker of it has given it too a home!——Neither are mirthful turns wanting: there is a great free human heart in this man. The common speech of him has a rugged nobleness, idiomatic, expressive, genuine; gleams here and there with beautiful poetic tints. One feels him to be a great brother man. His love of Music, indeed, is not this, as it were, the summary of all **His** these affections in him? Many a wild unuttera- **portrait** bility he spoke-forth from him in the tones of his flute. The Devils fled from his flute, he says. Death-defiance on the one hand, and such love of music on the other; I could call these the two opposite poles of a great soul; between these two all great things had room.

Luther's face is to me expressive of him; in Kranach's best portraits I find the true Luther. A rude plebeian face; with its huge crag-like brows and bones, the emblem of rugged energy; at first, almost a repulsive face. Yet in the eyes especially there is a wild silent sorrow; an unnamable melancholy, the element of all gentle and fine affections; giving to the rest the true stamp of nobleness. Laughter was in this Luther, as we said; but tears also were there. Tears also were appointed him; tears and hard toil. The basis of his life was Sadness, Earnestness. In his latter days, after all triumphs and victories, he expresses himself heartily weary of living; he considers that God alone can and will regulate the course things are taking, and that perhaps the Day of Judgment is not far. As for him, he longs for one thing: that God would release him from his labour, and let him depart and be at rest. They understand little of the man who cite this in *dis*credit of him!—I will call this Luther a true Great Man; great in intellect, in courage, affection and integrity; one of our most lovable and precious men. Great, not as a hewn obelisk; but as an Alpine mountain,—so simple, honest, spontaneous, not setting-up to be great at all; there for quite another purpose than being great! Ah yes, unsubduable granite, piercing

Puritan- far and wide into the Heavens; yet in the clefts
ism of it fountains, green beautiful valleys with flowers!
A right Spiritual Hero and Prophet; once more, a
true Son of Nature and Fact, for whom these
centuries, and many that are to come yet, will be
thankful to Heaven.

The most interesting phasis which the Reformation anywhere assumes, especially for us English,
is that of Puritanism. In Luther's own country
Protestantism soon dwindled into a rather barren
affair: not a religion or faith, but rather now a
theological jangling of argument, the proper seat
of it not the heart; the essence of it sceptical contention: which indeed has jangled more and more,
down to Voltaireism itself, — through Gustavus-
Adolphus contentions onward to French-Revolu-
tion ones! But in our Island there arose a
Puritanism, which even got itself established as
a Presbyterianism and National Church among the
Scotch; which came forth as a real business of the
heart; and has produced in the world very notable
fruit. In some senses, one may say it is the only
phasis of Protestantism that ever got to the rank of
being a Faith, a true heart-communication with
Heaven, and of exhibiting itself in History as such.
We must spare a few words for Knox; himself a
brave and remarkable man; but still more important
as Chief Priest and Founder, which one may consider him to be, of the Faith that became Scotland's,
New England's, Oliver Cromwell's. History will
have something to say about this, for some time to
come!

We may censure Puritanism as we please; and
no one of us, I suppose, but would find it a
very rough defective thing. But we, and all men,

may understand that it was a genuine thing; for Nature has adopted it, and it has grown, and grows. I say sometimes, that all goes by wager-of-battle in this world; that *strength*, well understood, is the measure of all worth. Give a thing time; if it can succeed, it is a right thing. Look now at American Saxondom; and at that little Fact of the sailing of the Mayflower, two hundred years ago, from Delft Haven in Holland! Were we of open sense as the Greeks were, we had found a Poem here; one of Nature's own Poems; such as she writes in broad facts over great continents. For it was properly the beginning of America: there were straggling settlers in America before, some material as of a body was there; but the soul of it was first this. These poor men, driven-out of their country, not able well to live in Holland, determine on settling in the New World. Black untamed forests are there, and wild savage creatures; but not so cruel as Starchamber hangmen. They thought the Earth would yield them food, if they tilled honestly; the everlasting heaven would stretch there too, overhead; they should be left in peace, to prepare for Eternity by living well in this world of Time; worshipping in what they thought the true, not the idolatrous way. They clubbed their small means together; hired a ship, the little ship Mayflower, and made ready to set sail.

In Neal's *History of the Puritans** is an account of the ceremony of their departure: solemnity, we might call it rather, for it was a real act of worship. Their minister went down with them to the beach, and their brethren whom they were to leave behind;

Sailing of the May- flower

* Neal (London, 1755), i. 490.

Scot-
land's
one epoch
all joined in solemn prayer, That God would have pity on His poor children, and *go* with them into that waste wilderness, for He also had made that, He was there also as well as here.—Hah! These men, I think, had a work! The weak thing, weaker than a child, becomes strong one day, if it be a true thing. Puritanism was only despicable, laughable then; but nobody can manage to laugh at it now. Puritanism has got weapons and sinews; it has fire-arms, war-navies; it has cunning in its ten fingers, strength in its right arm; it can steer ships, fell forests, remove mountains;—it is one of the strongest things under the sun at present!

In the history of Scotland, too, I can find properly but one epoch: we may say it contains nothing of world-interest at all but this Reformation by Knox. A poor barren country, full of continual broils, dissensions, massacrings; a people in the last state of rudeness and destitution, little better perhaps than Ireland at this day. Hungry fierce barons, not so much as able to form any arrangement with each other *how to divide* what they fleeced from these poor drudges; but obliged, as the Columbian Republics are at this day, to make of every alteration a revolution; no way of changing a ministry but by hanging the old ministers on gibbets: this is a historical spectacle of no very singular significance! 'Bravery' enough, I doubt not; fierce fighting in abundance: but not braver or fiercer than that of their old Scandinavian Sea-king ancestors; *whose* exploits we have not found worth dwelling on! It is a country as yet without a soul: nothing developed in it but what is rude, external, semi-animal. And now at the Reformation, the internal life is kindled, as it were, under the ribs of this outward material death. A cause, the noblest of causes kindles itself, like a beacon set on high; high as Heaven, yet attainable from Earth; — whereby the meanest man becomes not a Citizen only, but a Member of Christ's visible Church; a veritable Hero, if he prove a true man! A 'nation of heroes'

Well; this is what I mean by a whole 'nation of heroes;' a *believing* nation. There needs not a great soul to make a hero; there needs a god-created soul which will be true to its origin; that will be a great soul! The like has been seen, we find. The like will be again seen, under wider forms than the Presbyterian: there can be no lasting good done till then.—Impossible! say some. Possible? Has it not *been*, in this world, as a practised fact? Did Hero-worship fail in Knox's case? Or are we made of other clay now? Did the Westminster Confession of Faith add some new property to the soul of man? God made the soul of man. He did not doom any soul of man to live as a Hypothesis and Hearsay, in a world filled with such, and with the fatal work and fruit of such!——

But to return: This that Knox did for his Nation, I say, we may really call a resurrection as from death. It was not a smooth business; but it was welcome surely, and cheap at that price, had it been far rougher. On the whole, cheap at any price;—as life is. The people began to *live*: they needed first of all to do that, at what cost and costs soever. Scotch Literature and Thought, Scotch Industry; James Watt, David Hume, Walter Scott, Robert Burns: I find Knox and the Reformation acting in the heart's core of every one

What Scotland owes to Knox of these persons and phenomena; I find that without the Reformation they would not have been. Or what of Scotland? The Puritanism of Scotland became that of England, of New England. A tumult in the High Church of Edinburgh spread into a universal battle and struggle over all these realms;—there came out, after fifty years' struggling, what we call the '*Glorious* Revolution,' a *Habeas-Corpus* Act, Free Parliaments, and much else!—Alas, is it not too true what we said, That many men in the van do always, like Russian soldiers, march into the ditch of Schweidnitz, and fill it up with their dead bodies, that the rear may pass over them dry-shod and gain the honour? How many earnest rugged Cromwells, Knoxes, poor Peasant Covenanters, wrestling, battling for very life, in rough miry places, have to struggle, and suffer, and fall, greatly censured, *bemired*,—before a beautiful Revolution of Eighty-eight can step-over them in official pumps and silk-stockings, with universal three-times-three!

It seems to me hard measure that this Scottish man, now after three-hundred years, should have to plead like a culprit before the world; intrinsically for having been, in such way as it was then possible to be, the bravest of all Scotchmen! Had he been a poor Half-and-half, he could have crouched into the corner, like so many others; Scotland had not been delivered; and Knox had been without blame. He is the one Scotchman to whom, of all others, his country and the world owe a debt. He has to plead that Scotland would forgive him for having been worth to it any million 'unblamable' Scotchmen that need no forgiveness! He bared his breast to the battle; had to row in French galleys, wander forlorn in exile, in clouds and **Knox's** storms; was censured, shot-at through his windows; **call** had a right sore fighting life: if this world were his place of recompense, he had made but a bad venture of it. I cannot apologise for Knox. To him it is very indifferent, these two-hundred-and-fifty years or more, what men say of him. But we, having got above all those details of his battle, and living now in clearness on the fruits of his victory, we, for our own sake, ought to look through the rumours and controversies enveloping the man, into the man himself.

For one thing, I will remark that this post of Prophet to his Nation was not of his seeking; Knox had lived forty years quietly obscure, before he became conspicuous. He was the son of poor parents; had got a college education; become a Priest; adopted the Reformation, and seemed well content to guide his own steps by the light of it, nowise unduly intruding it on others. He had lived as Tutor in gentlemen's families; preaching when any body of persons wished to hear his doctrine: resolute he to walk by the truth, and speak the truth when called to do it; not ambitious of more; not fancying himself capable of more. In this entirely obscure way he had reached the age of forty; was with the small body of Reformers who were standing siege in St Andrew's Castle,—when one day in their chapel, the Preacher after finishing his exhortation to these fighters in the forlorn hope, said suddenly, That there ought to be other speakers, that all men who had a priest's heart and gift in them ought now to speak;— which gifts and heart one of their own number, John Knox the name of him, had: Had he not?

'A said the Preacher, appealing to all the audience:
pented what then is *his* duty? The people answered
bredd' affirmatively; it was a criminal forsaking of his
post, if such a man held the word that was in him
silent. Poor Knox was obliged to stand-up; he
attempted to reply; he could say no word;—burst
into a flood of tears, and ran out. It is worth
remembering, that scene. He was in grievous
trouble for some days. He felt what a small
faculty was his for this great work. He felt what
a baptism he was called to be baptised withal. He
' burst into tears.'

Our primary characteristic of a Hero, that he is
sincere, applies emphatically to Knox. It is not
denied anywhere that this, whatever might be his
other qualities or faults, is among the truest of men.
With a singular instinct he holds to the truth and
fact; the truth alone is there for him, the rest a
mere shadow and deceptive nonentity. However
feeble, forlorn the reality may seem, on that and
that only *can* he take his stand. In the Galleys of
the River Loire, whither Knox and the others,
after their Castle of St Andrew's was taken, had
been sent as Galley-slaves,—some officer or priest,
one day, presented them an Image of the Virgin
Mother, requiring that they, the blasphemous
heretics, should do it reverence. Mother? Mother
of God? said Knox, when the turn came to him:
This is no Mother of God: this is ' a *pented
bredd*,'—a piece of wood, I tell you, with paint on
it! She is fitter for swimming, I think, than for
being worshipped, added Knox, and flung the thing
into the river. It was not very cheap jesting there:
but come of it what might, this thing to Knox
was and must continue nothing other than the real

truth ; it was a *pented bredd* : worship it he would not.

He told his fellow-prisoners, in this darkest time, to be of courage ; the Cause they had was the true one, and must and would prosper ; the whole world could not put it down. Reality is of God's making ; it is alone strong. How many *pented bredds*, pretending to be real, are fitter to swim than to be worshipped !—This Knox cannot live but by fact : he clings to reality as the ship-wrecked sailor to the cliff. He is an instance to us how a man, by sincerity itself, becomes heroic : it is the grand gift he has. We find in Knox a good honest intellectual talent, no transcendent one ;—a narrow, inconsiderable man, as compared with Luther : but in heartfelt instinctive adherence to truth, in *sincerity*, as we say, he has no superior ; nay, one might ask, What equal he has? The heart of him is of the true Prophet cast. " He lies there," said the Earl of Morton at his grave, " who never feared the face of man." He resembles, more than any of the moderns, an Old-Hebrew Prophet. The same inflexibility, intoler-ance, rigid narrow-looking adherence to God's truth, stern rebuke in the name of God to all that forsake truth : an Old-Hebrew Prophet in the guise of an Edinburgh Minister of the Sixteenth Century. We are to take him for that ; not require him to be other.

Knox's conduct to Queen Mary, the harsh visits he used to make in her own palace, to reprove her there, have been much commented upon. Such cruelty, such coarseness fills us with indignation. On reading the actual narrative of the business, what Knox said, and what Knox meant, I must

Knox and the Queen say one's tragic feeling is rather disappointed. They are not so coarse, these speeches; they seem to me about as fine as the circumstances would permit! Knox was not there to do the courtier; he came on another errand. Whoever, reading these colloquies of his with the Queen, thinks they are vulgar insolences of a plebeian priest to a delicate high lady, mistakes the purport and essence of them altogether. It was unfortunately not possible to be polite with the Queen of Scotland, unless one proved untrue to the Nation and Cause of Scotland. A man who did not wish to see the land of his birth made a hunting-field for intriguing ambitious Guises, and the Cause of God trampled underfoot of Falsehoods, Formulas and the Devil's Cause, had no method of making himself agreeable! " Better that women weep," said Morton, "than that bearded men be forced to weep." Knox was the constitutional opposition-party in Scotland: the Nobles of the country, called by their station to take that post, were not found in it; Knox had to go or no one. The hapless Queen;—but the still more hapless Country, if *she* were made happy! Mary herself was not without sharpness enough, among her other qualities: " Who are you," said she once, " that presume to school the nobles and sovereign of this realm?"—"Madam, a subject born within the same," answered he. Reasonably answered! If the 'subject' have truth to speak, it is not the 'subject's' footing that will fail him here.—

We blame Knox for his intolerance. Well, surely it is good that each of us be as tolerant as possible. Yet, at bottom, after all the talk there is and has been about it, what is tolerance? Tolerance

has to tolerate the *un*essential; and to see well
what that is. Tolerance has to be noble, measured,
just in its very wrath, when it can tolerate no longer.
But, on the whole, we are not altogether here to
tolerate! We are here to resist, to control and
vanquish withal. We do not 'tolerate' Falsehoods, Thieveries, Iniquities, when they fasten on
us; we say to them, Thou art false, thou art not
tolerable! We are here to extinguish Falsehoods,
and put an end to them, in some wise way! I will
not quarrel so much with the way; the doing of
the thing is our great concern. In this sense Knox
was, full surely, intolerant.

A man sent to row in French Galleys, and suchlike, for teaching the Truth in his own land, cannot always be in the mildest humour! I am not
prepared to say that Knox had a soft temper; nor
do I know that he had what we call an ill-temper.
An ill nature he decidedly had not. Kind honest
affections dwell in the much-enduring, hard-worn,
ever-battling man. That he *could* rebuke Queens,
and had such weight among those proud turbulent
Nobles, proud enough whatever else they were; and
could maintain to the end a kind of virtual Presi-
dency and Sovereignty in that wild realm, he who
was only 'a subject born within the same:' this of
itself will prove to us that he was found, close at
hand, to be no mean acrid man; but at heart a
healthful, strong, sagacious man. Such alone can
bear rule in that kind. They blame him for
pulling-down cathedrals, and so forth, as if he were
a seditious rioting demagogue: precisely the reverse
is seen to be the fact, in regard to cathedrals and
the rest of it, if we examine! Knox wanted no
pulling-down of stone edifices; he wanted leprosy

Not a gloomy fanatic and darkness to be thrown out of the lives of men. Tumult was not his element; it was the tragic feature of his life that he was forced to dwell so much in that. Every such man is the born enemy of Disorder; hates to be in it: but what then? Smooth Falsehood is not Order; it is the general sumtotal of *Dis*order. Order is *Truth*,—each thing standing on the basis that belongs to it: Order and Falsehood cannot subsist together.

Withal, unexpectedly enough, this Knox has a vein of drollery in him; which I like much, in combination with his other qualities. He has a true eye for the ridiculous. His *History*, with its rough earnestness, is curiously enlivened with this. When the two Prelates, entering Glasgow Cathedral, quarrel about precedence; march rapidly up, take to hustling one another, twitching one another's rochets, and at last flourishing their crosiers like quarter-staves, it is a great sight for him everyway! Not mockery, scorn, bitterness alone; though there is enough of that too. But a true, loving, illuminating laugh mounts-up over the earnest visage; not a loud laugh; you would say, a laugh in the *eyes* most of all. An honest-hearted, brotherly man; brother to the high, brother also to the low; sincere in his sympathy with both. He has his pipe of Bourdeaux too, we find, in that old Edinburgh house of his; a cheery social man, with faces that loved him! They go far wrong who think this Knox was a gloomy, spasmodic, shrieking fanatic. Not at all: he is one of the solidest of men. Practical, cautious-hopeful, patient; a most shrewd, observing, quietly discerning man. In fact, he has very much the type of character we assign to the Scotch at present: a certain sardonic taci-

turnity is in him; insight enough; and a stouter 'Thy
heart than he himself knows of. He has the power **Kingdom**
of holding his peace over many things which do **come'**
not vitally concern him,—" They? what are they?"
But the thing which does vitally concern him, that
thing he will speak of; and in a tone the whole
world shall be made to hear: all the more emphatic
for his long silence.

This Prophet of the Scotch is to me no hateful
man!—He had a sore fight of an existence: wrestling with Popes and Principalities; in defeat, contention, life-long struggle; rowing as a galley-slave,
wandering as an exile. A sore fight: but he won
it. "Have you hope?" they asked him in his last
moment, when he could no longer speak. He
lifted his finger, 'pointed upwards with his finger,'
and so died. Honour to him! His works have
not died. The letter of his work dies, as of all
men's; but the spirit of it never.

One word more as to the letter of Knox's work.
The unforgivable offence in him is, that he wished
to set-up Priests over the head of Kings. In other
words he strove to make the Government of Scotland a *Theocracy*. This indeed is properly the sum
of his offences, the essential sin; for which what
pardon can there be? It is most true, he did, at
bottom, consciously or unconsciously, mean a Theocracy, or Government of God. He did mean that
Kings and Prime Ministers, and all manner of
persons, in public or private, diplomatising or whatever else they might be doing, should walk according to the Gospel of Christ, and understand that
this was their Law, supreme over all laws. He
hoped once to see such a thing realised; and the
Petition, *Thy Kingdom come*, no longer an empty

Theo-cracy word. He was sore grieved when he saw greedy worldly Barons clutch hold of the Church's property; when he expostulated that it was not secular property, that it was spiritual property, and should be turned to *true* churchly uses, education, schools, worship;—and the Regent Murray had to answer, with a shrug of the shoulders, "It is a devout imagination!" This was Knox's scheme of right and truth; this he zealously endeavoured after, to realise it. If we think this scheme of truth was too narrow, was not true, we may rejoice that he could not realise it; that it remained after two centuries of effort, unrealisable, and is a 'devout imagination' still. But how shall we blame *him* for struggling to realise it? Theocracy, Government of God, is precisely the thing to be struggled for! All Prophets, zealous Priests, are there for that purpose. Hildebrand wished a Theocracy; Cromwell wished it, fought for it; Mahomet attained it. Nay, is it not what all zealous men, whether called Priests, Prophets, or whatsoever else called, do essentially wish, and must wish? That right and truth, or God's Law, reign supreme among men, this is the Heavenly Ideal (well named in Knox's time, and namable in all times, a revealed 'Will of God') towards which the Reformer will insist that all be more and more approximated. All true Reformers, as I said, are by the nature of them Priests, and strive for a Theocracy.

How far such Ideals can ever be introduced into Practice, and at what point our impatience with their non-introduction ought to begin, is always a question. I think we may say safely, Let them introduce themselves as far as they can contrive to do it! If they are the true faith of men, all men ought to be more or less impatient always where they are not found **The Hero as Man of Letters** introduced. There will never be wanting Regent Murrays enough to shrug their shoulders, and say, "A devout imagination!" We will praise the Hero-priest, rather, who does what is in *him* to bring them in; and wears out, in toil, calumny, contradiction, a noble life, to make a God's Kingdom of this Earth. The Earth will not become too godlike!

LECTURE V

THE HERO AS A MAN OF LETTERS. JOHNSON, ROUSSEAU, BURNS.

[*Tuesday*, 19*th May* 1840]

HERO-GODS, Prophets, Poets, Priests are forms of Heroism that belong to the old ages, make their appearance in the remotest times; some of them have ceased to be possible long since, and cannot any more show themselves in this world. The Hero as *Man of Letters*, again, of which class we are to speak today, is altogether a product of these new ages; and so long as the wondrous art of *Writing*, or of Ready-writing which we call *Printing*, subsists, he may be expected to continue, as one of the main forms of Heroism for all future ages. He is, in various respects, a very singular phenomenon.

He is new, I say; he has hardly lasted above a century in the world yet. Never, till about a hundred years ago, was there seen any figure of a Great Soul living apart in that anomalous manner; endeavouring to speak-forth the inspiration that was in him by

Heroism in a strange shape Printed Books, and find place and subsistence by what the world would please to give him for doing that. Much had been sold and bought, and left to make its own bargain in the marketplace; but the inspired wisdom of a Heroic Soul never till then, in that naked manner. He, with his copy-rights and copy-wrongs, in his squalid garret, in his rusty coat; ruling (for this is what he does), from his grave, after death, whole nations and generations who would, or would not, give him bread while living, —is a rather curious spectacle! Few shapes of Heroism can be more unexpected.

Alas, the Hero from of old has had to cramp himself into strange shapes: the world knows not well at any time what to do with him, so foreign is his aspect in the world! It seemed absurd to us, that men, in their rude admiration, should take some wise great Odin for a god, and worship him as such; some wise great Mahomet for one god-inspired, and religiously follow his Law for twelve centuries: but that a wise great Johnson, a Burns, a Rousseau, should be taken for some idle nondescript, extant in the world to amuse idleness, and have a few coins and applauses thrown in, that he might live thereby; *this* perhaps, as before hinted, will one day seem a still absurder phasis of things!—Meanwhile, since it is the spiritual always that determines the material, this same Man-of-Letters Hero must be regarded as our most important modern person. He, such as he may be, is the soul of all. What he teaches, the whole world will do and make. The world's manner of dealing with him is the most significant feature of the world's general position. Looking well at his life, we may get a glance, as deep as is readily possible for us, into the life of those singular centuries which have produced him, in which we **The** ourselves live and work. **genuine**

There are genuine Men of Letters, and not **Man of** genuine; as in every kind there is a genuine and a **Letters** spurious. If *Hero* be taken to mean genuine, then I say the Hero as Man of Letters will be found discharging a function for us which is ever honourable, ever the highest; and was once well known to be the highest. He is uttering-forth, in such a way as he has, the inspired soul of him; all that a man, in any case, can do. I say *inspired;* for what we call 'originality,' 'sincerity,' 'genius,' the heroic quality we have no good name for, signifies that. The Hero is he who lives in the inward sphere of things, in the True, Divine and Eternal, which exists always, unseen to most, under the Temporary, Trivial: his being is in that; he declares that abroad, by act or speech as it may be, in declaring himself abroad. His life, as we said before, is a piece of the everlasting heart of Nature herself: all men's life is,—but the weak many know not the fact, and are untrue to it, in most times; the strong few are strong, heroic, perennial, because it cannot be hidden from them. The Man of Letters, like every Hero, is there to proclaim this in such sort as he can. Intrinsically it is the same function which the old generations named a man Prophet, Priest, Divinity for doing; which all manner of Heroes, by speech or by act, are sent into the world to do.

Fichte the German Philosopher delivered, some forty years ago at Erlangen, a highly remarkable Course of Lectures on this subject: '*Ueber das Wesen des Gelehrten*, On the Nature of the Literary Man.' Fichte, in conformity with the Transcen-

Fichte on the True Man of Letters dental Philosophy, of which he was a distinguished teacher, declares first: That all things which we see or work with in this Earth, especially we ourselves and all persons, are as a kind of vesture or sensuous Appearance: that under all there lies, as the essence of them, what he calls the 'Divine Idea of the World;' this is the Reality which 'lies at the bottom of all Appearance.' To the mass of men no such Divine Idea is recognisable in the world; they live merely, says Fichte, among the superficialities, practicalities and shows of the world, not dreaming that there is anything divine under them. But the Man of Letters is sent hither specially that he may discern for himself, and make manifest to us, this same Divine Idea: in every new generation it will manifest itself in a new dialect; and he is there for the purpose of doing that. Such is Fichte's phraseology; with which we need not quarrel. It is his way of naming what I here, by other words, am striving imperfectly to name; what there is at present no name for: The unspeakable Divine Significance, full of splendour, of wonder and terror, that lies in the being of every man, of every thing,—the Presence of the God who made every man and thing. Mahomet taught this in his dialect; Odin in his: it is the thing which all thinking hearts, in one dialect or another, are here to teach.

Fichte calls the Man of Letters, therefore, a Prophet, or as he prefers to phrase it, a Priest, continually unfolding the Godlike to men: Men of Letters are a perpetual Priesthood, from age to age, teaching all men that a God is still present in their life; that all 'Appearance,' whatsoever we see in the world, is but as a vesture for the 'Divine Idea of the World,' for 'that which lies at the bottom of **Goethe** Appearance.' In the true Literary Man there is thus ever, acknowledged or not by the world, a sacredness: he is the light of the world; the world's Priest:—guiding it, like a sacred Pillar of Fire, in its dark pilgrimage through the waste of Time. Fichte discriminates with sharp zeal the *true* Literary Man, what we here call the *Hero* as Man of Letters, from multitudes of false unheroic. Whoever lives not wholly in this Divine Idea, or living partially in it, struggles not, as for the one good, to live wholly in it,—he is, let him live where else he like, in what pomps and prosperities he like, no Literary Man; he is, says Fichte, a 'Bungler, *Stümper.*' Or at best, if he belong to the prosaic provinces, he may be a 'Hodman;' Fichte even calls him elsewhere a 'Nonentity,' and has in short no mercy for him, no wish that *he* should continue happy among us! This is Fichte's notion of the Man of Letters. It means, in its own form, precisely what we here mean.

In this point of view, I consider that, for the last hundred years, by far the notablest of all Literary Men is Fichte's countryman, Goethe. To that man too, in a strange way, there was given what we may call a life in the Divine Idea of the World; vision of the inward divine mystery: and strangely, out of his Books, the world rises imaged once more as godlike, the workmanship and temple of a God. Illuminated all, not in fierce impure fire-splendour as of Mahomet, but in mild celestial radiance;— really a Prophecy in these most unprophetic times; to my mind, by far the greatest, though one of the quietest, among all the great things that have come to pass in them. Our chosen specimen of the Hero

Johnson,　as Literary Man would be this Goethe. And it
　Burns,　were a very pleasant plan for me here to discourse
Rousseau　of his heroism : for I consider him to be a true
Hero ; heroic in what he said and did, and perhaps
still more in what he did not say and did not do ;
to me a noble spectacle : a great heroic ancient
man, speaking and keeping silence as an ancient
Hero, in the guise of a most modern, high-bred,
high-cultivated Man of Letters ! We have had no
such spectacle ; no man capable of affording such,
for the last hundred-and-fifty years.

But at present, such is the general state of knowledge about Goethe, it were worse than useless to
attempt speaking of him in this case. Speak as I
might, Goethe, to the great majority of you, would
remain problematic, vague ; no impression but a false
one could be realised. Him we must leave to future
times. Johnson, Burns, Rousseau, three great figures
from a prior time, from a far inferior state of circumstances, will suit us better here. Three men of the
Eighteenth Century ; the conditions of their life far
more resemble what those of ours still are in England, than what Goethe's in Germany were. Alas,
these men did not conquer like him ; they fought
bravely, and fell. They were not heroic bringers
of the light, but heroic seekers of it. They lived
under galling conditions ; struggling as under mountains of impediment, and could not unfold themselves into clearness, or victorious interpretation
of that 'Divine Idea.' It is rather the *Tombs* of
three Literary Heroes that I have to show you.
There are the monumental heaps, under which
three spiritual giants lie buried. Very mournful,
but also great and full of interest for us. We will
linger by them for a while.

Complaint is often made, in these times, of what The
we call the disorganised condition of society: how Man of
ill many arranged forces of society fulfil their work ; Letters
how many powerful forces are seen working in a an Ish-
wasteful, chaotic, altogether unarranged manner. maelite
It is too just a complaint, as we all know. But
perhaps if we look at this of Books and the Writers
of Books, we shall find here, as it were, the summary
of all other disorganisation ;—a sort of *heart*, from
which, and to which, all other confusion circulates
in the world ! Considering what Book-writers do
in the world, and what the world does with Book-
writers, I should say, It is the most anomalous thing
the world at present has to show.—We should get
into a sea far beyond sounding, did we attempt to
give account of this : but we must glance at it for
the sake of our subject. The worst element in the
life of these three Literary Heroes was, that they
found their business and position such a chaos. On
the beaten road there is tolerable travelling ; but it
is sore work, and many have to perish, fashioning a
path through the impassable !

Our pious Fathers, feeling well what importance
lay in the speaking of man to men, founded churches,
made endowments, regulations ; everywhere in the
civilised world there is a Pulpit, environed with
all manner of complex dignified appurtenances and
furtherances, that therefrom a man with the tongue
may, to best advantage, address his fellow-men.
They felt that this was the most important thing ;
that without this there was no good thing. It is a
right pious work, that of theirs; beautiful to behold ! But now with the art of Writing, with the
art of Printing, a total change has come over that
business. The Writer of a Book, is not he a

Miracles wrought by Books Preacher preaching not to this parish or that, on this day or that, but to all men in all times and places? Surely it is of the last importance that *he* do his work right, whoever do it wrong;—that the *eye* report not falsely, for then all the other members are astray! Well; how he may do his work, whether he do it right or wrong, or do it at all, is a point which no man in the world has taken the pains to think of. To a certain shopkeeper, trying to get some money for his books, if lucky, he is of some importance; to no other man of any. Whence he came, whither he is bound, by what ways he arrived, by what he might be furthered on his course, no one asks. He is an accident in society. He wanders like a wild Ishmaelite, in a world of which he is as the spiritual light, either the guidance or the misguidance!

Certainly the art of writing is the most miraculous of all things man has devised. Odin's *Runes* were the first form of the work of a Hero; *Books*, written words, are still miraculous *Runes*, of the latest form! In Books lies the *soul* of the whole Past Time; the articulate audible voice of the Past, when the body and material substance of it has altogether vanished like a dream. Mighty fleets and armies, harbours and arsenals, vast cities, high-domed, many-engined, —they are precious, great: but what do they become? Agamemnon, the many Agamemnons, Pericleses, and their Greece; all is gone now to some ruined fragments, dumb mournful wrecks and blocks: but the Books of Greece! There Greece, to every thinker, still very literally lives; can be called-up again into life. No magic *Rune* is stranger than a Book. All that Mankind has done, thought, gained or been: it is lying as in magic preservation in the pages of Books. They are the chosen **Miracles** possession of men. **wrought**

Do not Books still accomplish *miracles* as *Runes* **by Books** were fabled to do? They persuade men. Not the wretchedest circulating-library novel, which foolish girls thumb and con in remote villages but will help to regulate the actual practical weddings and households of those foolish girls. So 'Celia' felt, so 'Clifford' acted: the foolish Theorem of Life, stamped into those young brains, comes out as a solid Practice one day. Consider whether any *Rune* in the wildest imagination of Mythologist ever did such wonders as, on the actual firm Earth, some Books have done! What built St Paul's Cathedral? Look at the heart of the matter, it was that divine Hebrew Book,—the word partly of the man Moses, an outlaw tending his Midianitish herds, four thousand years ago, in the wildernesses of Sinai! It is the strangest of things, yet nothing is truer. With the art of Writing, of which Printing is a simple, an inevitable and comparatively insignificant corollary, the true reign of miracles for mankind commenced. It related, with a wondrous new contiguity and perpetual closeness, the Past and Distant with the Present in time and place; all times and all places with this our actual Here and Now. All things were altered for men; all modes of important work of men: teaching, preaching, governing, and all else.

To look at Teaching, for instance. Universities are a notable, respectable product of the modern ages. Their existence too is modified, to the very basis of it, by the existence of Books. Universities arose while there were yet no Books procurable; while a man, for a single Book, had to give an estate of land.   That, in those circumstances, when a man had some knowledge to communicate, he should do it by gathering the learners round him, face to face, was a necessity for him.   If you wanted to know what Abelard knew, you must go and listen to Abelard.   Thousands, as many as thirty-thousand, went to hear Abelard and that metaphysical theology of his.   And now for any other teacher who had something of his own to teach, there was a great convenience opened: so many thousands eager to learn were already assembled yonder; of all places the best place for him was that.   For any third teacher it was better still; and grew ever the better, the more teachers there came.   It only needed now that the King took notice of this new phenomenon; combined or agglomerated the various schools into one school; gave it edifices, privileges, encouragements, and named it *Universitas*, or School of all Sciences: the University of Paris, in its essential characters, was there.   The model of all subsequent Universities; which down even to these days, for six centuries now, have gone on to found themselves. Such, I conceive, was the origin of Universities.

It is clear, however, that with this simple circumstance, facility of getting Books, the whole conditions of the business from top to bottom were changed.   Once invent Printing, you metamorphosed all Universities, or superseded them!   The Teacher needed not now to gather men personally round him, that he might *speak* to them what he knew: print it in a Book, and all learners far and wide, for a trifle, had it each at his own fireside, much more effectually to learn it!—Doubtless there is still peculiar virtue in Speech; even writers of

Books may still, in some circumstances, find it convenient to speak also, — witness our present meeting here ! There is, one would say, and must ever remain while man has a tongue, a distinct province for Speech as well as for Writing and Printing. In regard to all things this must remain ; to Universities among others. But the limits of the two have nowhere yet been pointed out, ascertained; much less put in practice : the University which would completely take-in that great new fact, of the existence of Printed Books, and stand on a clear footing for the Nineteenth Century as the Paris one did for the Thirteenth, has not yet come into existence. If we think of it, all that a University, or final highest School can do for us, is still but what the first School began doing,— teach us to *read*. We learn to *read*, in various languages, in various sciences ; we learn the alphabet and letters of all manner of Books. But the place where we go to get knowledge, even theoretic knowledge, is the Books themselves ! It depends on what we read, after all manner of Professors have done their best for us. The true University of these days is a Collection of Books.

But to the Church itself, as I hinted already, all is changed, in its preaching, in its working, by the introduction of Books. The Church is the working recognised Union of our Priests or Prophets, of those who by wise teaching guide the souls of men. While there was no Writing, even while there was no Easy-writing or *Printing*, the preaching of the voice was the natural sole method of performing this. But now with Books !—He that can write a true Book, to persuade England, is not he the Bishop and Archbishop, the Primate of England

Books in place of Teachers

Books are the true Church and of All England? I many a time say, the writers of Newspapers, Pamphlets, Poems, Books, these *are* the real working effective Church of a modern country. Nay not only our preaching, but even our worship, is not it too accomplished by means of Printed Books? The noble sentiment which a gifted soul has clothed for us in melodious words, which brings melody into our hearts,—is not this essentially, if we will understand it, of the nature of worship? There are many, in all countries, who, in this confused time, have no other method of worship. He who, in any way, shows us better than we knew before that a lily of the fields is beautiful, does he not show it us as an effluence of the Fountain of all Beauty; as the *hand-writing*, made visible there, of the great Maker of the Universe? He has sung for us, made us sing with him, a little verse of a sacred Psalm. Essentially so. How much more he who sings, who says, or in any way brings home to our heart the noble doings, feelings, darings and endurances of a brother man! He has verily touched our hearts as with a live coal *from the altar*. Perhaps there is no worship more authentic.

Literature, so far as it is Literature, is an 'apocalypse of Nature,' a revealing of the 'open secret.' It may well enough be named, in Fichte's style, a 'continuous revelation' of the Godlike in the Terrestrial and Common. The Godlike does ever, in very truth, endure there; is brought out, now in this dialect, now in that, with various degrees of clearness: all true gifted Singers and Speakers are, consciously or unconsciously, doing so. The dark stormful indignation of a Byron, so wayward and perverse, may have touches of it; nay the withered mockery of a French sceptic,—his mockery of the **Books** False, a love and worship of the True. How **are our** much more the sphere-harmony of a Shakspeare, of **Parlia-** a Goethe; the cathedral-music of a Milton! They **ment** are something too, those humble genuine lark-notes of a Burns,—skylark, starting from the humble furrow, far overhead into the blue depths, and singing to us so genuinely there! For all true singing is of the nature of worship; as indeed all true *working* may be said to be,—whereof such *singing* is but the record, and fit melodious representation, to us. Fragments of a real 'Church Liturgy' and 'Body of Homilies,' strangely disguised from the common eye, are to be found weltering in that huge froth-ocean of Printed Speech we loosely call Literature! Books are our Church too.

Or turning now to the Government of men. Witenagemote, old Parliament, was a great thing. The affairs of the nation were there deliberated and decided; what we were to *do* as a nation. But does not, though the name Parliament subsists, the parliamentary debate go on now, everywhere and at all times, in a far more comprehensive way, *out* of Parliament altogether? Burke said there were Three Estates in Parliament; but, in the Reporters' Gallery yonder, there sat a *Fourth Estate* more important far than they all. It is not a figure of speech, or a witty saying; it is a literal fact,—very momentous to us in these times. Literature is our Parliament too. Printing, which comes necessarily out of Writing, I say often, is equivalent to Democracy: invent Writing, Democracy is inevitable. Writing brings Printing; brings universal every-day extempore Printing, as we see at present. Whoever can

Man's works the vesture of Thought speak, speaking now to the whole nation, becomes a power, a branch of government, with inalienable weight in law-making, in all acts of authority. It matters not what rank he has, what revenues or garnitures: the requisite thing is, that he have a tongue which others will listen to; this and nothing more is requisite. The nation is governed by all that has tongue in the nation: Democracy is virtually *there*. Add only, that whatsoever power exists will have itself, by and by, organised; working secretly under bandages, obscurations, obstructions, it will never rest till it get to work free, unencumbered, visible to all. Democracy virtually extant will insist on becoming palpably extant.—

On all sides, are we not driven to the conclusion that, of the things which man can do or make here below, by far the most momentous, wonderful and worthy are the things we call Books! Those poor bits of rag-paper with black ink on them;—from the Daily Newspaper to the sacred Hebrew Book, what have they not done, what are they not doing! —For indeed, whatever be the outward form of the thing (bits of paper, as we say, and black ink), is it not verily, at bottom, the highest act of man's faculty that produces a Book? It is the *Thought* of man; the true thaumaturgic virtue; by which man works all things whatsoever. All that he does, and brings to pass, is the vesture of a Thought. This London City, with all its houses, palaces, steam-engines, cathedrals, and huge immeasurable traffic and tumult, what is it but a Thought, but millions of Thoughts made into One;—a huge immeasurable Spirit of a THOUGHT, embodied in brick, in iron, smoke, dust, Palaces, Parliaments, Hackney Coaches, Katherine Docks, and the rest of it! Not a brick was made but some man had to *think* of the making of that brick.—The thing we called 'bits of paper with traces of black ink,' is the *purest* embodiment a Thought of man can have. No wonder it is, in all ways, the activest and noblest. **Organisation for Men of Letters**

All this, of the importance and supreme importance of the Man of Letters in modern Society, and how the Press is to such a degree superseding the Pulpit, the Senate, the *Senatus Academicus* and much else, has been admitted for a good while; and recognised often enough, in late times, with a sort of sentimental triumph and wonderment. It seems to me, the Sentimental by and by will have to give place to the Practical. If Men of Letters *are* so incalculably influential, actually performing such work for us from age to age, and even from day to day, then I think we may conclude that Men of Letters will not always wander like unrecognised unregulated Ishmaelites among us! Whatsoever thing, as I said above, has virtual unnoticed power will cast-off its wrappages, bandages, and step-forth one day with palpably articulated, universally visible power. That one man wear the clothes, and take the wages, of a function which is done by quite another: there can be no profit in this; this is not right, it is wrong. And yet, alas, the *making* of it right,—what a business, for long times to come! Sure enough, this that we call Organisation of the Literary Guild is still a great way off, encumbered with all manner of complexities. If you asked me what were the best possible organisation for the Men of Letters in modern society; the arrangement of furtherance and regulation, grounded the most accurately on the actual facts of their position and of the world's position,—I should beg to say that the problem far

Money
not the
chief
thing
wanted
exceeded my faculty! It is not one man's faculty; it is that of many successive men turned earnestly upon it, that will bring-out even an approximate solution. What the best arrangement were, none of us could say. But if you ask, Which is the worst? I answer: This which we now have, that Chaos should sit umpire in it; this is the worst. To the best, or any good one, there is yet a long way.

One remark I must not omit, That royal or parliamentary grants of money are by no means the chief thing wanted! To give our Men of Letters stipends, endowments and all furtherance of cash, will do little towards the business. On the whole, one is weary of hearing about the omnipotence of money. I will say rather that, for a genuine man, it is no evil to be poor; that there ought to be Literary Men poor,—to show whether they are genuine or not! Mendicant Orders, bodies of good men doomed to *beg*, were instituted in the Christian Church; a most natural and even necessary development of the spirit of Christianity. It was itself founded on Poverty, on Sorrow, Contradiction, Crucifixion, every species of worldly Distress and Degradation. We may say, that he who has not known those things, and learned from them the priceless lessons they have to teach, has missed a good opportunity of schooling. To beg, and go barefoot, in coarse woollen cloak with a rope round your loins, and be despised of all the world, was no beautiful business;—nor an honourable one in any eye, till the nobleness of those who did so had made it honoured of some!

Begging is not in our course at the present time: but for the rest of it, who will say that a Johnson is not perhaps the better for being poor? It is

needful for him, at all rates, to know that outward **The**
profit, that success of any kind is *not* the goal he has **Ordeal of**
to aim at. Pride, vanity, ill-conditioned egoism of all **struggle**
sorts, are bred in his heart, as in every heart ; need,
above all, to be cast-out of his heart,—to be, with
whatever pangs, torn-out of it, cast-forth from it, as
a thing worthless. Byron, born rich and noble, made-
out even less than Burns, poor and plebeian.   Who
knows but, in that same ' best possible organisation '
as yet far off, Poverty may still enter as an important
element ? What if our Men of Letters, Men setting-
up to be Spiritual Heroes, were still *then*, as they
now are, a kind of ' involuntary monastic order ; '
bound still to this same ugly Poverty,—till they had
tried what was in it too, till they had learned to
make it too do for them !   Money, in truth, can
do much, but it cannot do all. We must know the
province of it, and confine it ; and even spurn it
back, when it wishes to get farther.

Besides, were the money-furtherances, the proper
season for them, the fit assigner of them, all settled,
—how is the Burns to be recognised that merits
these ?   He must pass through the ordeal, and
prove himself. *This* ordeal ; this wild welter of
a chaos which is called Literary Life ; this too is
a kind of ordeal !   There is clear truth in the idea
that a struggle from the lower classes of society, towards the upper regions and rewards of society,
must ever continue. Strong men are born there,
who ought to stand elsewhere than there.   The
manifold, inextricably complex, universal struggle
of these constitutes, and must constitute, what is
called the progress of society. For Men of Letters,
as for all other sorts of men. How to regulate that
struggle ? There is the whole question. To leave

The Priest-hood of authors it as it is, at the mercy of blind Chance; a whirl of distracted atoms, one cancelling the other; one of the thousand arriving saved, nine-hundred-and-ninety-nine lost by the way; your royal Johnson languishing inactive in garrets, or harnessed to the yoke of Printer Cave; your Burns dying broken-hearted as a Gauger; your Rousseau driven into mad exasperation, kindling French Revolutions by his paradoxes: this, as we said, is clearly enough the *worst* regulation. The *best*, alas, is far from us!

And yet there can be no doubt but it is coming; advancing on us, as yet hidden in the bosom of centuries: this is a prophecy one can risk. For so soon as men get to discern the importance of a thing, they do infallibly set about arranging it, facilitating, forwarding it; and rest not till, in some approximate degree, they have accomplished that. I say, of all Priesthoods, Aristocracies, Governing Classes at present extant in the world, there is no class comparable for importance to that Priesthood of the Writers of Books. This is a fact which he who runs may read,—and draw inferences from. "Literature will take care of itself," answered Mr Pitt, when applied-to for some help for Burns. "Yes," adds Mr Southey, "it will take care of itself; *and of you too*, if you do not look to it!"

The result to individual Men of Letters is not the momentous one; they are but individuals, an infinitesimal fraction of the great body; they can struggle on, and live or else die, as they have been wont. But it deeply concerns the whole society, whether it will set its *light* on high places, to walk thereby; or trample it under foot, and scatter it in all ways of wild waste (not without conflagration), as heretofore! Light is the one thing wanted for the world. Put wisdom in the head of the world, the world will fight its battle victoriously, and be the best world man can make it. I call this anomaly of a disorganic Literary Class the heart of all other anomalies, at once product and parent; some good arrangement for that would be as the *punctum saliens* of a new vitality and just arrangement for all. Already, in some European countries, in France, in Prussia, one traces some beginnings of an arrangement for the Literary Class; indicating the gradual possibility of such. I believe that it is possible; that it will have to be possible.

By far the most interesting fact I hear about the Chinese is one on which we cannot arrive at clearness, but which excites endless curiosity even in the dim state: this namely, that they do attempt to make their Men of Letters their Governors! It would be rash to say, one understood how this was done, or with what degree of success it was done. All such things must be very *un*successful; yet a small degree of success is precious; the very attempt how precious! There does seem to be, all over China, a more or less active search everywhere to discover the men of talent that grow up in the young generation. Schools there are for every one: a foolish sort of training, yet still a sort. The youths who distinguish themselves in the lower school are promoted into favourable stations in the higher, that they may still more distinguish themselves,—forward and forward: it appears to be out of these that the Official Persons, and incipient Governors, are taken. These are they whom they *try* first, whether they can govern or not. And surely with the best hope: for they are the men that have already shown intellect. Try them:

End they have not governed or administered as yet;
of the perhaps they cannot; but there is no doubt they
Empire of *have* some Understanding, without which no man
Routine can! Neither is Understanding a *tool*, as we are
too apt to figure; 'it is a *hand* which can handle
any tool.' Try these men: they are of all others
the best worth trying.—Surely there is no kind of
government, constitution, revolution, social apparatus
or arrangement, that I know of in this world, so
promising to one's scientific curiosity as this. The
man of intellect at the top of affairs: this is the aim
of all constitutions and revolutions, if they have any
aim. For the man of true intellect, as I assert
and believe always, is the noblehearted man withal,
the true, just, humane and valiant man. Get *him*
for governor, all is got; fail to get him, though
you had Constitutions plentiful as blackberries, and
a Parliament in every village, there is nothing yet
got!—

These things look strange, truly; and are not
such as we commonly speculate upon. But we are
fallen into strange times; these things will require
to be speculated upon; to be rendered practicable,
to be in some way put in practice. These and
many others. On all hands of us, there is the
announcement, audible enough, that the old Empire
of Routine has ended; that to say a thing has long
been, is no reason for its continuing to be. The
things which have been are fallen into decay, are
fallen into incompetence; large masses of mankind,
in every society of our Europe, are no longer capable
of living at all by the things which have been.
When millions of men can no longer by their
utmost exertion gain food for themselves, and 'the
third man for thirty-six weeks each year is short of

third-rate potatoes,' the things which have been **The** must decidedly prepare to alter themselves!—I will **sceptical** now quit this of the organisation of Men of Letters. **century**

Alas, the evil that pressed heaviest on those Literary Heroes of ours was not the want of organisation for Men of Letters, but a far deeper one; out of which, indeed, this and so many other evils for the Literary Man, and for all men, had, as from their fountain, taken rise. That our Hero as Man of Letters had to travel without highway, companionless, through an inorganic chaos,—and to leave his own life and faculty lying there, as a partial contribution towards *pushing* some highway through it: this, had not his faculty itself been so perverted and paralysed, he might have put up with, might have considered to be but the common lot of Heroes. His fatal misery was the *spiritual paralysis*, so we may name it, of the Age in which his life lay; whereby his life too, do what he might, was half-paralysed! The Eighteenth was a *Sceptical* Century; in which little word there is a whole Pandora's Box of miseries. Scepticism means not intellectual Doubt alone, but moral Doubt; all sorts of *in*fidelity, insincerity, spiritual paralysis. Perhaps, in few centuries that one could specify since the world began, was a life of Heroism more difficult for a man. That was not an age of Faith,—an age of Heroes! The very possibility of Heroism had been, as it were, formally abnegated in the minds of all. Heroism was gone forever; Triviality, Formulism and Commonplace were come forever. The 'age of miracles' had been, or perhaps had not been; but it was not any longer. An effete world; wherein Wonder,

Machine-sceptics Greatness, Godhood could not now dwell;—in one word, a godless world!

How mean, dwarfish are their ways of thinking, in this time,—compared not with the Christian Shakspeares and Miltons, but with the old Pagan Skalds, with any species of believing men! The living TREE Igdrasil, with the melodious prophetic waving of its world-wide boughs, deep-rooted as Hela, has died-out into the clanking of a World-MACHINE. 'Tree' and 'Machine': contrast these two things. I, for my share, declare the world to be no machine! I say that it does not go by wheel-and-pinion 'motives,' self-interests, checks, balances; that there is something far other in it than the clank of spinning-jennies, and parliamentary majorities; and, on the whole, that it is not a machine at all!—The old Norse Heathen had a truer notion of God's-world than these poor Machine-Sceptics: the old Heathen Norse were *sincere* men. But for these poor Sceptics there was no sincerity, no truth. Half-truth and hearsay was called truth. Truth, for most men, meant plausibility; to be measured by the number of votes you could get. They had lost any notion that sincerity was possible, or of what sincerity was. How many Plausibilities asking, with unaffected surprise and the air of offended virtue, What! am not I sincere? Spiritual Paralysis, I say, nothing left but a Mechanical life, was the characteristic of that century. For the common man, unless happily he stood *below* his century and belonged to another prior one, it was impossible to be a Believer, a Hero; he lay buried, unconscious, under these baleful influences. To the strongest man, only with infinite struggle and confusion was it possible to work himself half-loose; and lead as it were, in an enchanted, most tragical way, a spiritual death-in-life, and be a Half-Hero.

Scepti-cism a begin-ning not an end

Scepticism is the name we give to all this; as the chief symptom, as the chief origin of all this. Concerning which so much were to be said! It would take many Discourses, not a small fraction of one Discourse, to state what one feels about that Eighteenth Century and its ways. As indeed this, and the like of this, which we now call Scepticism, is precisely the black malady and life-foe, against which all teaching and discoursing since man's life began has directed itself: the battle of Belief against Unbelief is the never-ending battle! Neither is it in the way of crimina-tion that one would wish to speak. Scepticism, for that century, we must consider as the decay of old ways of believing, the preparation afar off for new better and wider ways,—an inevitable thing. We will not blame men for it; we will lament their hard fate. We will understand that destruc-tion of old *forms* is not destruction of everlasting *substances*; that Scepticism, as sorrowful and hate-ful as we see it, is not an end but a beginning.

The other day speaking, without prior purpose that way, of Bentham's theory of man and man's life, I chanced to call it a more beggarly one than Mahomet's. I am bound to say, now when it is once uttered, that such is my deliberate opinion. Not that one would mean offence against the man Jeremy Bentham, or those who respect and believe him. Bentham himself, and even the creed of Bentham, seems to me comparatively worthy of praise. It is a determinate *being* what all the world, in a cowardly, half-and-half manner, was tending

Bentham-ism to be. Let us have the crisis; we shall either have death or the cure. I call this gross, steam-engine Utilitarianism an approach towards new Faith. It was a laying down of cant; a saying to oneself: "Well then, this world is a dead iron machine, the god of it Gravitation and selfish Hunger; let us see what, by checking and balancing, and good adjustment of tooth and pinion, can be made of it!" Bentham-ism has something complete, manful, in such fear-less committal of itself to what it finds true; you may call it Heroic, though a Heroism with its *eyes* put out! It is the culminating point, and fearless ultimatum, of what lay in the half-and-half state, pervading man's whole existence in that Eighteenth Century. It seems to me, all deniers of Godhood, and all lip-believers of it, are bound to be Ben-thamites, if they have courage and honesty. Ben-thamism is an *eyeless* Heroism : the Human Species, like a hapless blinded Samson grinding in the Philistine Mill, clasps convulsively the pillars of its Mill; brings huge ruin down, but ultimately deliverance withal. Of Bentham I meant to say no harm.

But this I do say, and would wish all men to know and lay to heart, that he who discerns nothing but Mechanism in the Universe has in the fatalest way missed the secret of the Universe altogether. That all Godhood should vanish out of men's conception of this Universe seems to me precisely the most brutal error, — I will not disparage Heathenism by calling it a Heathen error,—that men could fall into. It is not true; it is false at the very heart of it. A man who thinks so will think *wrong* about all things in the world; this original sin will vitiate all other conclusions he can form.   One might call it the most lamentable **of Belief** delusions,—not forgetting Witchcraft itself! Witchcraft worshipped at least a living Devil: but this worships a dead iron Devil; no God, not even a Devil!—Whatsoever is noble, divine, inspired, drops thereby out of life.   There remains everywhere in life a despicable *caput-mortuum ;* the mechanical hull, all soul fled out of it.   How can a man act heroically ?   The 'Doctrine of Motives' will teach him that it is, under more or less disguise, nothing but a wretched love of Pleasure, fear of Pain ; that Hunger, of applause, of cash, of whatsoever victual it may be, is the ultimate fact of man's life.   Atheism, in brief;—which does indeed frightfully punish itself.   The man, I say, is become spiritually a paralytic man; this god-like Universe a dead mechanical steam-engine, all working by motives, checks, balances, and I know not what; wherein, as in the detestable belly of some Phalaris'-Bull of his own contriving, he the poor Phalaris sits miserably dying!

Belief I define to be the healthy act of a man's mind.   It is a mysterious indescribable process, that of getting to believe;—indescribable, as all vital acts are.   We have our mind given us, not that it may cavil and argue, but that it may see into something, give us clear belief and understanding about something, whereon we are then to proceed to act.   Doubt, truly, is not itself a crime.   Certainly we do not rush out, clutch-up the first thing we find, and straightway believe that !   All manner of doubt, inquiry, σκέψις as it is named, about all manner of objects, dwells in every reasonable mind.   It is the mystic working of the mind, on the object it is *getting* to know and believe.   Belief comes out of

Scepti-
cism

all this, above ground, like the tree from its hidden *roots.* But now if, even on common things, we require that a man keep his doubts *silent,* and not babble of them till they in some measure become affirmations or denials; how much more in regard to the highest things, impossible to speak of in words at all! That a man parade his doubt, and get to imagine that debating and logic (which means at best only the manner of *telling* us your thought, your belief or disbelief, about a thing) is the triumph and true work of what intellect he has: alas, this is as if you should *overturn* the tree, and instead of green boughs, leaves, and fruits, show us ugly taloned roots turned-up into the air,—and no growth, only death and misery going on!

For the Scepticism, as I said, is not intellectual only; it is moral also; a chronic atrophy and disease of the whole soul. A man lives by believing something; not by debating and arguing about many things. A sad case for him when all that he can manage to believe is something he can button in his pocket, and with one or the other organ eat and digest! Lower than that he will not get. We call those ages in which he gets so low the mournfulest, sickest, and meanest of all ages. The world's heart is palsied, sick: how can any limb of it be whole? Genuine Acting ceases in all departments of the world's work; dextrous Similitude of Acting begins. The world's wages are pocketed, the world's work is not done. Heroes have gone out; quacks have come in. Accordingly, what Century, since the end of the Roman world, which also was a time of scepticism, simulacra and universal decadence, so abounds with Quacks as that Eighteenth! Consider them, with their tumid sentimental vapour-ing about virtue, benevolence,—the wretched Quack- squadron, Cagliostro at the head of them! Few men were without quackery; they had got to consider it a necessary ingredient and amalgam for truth. Chatham, our brave Chatham himself, comes down to the House, all wrapt and bandaged; he 'has crawled out in great bodily suffering,' and so on; —*forgets*, says Walpole, that he is acting the sick man; in the fire of debate, snatches his arm from the sling, and oratorically swings and brandishes it! Chatham himself lives the strangest mimetic life, half hero, half quack, all along. For indeed the world is full of dupes; and you have to gain the *world's* suffrage! How the duties of the world will be done in that case, what quantities of error, which means failure, which means sorrow and misery, to some and to many, will gradually accumulate in all provinces of the world's business, we need not compute.

It seems to me, you lay your finger here on the heart of the world's maladies, when you call it a Sceptical World. An insincere world; a godless untruth of a world! It is out of this, as I consider, that the whole tribe of social pestilences, French Revolutions, Chartisms, and what not, have derived their being, their chief necessity to be. This must alter. Till this alter, nothing can beneficially alter. My one hope of the world, my inexpugnable consolation in looking at the miseries of the world, is that this is altering. Here and there one does now find a man who knows, as of old, that this world is a Truth, and no Plausibility and Falsity; that he himself is alive, not dead or paralytic; and that the world is alive, instinct with Godhood, beautiful and awful, even as in the beginning of days! One man once knowing this, many men, all men, must by and

'**Saving** by come to know it. It lies there clear, for who-
worlds' soever will take the *spectacles* off his eyes and
honestly look, to know! For such a man, the
Unbelieving Century, with its unblessed Products,
is already past: a new century is already come.
The old unblessed Products and Performances, as
solid as they look, are Phantasms, preparing speedily
to vanish. To this and the other noisy, very great-
looking Simulacrum with the whole world huzzah-
ing at its heels, he can say, composedly stepping
aside: Thou art not *true ;* thou art not extant, only
semblant; go thy way!—Yes, hollow Formulism,
gross Benthamism, and other unheroic atheistic Insincerity is visibly and even rapidly declining. An
unbelieving Eighteenth Century is but an exception,
—such as now and then occurs. I prophesy that
the world will once more become *sincere;* a believing world : with *many* Heroes in it, a heroic
world ! It will then be a victorious world; never
till then !

Or indeed what of the world and its victories?
Men speak too much about the world. Each one
of us here, let the world go how it will, and be
victorious or not victorious, has he not a Life of
his own to lead? One Life; a little gleam of
Time between two Eternities; no second chance
to us forevermore ! It were well for *us* to live not
as fools and simulacra, but as wise and realities.
The world's being saved will not save us; nor the
world's being lost destroy us. We should look to
ourselves : there is great merit here in the 'duty of
staying at home'! And, on the whole, to say
truth, I never heard of 'worlds' being 'saved' in
any other way. That mania of saving worlds is
itself a piece of the Eighteenth Century with its

windy sentimentalism. Let us not follow it too
far. For the saving of the *world* I will trust
confidently to the Maker of the world; and look
a little to my own saving, which I am more
competent to!—In brief, for the world's sake, and
for our own, we will rejoice greatly that Scepticism,
Insincerity, Mechanical Atheism, with all their
poison-dews, are going, and as good as gone.—

Now it was under such conditions, in those
times of Johnson, that our Men of Letters had to
live. Times in which there was properly no truth
in life. Old truths had fallen nigh dumb; the new
lay yet hidden, not trying to speak. That Man's
Life here below was a Sincerity and Fact, and
would forever continue such, no new intimation,
in that dusk of the world, had yet dawned. No
intimation; not even any French Revolution,—
which we define to be a Truth once more, though
a Truth clad in hellfire! How different was the
Luther's Pilgrimage, with its assured goal, from
the Johnson's, girt with mere traditions, suppositions,
grown now incredible, unintelligible! Mahomet's
Formulas were of 'wood waxed and oiled,' and
could be *burnt* out of one's way: poor Johnson's
were far more difficult to burn.—The strong man
will ever find *work*, which means difficulty, pain,
to the full measure of his strength. But to make-
out a victory, in those circumstances of our poor
Hero as Man of Letters, was perhaps more
difficult than in any. Not obstruction, disorganisation, Bookseller Osborne and Fourpence-halfpenny
a day; not this alone; but the light of his own
soul was taken from him. No landmark on the
Earth; and, alas, what is that to having no loadstar in the Heaven! We need not wonder that

Fallen Heroes none of those Three men rose to victory. That they fought truly is the highest praise. With a mournful sympathy we will contemplate, if not three living victorious Heroes, as I said, the Tombs of three fallen Heroes! They fell for us too; making a way for us. There are the mountains which they hurled abroad in their confused War of the Giants; under which, their strength and life spent, they now lie buried.

I have already written of these three Literary Heroes, expressly or incidentally; what I suppose is known to most of you; what need not be spoken or written a second time. They concern us here as the singular *Prophets* of that singular age; for such they virtually were; and the aspect they and their world exhibit, under this point of view, might lead us into reflections enough! I call them, all three, Genuine Men more or less; faithfully, for most part unconsciously, struggling to be genuine, and plant themselves on the everlasting truth of things. This to a degree that eminently distinguishes them from the poor artificial mass of their contemporaries; and renders them worthy to be considered as Speakers, in some measure, of the everlasting truth, as Prophets in that age of theirs. By Nature herself, a noble necessity was laid on them to be so. They were men of such magnitude that they could not live on unrealities,—clouds, froth and all inanity gave-way under them: there was no footing for them but on firm earth; no rest or regular motion for them, if they got not footing there. To a certain extent, they were Sons of Nature once more in an age of Artifice; once more, Original Men.

As for Johnson, I have always considered him Johnson's to be, by nature, one of our great English souls. Nessus'- A strong and noble man; so much left undeveloped shirt in him to the last: in a kindlier element what might he not have been,—Poet, Priest, sovereign Ruler! On the whole, a man must not complain of his 'element,' of his 'time,' or the like; it is thriftless work doing so. His time is bad: well then, he is there to make it better!—Johnson's youth was poor, isolated, hopeless, very miserable. Indeed, it does not seem possible that, in any the favourablest outward circumstances, Johnson's life could have been other than a painful one. The world might have had more of profitable *work* out of him, or less; but his *effort* against the world's work could never have been a light one. Nature, in return for his nobleness, had said to him, Live in an element of diseased sorrow. Nay, perhaps the sorrow and the nobleness were intimately and even inseparably connected with each other. At all events, poor Johnson had to go about girt with continual hypo-chondria, physical and spiritual pain. Like a Hercules with the burning Nessus'-shirt on him, which shoots-in on him dull incurable misery: the Nessus'-shirt not to be stript-off, which is his own natural skin! In this manner *he* had to live. Figure him there, with his scrofulous diseases, with his great greedy heart, and unspeakable chaos of thoughts; stalking mournful as a stranger in this Earth; eagerly devouring what spiritual thing he could come at: school-languages and other merely grammatical stuff, if there were nothing better! The largest soul that was in all England; and pro-vision made for it of 'fourpence-halfpenny a day.' Yet a giant invincible soul; a true man's. One

An original man remembers always that story of the shoes at Oxford: the rough, seamy-faced, rawboned College Servitor stalking about, in winter-season, with his shoes worn-out; how the charitable Gentleman Commoner secretly places a new pair at his door; and the rawboned Servitor, lifting them, looking at them near, with his dim eyes, with what thoughts,— pitches them out of window! Wet feet, mud, frost, hunger or what you will; but not beggary: we cannot stand beggary! Rude stubborn self-help here; a whole world of squalor, rudeness, confused misery and want, yet of nobleness and man-fulness withal. It is a type of the man's life, this pitching-away of the shoes. An original man;— not a secondhand, borrowing or begging man. Let us stand on our own basis, at any rate! On such shoes as we ourselves can get. On frost and mud, if you will, but honestly on that;—on the reality and substance which Nature gives *us*, not on the semblance, on the thing she has given another than us!—

And yet with all this rugged pride of manhood and self-help was there ever soul more tenderly affectionate, loyally submissive to what was really higher than he? Great souls are always loyally submissive, reverent to what is over them; only small mean souls are otherwise. I could not find a better proof of what I said the other day, That the sincere man was by nature the obedient man; that only in a World of Heroes was there loyal Obedience to the Heroic. The essence of *originality* is not that it be *new*: Johnson believed altogether in the old; he found the old opinions credible for him, fit for him; and in a right heroic manner lived under them. He is well worth study in regard to that. For we are to say that Johnson was far **Origin of** other than a mere man of words and formulas; he **Formulas** was a man of truths and facts. He stood by the old formulas; the happier was it for him that he could so stand: but in all formulas that *he* could stand by, there needed to be a most genuine substance. Very curious how, in that poor Paper-age, so barren, artificial, thick-quilted with Pedantries, Hearsays, the great Fact of this Universe glared in, forever wonderful, indubitable, unspeakable, divine-infernal, upon this man too! How he harmonised his Formulas with it, how he managed at all under such circumstances: that is a thing worth seeing. A thing 'to be looked at with reverence, with pity, with awe.' That Church of St. Clement Danes, where Johnson still *worshipped* in the era of Voltaire, is to me a venerable place.

It was in virtue of his *sincerity*, of his speaking still in some sort from the heart of Nature, though in the current artificial dialect, that Johnson was a Prophet. Are not all dialects 'artificial'? Artificial things are not all false;—nay every true Product of Nature will infallibly *shape* itself; we may say all artificial things are, at the starting of them, *true*. What we call 'Formulas' are not in their origin bad; they are indispensably good. Formula is *method*, habitude; found wherever man is found. Formulas fashion themselves as Paths do, as beaten Highways, leading towards some sacred or high object, whither many men are bent. Consider it. One man, full of heartfelt earnest impulse, finds-out a way of doing somewhat,—were it of uttering his soul's reverence for the Highest, were it but of fitly saluting his fellow-man. An inventor was needed to do that, a *poet*; he has articulated the dim-struggling thought

All formulas once true that dwelt in his own and many hearts. This is his way of doing that; these are his footsteps, the beginning of a 'Path.' And now see: the second man travels naturally in the footsteps of his foregoer, it is the *easiest* method. In the footsteps of his foregoer; yet with improvements, with changes where such seem good; at all events with enlargements, the Path ever *widening* itself as more travel it;—till at last there is a broad Highway whereon the whole world may travel and drive. While there remains a City or Shrine, or any Reality to drive to, at the farther end, the Highway shall be right welcome! When the City is gone, we will forsake the Highway. In this manner all Institutions, Practices, Regulated Things in the world have come into existence, and gone out of existence. Formulas all begin by being *full* of substance; you may call them the *skin*, the articulation into shape, into limbs and skin, of a substance that is already there: *they* had not been there otherwise. Idols, as we said, are not idolatrous till they become doubtful, empty for the worshipper's heart. Much as we talk against Formulas, I hope no one of us is ignorant withal of the high significance of *true* Formulas; that they were, and will ever be, the indispensablest furniture of our habitation in this world.——

Mark, too, how little Johnson boasts of his 'sincerity.' He has no suspicion of his being particularly sincere,—of his being particularly anything! A hard-struggling, weary-hearted man, or 'scholar' as he calls himself, trying hard to get some honest livelihood in the world, not to starve, but to live—without stealing! A noble unconsciousness is in him. He does not 'engrave *Truth*

on his watch-seal;' no, but he stands by truth, **Uncon-**
speaks by it, works and lives by it. Thus it ever **scious**
is. Think of it once more. The man whom **sincerity**
Nature has appointed to do great things is, first of **Johnson**
all, furnished with that openness to Nature which
renders him incapable of being *in*sincere ! To his
large, open, deep-feeling heart Nature is a Fact:
all hearsay is hearsay ; the unspeakable greatness of
this Mystery of Life, let him acknowledge it or
not, nay even though he seem to forget it or deny
it, is ever present to *him*,—fearful and wonderful,
on this hand and on that. He has a basis of
sincerity ; unrecognised, because never questioned or
capable of question. Mirabeau, Mahomet, Cromwell, Napoleon : all the Great Men I ever heard-
of have this as the primary material of them.
Innumerable commonplace men are debating, are
talking everywhere their commonplace doctrines,
which they have learned by logic, by rote, at secondhand : to that kind of man all this is still nothing.
He must have truth; truth which *he* feels to be
true. How shall he stand otherwise ? His whole
soul, at all moments, in all ways, tells him that there
is no standing. He is under the noble necessity of
being true. Johnson's way of thinking about this
world is not mine, any more than Mahomet's was :
but I recognise the everlasting element of heart-
sincerity in both ; and see with pleasure how neither
of them remains ineffectual. Neither of them is as
chaff sown ; in both of them is something which
the seed-field will *grow*.

Johnson was a Prophet to his people ; preached
a Gospel to them,—as all like him always do.
The highest Gospel he preached we may describe
as a kind of Moral Prudence : 'in a world where

His much is to be done, and little is to be known,' see
Gospel how you will *do* it! A thing well worth preaching.
'A world where much is to be done, and little is to
be known:' do not sink yourselves in boundless
bottomless abysses of Doubt, of wretched god-for-
getting Unbelief;—you were miserable then, powerless, mad: how could you *do* or work at all? Such
Gospel Johnson preached and taught;—coupled,
theoretically and practically, with this other great
Gospel, 'Clear your mind of Cant!' Have no
trade with Cant: stand on the cold mud in the
frosty weather, but let it be in your own *real* torn
shoes: 'that will be better for you,' as Mahomet
says! I call this, I call these two things *joined
together*, a great Gospel, the greatest perhaps that
was possible at that time.

Johnson's Writings, which once had such currency
and celebrity, are now, as it were, disowned by the
young generation. It is not wonderful; Johnson's
opinions are fast becoming obsolete: but his style
of thinking and of living, we may hope, will never
become obsolete. I find in Johnson's Books the
indisputablest traces of a great intellect and great
heart:—ever welcome, under what obstructions and
perversions soever. They are *sincere* words, those
of his; he means things by them. A wondrous
buckram style,—the best he could get to then; a
measured grandiloquence, stepping or rather stalking
along in a very solemn way, grown obsolete now;
sometimes a tumid *size* of phraseology not in proportion to the contents of it: all this you will put-
up with. For the phraseology, tumid or not, has
always *something within it*. So many beautiful styles
and books, with *nothing* in them;—a man is a *male-
factor* to the world who writes such! *They* are

the avoidable kind!—Had Johnson left nothing **Boswell** but his *Dictionary*, one might have traced there a great intellect, a genuine man. Looking to its clearness of definition, its general solidity, honesty, insight, and successful method, it may be called the best of all Dictionaries. There is in it a kind of architectural nobleness; it stands there like a great solid square-built edifice, finished, symmetrically complete: you judge that a true Builder did it.

One word, in spite of our haste, must be granted to poor Bozzy. He passes for a mean, inflated, gluttonous creature; and was so in many senses. Yet the fact of his reverence for Johnson will ever remain noteworthy. The foolish conceited Scotch Laird, the most conceited man of his time, approaching in such awestruck attitude the great dusty irascible Pedagogue in his mean garret there: it is a genuine reverence for Excellence; a *worship* for Heroes, at a time when neither Heroes nor worship were surmised to exist. Heroes, it would seem, exist always, and a certain worship of them! We will also take the liberty to deny altogether that of the witty Frenchman, that no man is a Hero to his valet-de-chambre. Or if so, it is not the Hero's blame, but the Valet's: that his soul, namely, is a mean *valet*-soul! He expects his Hero to advance in royal stage-trappings, with measured step, trains borne behind him, trumpets sounding before him. It should stand rather, No man can be a *Grand-Monarque* to his valet-de-chambre. Strip your Louis Quatorze of his king-gear, and there *is* left nothing but a poor forked radish with a head fantastically carved;—admirable to no valet. The Valet does not know a Hero when he sees him! Alas, no: it requires a kind of *Hero* to do that;—

and one of the world's wants, in *this* as in other senses, is for the most part want of such.

On the whole, shall we not say, that Boswell's admiration was well bestowed; that he could have found no soul in all England so worthy of bending down before? Shall we not say, of this great mournful Johnson too, that he guided his difficult confused existence wisely; led it *well*, like a right-valiant man? That waste chaos of Authorship by trade; that waste chaos of Scepticism in religion and politics, in life-theory and life-practice; in his poverty, in his dust and dimness, with the sick body and the rusty coat: he made it do for him, like a brave man. Not wholly without a loadstar in the Eternal; he had still a loadstar, as the brave all need to have: with his eye set on that, he would change his course for nothing in these confused vortices of the lower sea of Time. 'To the Spirit of Lies, bearing death and hunger, he would in no wise strike his flag.' Brave old Samuel: *ultimus Romanorum !*

Of Rousseau and his Heroism I cannot say so much. He is not what I call a strong man. A morbid, excitable, spasmodic man; at best, intense rather than strong. He had not 'the talent of Silence,' an invaluable talent; which few Frenchmen, or indeed men of any sort in these times, excel in! The suffering man ought really 'to consume his own smoke;' there is no good in emitting *smoke* till you have made it into *fire*,— which, in the metaphorical sense too, all smoke is capable of becoming! Rousseau has not depth or width, not calm force for difficulty; the first characteristic of true greatness. A fundamental mistake

to call vehemence and rigidity strength! A man is
not strong who takes convulsion-fits; though six
men cannot hold him then. He that can walk
under the heaviest weight without staggering, he
is the strong man. We need forever, especially in
these loud-shrieking days, to remind ourselves of
that. A man who cannot *hold his peace*, till the
time come for speaking and acting, is no right
man.

Poor Rousseau's face is to me expressive of him.
A high but narrow contracted intensity in it: bony
brows; deep, straight-set eyes, in which there is
something bewildered-looking,—bewildered, peer-
ing with lynx-eagerness. A face full of misery,
even ignoble misery, and also of the antagonism
against that; something mean, plebeian there, re-
deemed only by *intensity* : the face of what is called
a Fanatic,—a sadly *contracted* Hero! We name
him here because, with all his drawbacks, and they
are many, he has the first and chief characteristic of
a Hero: he is heartily *in earnest*. In earnest, if
ever man was; as none of these French Philo-
sophes were. Nay, one would say, of an earnestness too great for his otherwise sensitive, rather
feeble nature; and which indeed in the end drove
him into the strangest incoherences, almost delira-
tions. There had come, at last, to be a kind of
madness in him: his Ideas *possessed* him like
demons; hurried him so about, drove him over
steep places!—

The fault and misery of Rousseau was what we
easily name by a single word *Egoism*; which is
indeed the source and summary of all faults and
miseries whatsoever. He had not perfected himself into victory over mere Desire; a mean hunger,

Rousseau a 'con-tracted hero'

His
egoism in many sorts, was still the motive principle of him. I am afraid he was a very vain man; hungry for the praises of men. You remember Genlis's experience of him. She took Jean Jacques to the Theatre; he bargaining for a strict incognito,— "*He* would not be seen there for the world!" The curtain did happen nevertheless to be drawn aside: the Pit recognised Jean Jacques, but took no great notice of him! He expressed the bitterest indignation; gloomed all evening, spake no other than surly words. The glib Countess remained entirely convinced that his anger was not at being seen, but at not being applauded when seen. How the whole nature of the man is poisoned; nothing but suspicion, self-isolation, fierce moody ways! He could not live with anybody. A man of some rank from the country, who visited him often, and used to sit with him, expressing all reverence and affection for him, comes one day, finds Jean Jacques full of the sourest unintelligible humour. "Monsieur," said Jean Jacques, with flaming eyes, "I know why you come here. You come to see what a poor life I lead; how little is in my poor pot that is boiling there. Well, look into the pot! There is half a pound of meat, one carrot and three onions; that is all: go and tell the whole world that, if you like, Monsieur!"—A man of this sort was far gone. The whole world got itself supplied with anecdotes for light laughter, for a certain theatrical interest, from these perversions and contortions of poor Jean Jacques. Alas, to him they were not laughing or theatrical; too real to him! The contortions of a dying gladiator: the crowded amphitheatre looks-on with entertainment; but the gladiator is in agonies and dying.

And yet this Rousseau, as we say, with his **A prophet** passionate appeals to Mothers, with his *Contrat-* **spite of all** *social*, with his celebrations of Nature, even of savage life in Nature, did once more touch upon Reality, struggle towards Reality ; was doing the function of a Prophet to his Time. As *he* could, and as the Time could ! Strangely through all that defacement, degradation and almost madness, there is in the inmost heart of poor Rousseau a spark of real heavenly fire. Once more, out of the element of that withered mocking Philosophism, Scepticism and Persiflage, there has arisen in that man the ineradicable feeling and knowledge that this Life of ours is *true;* not a Scepticism, Theorem, or Persiflage, but a Fact, an awful Reality. Nature had made that revelation to him ; had ordered him to speak it out. He got it spoken out ; if not well and clearly, then ill and dimly,—as clearly as he could. Nay what are all errors and perversities of his, even those stealings of ribbons, aimless confused miseries and vagabondisms, if we will interpret them kindly, but the blinkard dazzlements and staggerings to and fro of a man sent on an errand he is too weak for, by a path he cannot yet find ? Men are led by strange ways. One should have tolerance for a man, hope of him ; leave him to try yet what he will do. While life lasts, hope lasts for every man.

Of Rousseau's literary talents, greatly celebrated still among his countrymen, I do not say much. His Books, like himself, are what I call unhealthy; not the good sort of Books. There is a sensuality in Rousseau. Combined with such an intellectual gift as his, it makes pictures of a certain gorgeous attractiveness : but they are not genuinely poetical.

The Evangel-
ist of the
Revolu-
tion
Not white sunlight: something *operatic ;* a kind of rosepink, artificial bedizenment. It is frequent, or rather it is universal, among the French since his time. Madame de Staël has something of it; St. Pierre; and down onwards to the present astonishing convulsionary 'Literature of Desperation,' it is everywhere abundant. That same *rosepink* is not the right hue. Look at a Shakspeare, at a Goethe, even at a Walter Scott! He who has once seen into this, has seen the difference of the True from the Sham-True, and will discriminate them ever afterwards.

We had to observe in Johnson how much good a Prophet, under all disadvantages and disorganisations, can accomplish for the world. In Rousseau we are called to look rather at the fearful amount of evil which, under such disorganisation, may accompany the good. Historically it is a most pregnant spectacle, that of Rousseau. Banished into Paris garrets, in the gloomy company of his own Thoughts and Necessities there; driven from post to pillar; fretted, exasperated till the heart of him went mad, he had grown to feel deeply that the world was not his friend nor the world's law. It was expedient, if anyway possible, that such a man should *not* have been set in flat hostility with the world. He could be cooped into garrets, laughed at as a maniac, left to starve like a wild beast in his cage;—but he could not be hindered from setting the world on fire. The French Revolution found its Evangelist in Rousseau. His semi-delirious speculations on the miseries of civilised life, the preferability of the savage to the civilised, and suchlike, helped well to produce a whole delirium in France generally. True, you may well ask, What could the world, the governors of **Burns** the world, do with such a man? Difficult to say what the governors of the world could do with him! What he could do with them is unhappily clear enough,—*guillotine* a great many of them! Enough now of Rousseau.

It was a curious phenomenon, in the withered, unbelieving, secondhand Eighteenth Century, that of a Hero starting up, among the artificial pasteboard figures and productions, in the guise of a Robert Burns. Like a little well in the rocky desert places,—like a sudden splendour of Heaven in the artificial Vauxhall! People knew not what to make of it. They took it for a piece of the Vauxhall fire-work; alas, it *let* itself be so taken, though struggling half-blindly, as in bitterness of death, against that! Perhaps no man had such a false reception from his fellow-men. Once more a very wasteful life-drama was enacted under the sun.

The tragedy of Burns's life is known to all of you. Surely we may say, if discrepancy between place held and place merited constitute perverseness of lot for a man, no lot could be more perverse than Burns's. Among those secondhand acting-figures, *mimes* for most part, of the Eighteenth Century, once more a giant Original man; one of those men who reach down to the perennial Deeps, who take rank with the Heroic among men: and he was born in a poor Ayrshire hut. The largest soul of all the British lands came among us in the shape of a hard-handed Scottish Peasant.

His Father, a poor toiling man, tried various things; did not succeed in any; was involved in continual difficulties. The Steward, Factor as the

Burns's father Scotch call him, used to send letters and threaten-ings, Burns says, 'which threw us all into tears.' The brave, hard-toiling, hard-suffering Father, his brave heroine of a wife; and those children, of whom Robert was one! In this Earth, so wide otherwise, no shelter for *them*. The letters 'threw us all into tears·' figure it. The brave Father, I say always;—a *silent* Hero and Poet; without whom the son had never been a speaking one! Burns's Schoolmaster came afterwards to London, learnt what good society was; but declares that in no meeting of men did he ever enjoy better dis-course than at the hearth of this peasant. And his poor 'seven acres of nursery-ground,'—not that, nor the miserable patch of clay-farm, nor anything he tried to get a living by, would prosper with him; he had a sore unequal battle all his days. But he stood to it valiantly; a wise, faithful, unconquerable man;—swallowing-down how many sore sufferings daily into silence; fighting like an unseen Hero,—nobody publishing newspaper paragraphs about his nobleness; voting pieces of plate to him! How-ever, he was not lost: nothing is lost. Robert is there; the outcome of him,—and indeed of many generations of such as him.

This Burns appeared under every disadvantage: uninstructed, poor, born only to hard manual toil; and writing, when it came to that, in a rustic special dialect, known only to a small province of the country he lived in. Had he written, even what he did write, in the general language of England, I doubt not he had already become universally re-cognised as being, or capable to be, one of our greatest men. That he should have tempted so many to penetrate through the rough husk of that

dialect of his, is proof that there lay something far A 'basis
from common within it. He has gained a certain of mirth'
recognition, and is continuing to do so over all in Burns
quarters of our wide Saxon world: wheresoever
a Saxon dialect is spoken, it begins to be understood,
by personal inspection of this and the other, that
one of the most considerable Saxon men of
the Eighteenth century was an Ayrshire Peasant
named Robert Burns. Yes, I will say, here too
was a piece of the right Saxon stuff: strong as
the Harz-rock, rooted in the depths of the world ;
—rock, yet with wells of living softness in it ! A
wild impetuous whirlwind of passion and faculty
slumbered quiet there ; such heavenly *melody* dwelling in the heart of it. A noble rough genuineness;
homely, rustic, honest ; true simplicity of strength :
with its lightning-fire, with its soft dewy pity ;—
like the old Norse Thor, the Peasant-god !—

Burns's Brother Gilbert, a man of much sense
and worth, has told me that Robert, in his young
days, in spite of their hardship, was usually the
gayest of speech ; a fellow of infinite frolic, laughter,
sense and heart ; far pleasanter to hear there, stript
cutting peats in the bog, or suchlike, than he ever
afterwards knew him. I can well believe it. This
basis of mirth ('*fond gaillard*,' as old Marquis
Mirabeau calls it), a primal-element of sunshine
and joyfulness, coupled with his other deep and
earnest qualities, is one of the most attractive characteristics of Burns. A large fund of Hope dwells
in him ; spite of his tragical history, he is not a
mourning man. He shakes his sorrows gallantly
aside ; bounds forth victorious over them. It is as
the lion shaking 'dew-drops from his mane ; ' as
the swift-bounding horse, that *laughs* at the shaking

Burns's
conver-
sation of the spear.—But indeed, Hope, Mirth, of the sort like Burns's, are they not the outcome properly of warm generous affection,—such as is the beginning of all to every man?

You would think it strange if I called Burns the most gifted British soul we had in all that century of his: and yet I believe the day is coming when there will be little danger in saying so. His writings, all that he *did* under such obstructions, are only a poor fragment of him. Professor Stewart remarked very justly, what indeed is true of all Poets good for much, that his poetry was not any particular faculty; but the general result of a naturally vigorous original mind expressing itself in that way. Burns's gifts, expressed in conversation, are the theme of all that ever heard him. All kinds of gifts: from the gracefulest utterances of courtesy, to the highest fire of passionate speech; loud floods of mirth, soft wailings of affection, laconic emphasis, clear piercing insight; all was in him. Witty duchesses celebrate him as a man whose speech 'led them off their feet.' This is beautiful: but still more beautiful that which Mr Lockhart has recorded, which I have more than once alluded to, How the waiters and ostlers at inns would get out of bed, and come crowding to hear this man speak! Waiters and ostlers:—they too were men, and here was a man! I have heard much about his speech; but one of the best things I ever heard of it was, last year, from a venerable gentleman long familiar with him. That it was speech distinguished by always *having something in it.* "He spoke rather little than much," this old man told me; "sat rather silent in those early days, as in the company of persons above him; and always when he did speak, it was to throw new

light on the matter." I know not why any one Burns and Mirabeau
should ever speak otherwise !—But if we look at
his general force of soul, his healthy *robustness*
everyway, the rugged down-rightness, penetration,
generous valour and manfulness that was in him,
— where shall we readily find a better-gifted
man ?

Among the great men of the Eighteenth Century,
I sometimes feel as if Burns might be found to resemble Mirabeau more than any other. They differ
widely in vesture ; yet look at them intrinsically.
There is the same burly thick-necked strength of
body as of soul ;—built, in both cases, on what the
old Marquis calls a *fond gaillard.* By nature, by
course of breeding, indeed by nation, Mirabeau has
much more of bluster ; a noisy, forward, unresting
man. But the characteristic of Mirabeau too is
veracity and sense, power of true *insight*, superiority
of vision. The thing that he says is worth remembering. It is a flash of insight into some object or
other : so do both these men speak. The same
raging passions ; capable too in both of manifesting
themselves as the tenderest noble affections. Wit,
wild laughter, energy, directness, sincerity : these
were in both. The types of the two men are not
dissimilar. Burns too could have governed, debated
in National Assemblies ; politicised, as few could.
Alas, the courage which had to exhibit itself in
capture of smuggling schooners in the Solway Frith ;
in keeping *silence* over so much, where no good speech,
but only inarticulate rage was possible : this might
have bellowed forth Ushers de Brézé and the like ;
and made itself visible to all men, in managing of
kingdoms, in ruling of great ever-memorable epochs !
But they said to him reprovingly, his Official Superiors

Burns denied his arena said, and wrote : 'You are to work, not think.' Of your *thinking*-faculty, the greatest in this land, we have no need ; you are to gauge beer there ; for that only are *you* wanted. Very notable ;—and worth mentioning, though we know what is to be said and answered ! As if Thought, Power of Thinking, were not, at all times, in all places and situations of the world, precisely the thing that *was* wanted. The fatal man, is he not always the *un*thinking man, the man who cannot think and *see ;* but only grope, and hallucinate, and *mis*see the nature of the thing he works with ? He missees it, mis*takes* it as we say ; takes it for one thing, and it *is* another thing,—and leaves him standing like a Futility there ! He is the fatal man ; unutterably fatal, put in the high places of men.— "Why complain of this ? " say some : " Strength is mournfully denied its arena ; that was true from of old." Doubtless ; and the worse for the *arena*, answer I ! *Complaining* profits little ; stating of the truth may profit. That a Europe, with its French Revolution just breaking out, finds no need of a Burns except for gauging beer,—is a thing I, for one, cannot *rejoice* at !—

Once more we have to say here, that the chief quality of Burns is the *sincerity* of him. So in his Poetry, so in his Life. The Song he sings is not of fantasticalities ; it is of a thing felt, really there ; the prime merit of this, as of all in him, and of his Life generally, is truth. The Life of Burns is what we may call a great tragic sincerity. A sort of savage sincerity,—not cruel, far from that ; but wild, wrestling naked with the truth of things. In that sense, there is something of the savage in all great men.

Hero-worship,—Odin, Burns? Well; these Men of Letters too were not without a kind of Hero-worship: but what a strange condition has that got into now! The waiters and ostlers of Scotch inns, prying about the door, eager to catch any word that fell from Burns, were doing unconscious reverence to the Heroic. Johnson had his Boswell for worshipper. Rousseau had worshippers enough; princes calling on him in his mean garret; the great, the beautiful doing reverence to the poor moonstruck man. For himself a most portentous contradiction; the two ends of his life not to be brought into harmony. He sits at the tables of grandees; and has to copy music for his own living. He cannot even get his music copied. " By dint of dining out," says he, " I run the risk of dying by starvation at home." For his worshippers too a most questionable thing! If doing Hero-worship well or badly be the test of vital wellbeing or ill-being to a generation, can we say that *these* generations are very first-rate?—And yet our heroic Men of Letters do teach, govern, are kings, priests, or what you like to call them; intrinsically there is no preventing it by any means whatever. The world *has* to obey him who thinks and sees in the world. The world can alter the manner of that; can either have it as blessed continuous summer sunshine, or as unblessed black thunder and tornado,—with unspeakable difference of profit for the world! The manner of it is very alterable; the matter and fact of it is not alterable by any power under the sky. Light; or, failing that, lightning: the world can take its choice. Not whether we call an Odin god, prophet, priest, or what we call him; but whether we believe the word he tells us: there it all lies. If it be a true word, we shall have to believe it; believing it, we shall have to do it. What *name* or welcome we give him or it, is a point that concerns ourselves mainly. *It*, the new Truth, new deeper revealing of the Secret of this Universe, is verily of the nature of a message from on high; and must and will have itself obeyed.—

My last remark is on that notablest phasis of Burns's history,—his visit to Edinburgh. Often it seems to me as if his demeanour there were the highest proof he gave of what a fund of worth and genuine manhood was in him. If we think of it, few heavier burdens could be laid on the strength of a man. So sudden; all common *Lionism*, which ruins innumerable men, was as nothing to this. It is as if Napoleon had been made a King of, not gradually, but at once from the Artillery Lieutenancy in the Regiment La Fère. Burns, still only in his twenty-seventh year, is no longer even a ploughman; he is flying to the West Indies to escape disgrace and a jail. This month he is a ruined peasant, his wages seven pounds a year, and these gone from him: next month he is in the blaze of rank and beauty, handing down jewelled Duchesses to dinner; the cynosure of all eyes! Adversity is sometimes hard upon a man; but for one man who can stand prosperity, there are a hundred that will stand adversity. I admire much the way in which Burns met all this. Perhaps no man one could point out, was ever so sorely tried, and so little forgot himself. Tranquil, unastonished; not abashed, not inflated, neither awkwardness nor affectation: he feels that *he* there is the man Robert Burns; that the 'rank is but the guinea-stamp;' that the celebrity is but the candle-light, which will show *what* man, not in **Ruined** the least make him a better or other man! Alas, **by Lion-** it may readily, unless he look to it, make him a **Hunters** *worse* man; a wretched inflated wind-bag,—inflated till he *burst* and become a *dead* lion; for whom, as some one has said, 'there is no resurrection of the body;' worse than a living dog!—Burns is admirable here.

And yet, alas, as I have observed elsewhere, these Lion-hunters were the ruin and death of Burns. It was they that rendered it impossible for him to live! They gathered round him in his Farm; hindered his industry; no place was remote enough from them. He could not get his Lionism forgotten, honestly as he was disposed to do so. He falls into discontents, into miseries, faults; the world getting ever more desolate for him; health, character, peace of mind all gone;—solitary enough now. It is tragical to think of! These men came but to *see* him; it was out of no sympathy with him, nor no hatred to him. They came to get a little amusement: they got their amusement;—and the Hero's life went for it!

Richter says, in the Island of Sumatra there is a kind of 'Light-chafers,' large Fire-flies, which people stick upon spits, and illuminate the ways with at night. Persons of condition can thus travel with a pleasant radiance, which they much admire. Great honour to the Fire-flies! But—!—

LECTURE VI

THE HERO AS KING.   CROMWELL, NAPOLEON :
MODERN REVOLUTIONISM.

[*Friday, 22nd May* 1840]

The Hero as king WE come now to the last form of Heroism; that which we call Kingship. The Commander over men ; he to whose will our wills are to be subordinated, and loyally surrender themselves, and find their welfare in doing so, may be reckoned the most important of Great Men. He is practically the summary for us of *all* the various figures of Heroism ; Priest, Teacher, whatsoever of earthly or of spiritual dignity we can fancy to reside in a man, embodies itself here, to *command* over us, to furnish us with constant practical teaching, to tell us for the day and hour what we are to *do*. He is called *Rex*, Regulator, *Roi :* our own name is still better ; King, *Könning*, which means *Can*-ning, Able-man.

Numerous considerations, pointing towards deep, questionable, and indeed unfathomable regions, present themselves here : on the most of which we must resolutely for the present forbear to speak at all. As Burke said that perhaps fair *Trial by Jury* was the Soul of Government, and that all legislation, administration, parliamentary debating, and the rest of it, went on, in ' order to bring twelve impartial men into a jury-box ; '—so, by much stronger reason, may I say here, that the finding of your *Ableman* and getting him invested with the *symbols of ability*, with dignity, worship (*worth*-ship), royalty, kinghood, or whatever we call it, so that *he* may actually **The** have room to guide according to his faculty of **perfect** doing it,—is the business, well or ill accomplished, **form of govern-** of all social procedure whatsoever in this world! **ment** Hustings-speeches, Parliamentary motions, Reform Bills, French Revolutions, all mean at heart this ; or else nothing. Find in any country the Ablest Man that exists there ; raise *him* to the supreme place, and loyally reverence him : you have a perfect government for that country ; no ballot-box, parliamentary eloquence, voting, constitution-building, or other machinery whatsoever can improve it a whit. It is in the perfect state : an ideal country. The Ablest Man ; he means also the truest-hearted, justest, the Noblest Man : what he *tells us to do* must be precisely the wisest, fittest, that we could anywhere or anyhow learn ;—the thing which it will in all ways behove us, with right loyal thankfulness, and nothing doubting, to do ! Our *doing* and life were then, so far as government could regulate it, well regulated ; that were the ideal of constitutions.

Alas, we know very well that Ideals can never be completely embodied in practice. Ideals must ever lie a very great way off; and we will right thankfully content ourselves with any not intolerable approximation thereto ! Let no man, as Schiller says, too querulously ' measure by a scale of perfection the meagre product of reality' in this poor world of ours. We will esteem him no wise man ; we will esteem him a sickly, discontented, foolish man. And yet, on the other hand, it is never to be forgotten that Ideals do exist; that if they be not approximated to at all, the whole matter goes to wreck ! Infallibly. No bricklayer builds a wall

The History of all rebellions

perfectly perpendicular, mathematically this is not possible; a certain degree of perpendicularity suffices him; and he, like a good bricklayer, who must have done with his job, leaves it so. And yet if he sway *too much* from the perpendicular; above all, if he throw plummet and level quite away from him, and pile brick on brick heedless, just as it comes to hand—! Such bricklayer, I think, is in a bad way. *He* has forgotten himself: but the Law of Gravitation does not forget to act on him; he and his wall rush-down into confused welter of ruin!—

This is the history of all rebellions, French Revolutions, social explosions in ancient or modern times. You have put the too *Un*able man at the head of affairs! The too ignoble, unvaliant, fatuous man. You have forgotten that there is any rule, or natural necessity whatever, of putting the Able Man there. Brick must lie on brick as it may and can. Unable Simulacrum of Ability, *quack*, in a word, must adjust himself with quack, in all manner of administration of human things;—which accordingly lie unadministered, fermenting into unmeasured masses of failure, of indigent misery: in the outward, and in the inward or spiritual, miserable millions stretch-out the hand for their due supply, and it is not there. The 'law of gravitation' acts; Nature's laws do none of them forget to act. The miserable millions burst-forth into Sansculottism, or some other sort of madness; bricks and bricklayers lie as a fatal chaos!—

Much sorry stuff, written some hundred years ago or more, about the 'Divine right of Kings,' moulders unread now in the Public Libraries of this country. Far be it from us to disturb the calm process by which it is disappearing harmlessly from the earth, in those repositories! At the same time, not to **Divine** let the immense rubbish go without leaving us, as **right of** it ought, some soul of it behind—I will say that it **kings** did mean something; something true, which it is important for us and all men to keep in mind. To assert that in whatever man you chose to lay hold of (by this or the other plan of clutching at him); and clapt a round piece of metal on the head of, and called King,—there straightway came to reside a divine virtue, so that *he* became a kind of God, and a Divinity inspired him with faculty and right to rule over you to all lengths: this,—what can we do with this but leave it to rot silently in the Public Libraries? But I will say withal, and that is what these Divine-right men meant, That in Kings, and in all human Authorities, and relations that men god-created can form among each other, there is verily either a Divine Right or else a Diabolic Wrong; one or the other of these two! For it is false altogether, what the last Sceptical Century taught us, that this world is a steamengine. There is a God in this world; and a God's-sanction, or else the violation of such, does look-out from all ruling and obedience, from all moral acts of men. There is no act more moral between men than that of rule and obedience. Woe to him that claims obedience when it is not due; woe to him that refuses it when it is! God's law is in that, I say, however the Parchment-laws may run: there is a Divine Right or else a Diabolic Wrong at the heart of every claim that one man makes upon another.

It can do none of us harm to reflect on this: in all the relations of life it will concern us; in Loyalty and Royalty, the highest of these. I

The true king to seek esteem the modern error, That all goes by self-interest and the checking and balancing of greedy knaveries, and that, in short, there is nothing divine whatever in the association of men, a still more despicable error, natural as it is to an unbelieving century, than that of a 'divine right' in people *called* Kings. I say, Find me the true *Könning*, King, or Able-man, and he *has* a divine right over me. That we knew in some tolerable measure how to find him, and that all men were ready to acknowledge his divine right when found : this is precisely the healing which a sick world is every-where, in these ages, seeking after ! The true King, as guide of the practical, has ever something of the Pontiff in him,—guide of the spiritual, from which all practice has its rise. This too is a true saying, That the *King* is head of the *Church*.—But we will leave the Polemic stuff of a dead century to lie quiet on its bookshelves.

Certainly it is a fearful business, that of having your Ableman to *seek*, and not knowing in what manner to proceed about it ! That is the world's sad predicament in these times of ours. They are times of Revolution, and have long been. The bricklayer with his bricks, no longer heedful of plummet or the law of gravitation, have toppled, tumbled, and it all welters as we see ! But the beginning of it was not the French Revolution ; that is rather the *end*, we can hope. It were truer to say, the *beginning* was three centuries farther back : in the Reformation of Luther. That the thing which still called itself Christian Church had become a Falsehood, and brazenly went about pretending to pardon men's sins for metallic coined money, and to do much else which in the everlasting **Era of** truth of Nature it did *not* now do: here lay the **Revolu-** vital malady. The inward being wrong, all out- **tion** ward went ever more and more wrong. Belief died away; all was Doubt, Disbelief. The builder *cast away* his plummet; said to himself, "What is gravitation? Brick lies on brick there!" Alas, does it not still sound strange to many of us, the assertion that there *is* a God's truth in the business of god-created men; that all is not a kind of grimace, an 'expediency,' diplomacy, one knows not what!—

From that first necessary assertion of Luther's, "You, self-styled *Papa*, you are no Father in God at all; you are—a Chimera, whom I know not how to name in polite language!"—from that onwards to the shout which rose round Camille Desmoulins in the Palais-Royal, "*Aux armes!*" when the people had burst-up against *all* manner of Chimeras,—I find a natural historical sequence. That shout too, so frightful, half-infernal, was a great matter. Once more the voice of awakened nations; starting confusedly, as out of nightmare, as out of death-sleep, into some dim feeling that Life was real; that God's-world was not an expediency and diplomacy! Infernal;—yes, since they would not have it otherwise. Infernal, since not celestial or terrestrial!—Hollowness, insincerity *has* to cease;—sincerity of some sort has to begin. Cost what it may, reigns of terror, horrors of French Revolution or what else, we have to return to truth. Here is a Truth, as I said: a Truth clad in hell-fire, since they would not but have it so!—

A common theory among considerable parties of men in England and elsewhere used to be, that the

The French Nation had, in those days, as it were gone
Three *mad ;* that the French Revolution was a general
Days act of insanity, a temporary conversion of France
and large sections of the world into a kind of
Bedlam. The Event had risen and raged ; but was
a madness and nonentity,—gone now happily into
the region of Dreams and the Picturesque !—To
such comfortable philosophers, the Three Days of
July 1830 must have been a surprising phenomenon.
Here is the French Nation risen again, in musketry
and death-struggle, out shooting and being shot, to
make that same mad French Revolution good !
The sons and grandsons of those men, it would
séem, persist in the enterprise : they do not disown
it ; they will have it made good ; will have themselves shot, if it be not made good ! To philosophers
who had made-up their life-system on that 'madness'
quietus, no phenomenon could be more alarming.
Poor Niebuhr, they say, the Prussian Professor and
Historian, fell broken-hearted in consequence ;
sickened, if we can believe it, and died of the
Three Days ! It was surely not a very heroic
death ;—little better than Racine's, dying because
Louis Fourteenth looked sternly on him once.
The world had stood some considerable shocks, in
its time ; might have been expected to survive the
Three Days too, and be found turning on its axis
after even them ! The Three Days told all mortals
that the old French Revolution, mad as it might
look, was not a transitory ebullition of Bedlam, but
a genuine product of this Earth where we all live ;
that it was verily a Fact, and that the world in
general would do well everywhere to regard it as
such.

Truly, without the French Revolution, one would

not know what to make of an age like this at all. We will hail the French Revolution, as shipwrecked mariners might the sternest rock, in a world otherwise all of baseless sea and waves. A true Apocalypse, though a terrible one, to this false withered artificial time; testifying once more that Nature is *preter*natural; if not divine, then diabolic; that Semblance is not reality; that it has to become reality, or the world will take-fire under it,—burn *it* into what it is, namely Nothing! Plausibility has ended; empty Routine has ended; much has ended. This, as with a Trump of Doom, has been proclaimed to all men. They are the wisest who will learn it soonest. Long confused generations before it be learned; peace impossible till it be! The earnest man, surrounded, as ever, with a world of inconsistencies, can await patiently, patiently strive to do *his* work, in the midst of that. Sentence of Death is written down in Heaven against all that; sentence of Death is now proclaimed on the Earth against it: this he with his eyes may see. And surely, I should say, considering the other side of the matter, what enormous difficulties lie there, and how fast, fearfully fast, in all countries, the inexorable demand for solution of them is pressing on,—he may easily find other work to do than labouring in the Sansculottic province at this time of day!

To me, in these circumstances, that of 'Hero-worship' becomes a fact inexpressibly precious; the most solacing fact one sees in the world at present. There is an everlasting hope in it for the management of the world. Had all traditions, arrangements, creeds, societies that men ever instituted, sunk away, this would remain. The

Liberty and Equality certainty of Heroes being sent us; our faculty, our necessity, to reverence Heroes when sent: it shines like a polestar through smoke-clouds, dust-clouds, and all manner of down-rushing and conflagration.

Hero-worship would have sounded very strange to those workers and fighters in the French Revolution. Not reverence for Great Men; not any hope or belief, or even wish, that Great Men could again appear in the world! Nature, turned into a 'Machine,' was as if effete now; could not any longer produce Great Men:—I can tell her, she may give-up the trade altogether, then; we cannot do without Great Men!—But neither have I any quarrel with that of 'Liberty and Equality;' with the faith that, wise great men being impossible, a level immensity of foolish small men would suffice. It was a natural faith then and there. "Liberty and Equality; no Authority needed any longer. Hero-worship, reverence for *such* Authorities, has proved false, is itself a falsehood; no more of it! We have had such *forgeries*, we will now trust nothing. So many base plated coins passing in the market, the belief has now become common that no gold any longer exists,—and even that we can do very well without gold!" I find this, among other things, in that universal cry of Liberty and Equality; and find it very natural, as matters then stood.

And yet surely it is but the *transition* from false to true. Considered as the whole truth, it is false altogether;—the product of entire sceptical blindness, as yet only *struggling* to see. Hero-worship exists forever, and everywhere: not Loyalty alone; it extends from divine adoration down to the

lowest practical regions of life. 'Bending before The
men,' if it is not to be a mere empty grimace, Great
better dispensed with than practised, is Hero- Man a
worship,—a recognition that there does dwell in order
that presence of our brother something divine; that
every created man, as Novalis said, is a 'revelation
in the Flesh.' They were Poets too, that devised
all those graceful courtesies which make life noble!
Courtesy is not a falsehood or grimace; it need not
be such. And Loyalty, religious Worship itself,
are still possible; nay still inevitable.

May we not say, moreover, while so many of
our late Heroes have worked rather as revolutionary
men, that nevertheless every Great Man, every
genuine man, is by the nature of him a son of
Order, not of Disorder? It is a tragical position
for a true man to work in revolutions. He seems
an anarchist; and indeed a painful element of
anarchy does encumber him at every step,—him to
whose whole soul anarchy is hostile, hateful. His
mission is Order; every man's is. He is here to
make what was disorderly, chaotic, into a thing
ruled, regular. He is the missionary of Order.
Is not all work of man in this world a *making of
Order?* The carpenter finds rough trees: shapes
them, constrains them into square fitness, into
purpose and use. We are all born enemies of
Disorder: it is tragical for us all to be concerned
in image-breaking and down-pulling; for the Great
Man, *more* a man than we, it is doubly tragical.

Thus too all human things, maddest French
Sansculottisms, do and must work towards Order.
I say, there is not a *man* in them, raging in the
thickest of the madness, but is impelled withal, at
all moments, towards Order. His very life means

The war of the Puritans that; Disorder is dissolution, death. No chaos but it seeks a *centre* to revolve round. While man is man, some Cromwell or Napoleon is the necessary finish of a Sansculottism.—Curious: in those days when Hero-worship was the most incredible thing to every one, how it does come-out nevertheless, and assert itself practically, in a way which all have to credit. Divine *right*, take it on the great scale, is found to mean divine *might* withal! While old false Formulas are getting trampled everywhere into destruction, new genuine Substances unexpectedly unfold themselves indestructible. In rebellious ages, when Kingship itself seems dead and abolished, Cromwell, Napoleon step-forth again as Kings. The history of these men is what we have now to look at, as our last phasis of Heroism. The old ages are brought back to us; the manner in which Kings were made, and Kingship itself first took rise, is again exhibited in the history of these Two.

We have had many civil-wars in England; wars of Red and White Roses, wars of Simon de Montfort; wars enough, which are not very memorable. But that war of the Puritans has a significance which belongs to no one of the others. Trusting to your candour, which will suggest on the other side what I have not room to say, I will call it a section once more of that great universal war which alone makes-up the true History of the World,—the war of Belief against Unbelief! The struggle of men intent on the real essence of things, against men intent on the semblances and forms of things. The Puritans, to many, seem mere savage Iconoclasts, fierce destroyers of Forms; but it were more just to call them haters of *untrue* Forms. **Laud a** I hope we know how to respect Laud and his King **pedant** as well as them. Poor Laud seems to me to have been weak and ill-starred, not dishonest; an unfortunate Pedant rather than anything worse. His 'Dreams' and superstitions, at which they laugh so, have an affectionate, lovable kind of character. He is like a College-Tutor, whose whole world is forms, College-rules; whose notion is that these are the life and safety of the world. He is placed suddenly, with that unalterable luckless notion of his, at the head not of a College but of a Nation, to regulate the most complex deep-reaching interests of men. He thinks they ought to go by the old decent regulations; nay that their salvation will lie in extending and improving these. Like a weak man, he drives with spasmodic vehemence towards his purpose; cramps himself to it, heeding no voice of prudence, no cry of pity: He will have his College-rules obeyed by his Collegians; that first; and till that, nothing. He is an ill-starred Pedant, as I said. He would have it the world was a College of that kind, and the world *was not* that. Alas, was not his doom stern enough? Whatever wrongs he did, were they not all frightfully avenged on him?

It is meritorious to insist on forms; Religion and all else naturally clothes itself in forms. Everywhere the *formed* world is the only habitable one. The naked formlessness of Puritanism is not the thing I praise in the Puritans; it is the thing I pity,—praising only the spirit which had rendered that inevitable! All substances clothe themselves in forms: but there are suitable true forms, and then there are untrue unsuitable. As the briefest

True
forms and
false
definition, one might say, Forms which *grow* round a substance, if we rightly understand that, will correspond to the real nature and purport of it, will be true, good; forms which are consciously *put* round a substance, bad. I invite you to reflect on this. It distinguishes true from false in Ceremonial Form, earnest solemnity from empty pageant, in all human things.

There must be a veracity, a natural spontaneity in forms. In the commonest meeting of men, a person making, what we call, ' set speeches,' is not he an offence? In the mere drawing-room, whatsoever courtesies you see to be grimaces, prompted by no spontaneous reality within, are a thing you wish to get away from. But suppose now it were some matter of vital concernment, some transcendent matter (as Divine Worship is), about which your whole soul, struck dumb with its excess of feeling, knew not how to *form* itself into utterance at all, and preferred formless silence to any utterance there possible,—what should we say of a man coming forward to represent or utter it for you in the way of upholsterer-mummery? Such a man,—let him depart swiftly, if he love himself! You have lost your only son; are mute, struck down, without even tears: an importunate man importunately offers to celebrate Funeral Games for him in the manner of the Greeks! Such mummery is not only not to be accepted,—it is hateful, unendurable. It is what the old Prophets called ' Idolatry,' worshipping of hollow *shows*; what all earnest men do and will reject. We can partly understand what those poor Puritans meant. Laud dedicating that St. Catherine Creed's Church, in the manner we have it described; with his multiplied ceremonial bowings, gesticulations, exclamations: surely it is rather the rigorous **Laud** formal *Pedant*, intent on his 'College-rules,' than **and the** the earnest Prophet, intent on the essence of the **Puritans** matter!

Puritanism found *such* forms insupportable; trampled on such forms;—we have to excuse it for saying, No form at all rather than such! It stood preaching in its bare pulpit, with nothing but the Bible in its hand. Nay, a man preaching from his earnest *soul* into the earnest *souls* of men: is not this virtually the essence of all Churches whatsoever? The nakedest, savagest reality, I say, is preferable to any semblance, however dignified. Besides, it will clothe itself with *due* semblance by and by, if it be real. No fear of that; actually no fear at all. Given the living *man*, there will be found *clothes* for him; he will find himself clothes. But the suit-of-clothes pretending that *it* is both clothes and man—!—We cannot 'fight the French' by three-hundred-thousand red uniforms; there must be *men* in the inside of them! Semblance, I assert, must actually *not* divorce itself from Reality. If Semblance do,—why then there must be men found to rebel against Semblance, for it has become a lie! These two Antagonisms at war here, in the case of Laud and the Puritans, are as old nearly as the world. They went to fierce battle over England in that age; and fought-out their confused controversy to a certain length, with many results for all of us.

In the age which directly followed that of the Puritans, their cause or themselves were little likely to have justice done them. Charles Second and his Rochesters were not the kind of men you would

Canon-
ised
Puritans
set to judge what the worth or meaning of such men might have been. That there could be any faith or truth in the life of a man, was what these poor Rochesters, and the age they ushered-in, had forgotten. Puritanism was hung on gibbets,—like the bones of the leading Puritans. Its work nevertheless went on accomplishing itself. All true work of a man, hang the author of it on what gibbet you like, must and will accomplish itself. We have our *Habeas-Corpus*, our free Representation of the People; acknowledgment, wide as the world, that all men are, or else must, shall, and will become, what we call *free* men;—men with their life grounded on reality and justice, not on tradition, which has become unjust and a chimera! This in part and much besides this, was the work of the Puritans.

And indeed, as these things became gradually manifest, the character of the Puritans began to clear itself. Their memories were, one after another, taken *down* from the gibbet; nay a certain portion of them are now, in these days, as good as canonised. Eliot, Hampden, Pym, nay Ludlow, Hutchinson, Vane himself, are admitted to be a kind of Heroes; political Conscript Fathers, to whom in no small degree we owe what makes us a free England: it would not be safe for anybody to designate these men as wicked now. Few Puritans of note but find their apologists somewhere, and have a certain reverence paid them by earnest men. One Puritan, I think, and almost he alone, our poor Cromwell, seems to hang yet on the gibbet, and find no hearty apologist anywhere. Him neither saint nor sinner will acquit of great wickedness. A man of ability, infinite talent, courage, and so forth: but he betrayed the Cause. Selfish ambition, dishonesty, duplicity; a fierce, coarse, hypocritical *Tartufe*; turning all that noble Struggle for constitutional Liberty into a sorry farce played for his own benefit: this and worse is the character they give of Cromwell. And then there come contrasts with Washington and others; above all, with these noble Pyms and Hampdens, whose noble work he stole for himself, and ruined into a futility and deformity.

18th Century view of Cromwell

This view of Cromwell seems to me the not unnatural product of a century like the Eighteenth. As we said of the Valet, so of the Sceptic: He does not know a Hero when he sees him! The Valet expected purple mantles, gilt sceptres, body-guards and flourishes of trumpets: the Sceptic of the Eighteenth century looks for regulated respectable Formulas, 'Principles,' or what else he may call them; a style of speech and conduct which has got to seem 'respectable,' which can plead for itself in a handsome articulate manner, and gain the suffrages of an enlightened sceptical Eighteenth century! It is, at bottom, the same thing that both the Valet and he expect: the garnitures of some *acknowledged* royalty, which *then* they will acknowledge! The King coming to them in the rugged *un*formulistic state shall be no King.

For my own share, far be it from me to say or insinuate a word of disparagement against such characters as Hampden, Eliot, Pym; whom I believe to have been right worthy and useful men. I have read diligently what books and documents about them I could come at;—with the honestest wish to admire, to love and worship them like Heroes; but I am sorry to say, if the real truth

Cromwell the greatest of the Puritans must be told, with very indifferent success! At bottom, I found that it would not do. They are very noble men, these; step along in their stately way, with their measured euphemisms, philosophies, parliamentary eloquences, Ship-moneys, *Monarchies of Man;* a most constitutional, unblamable, dignified set of men. But the heart remains cold before them; the fancy alone endeavours to get-up some worship of them. What man's heart does, in reality, break-forth into any fire of brotherly love for these men? They are become dreadfully dull men! One breaks-down often enough in the constitutional eloquence of the admirable Pym, with his 'seventhly and lastly.' You find that it may be the admirablest thing in the world, but that it is heavy,—heavy as lead, barren as brick-clay; that, in a word, for you there is little or nothing now surviving there! One leaves all these Nobilities standing in their niches of honour: the rugged outcast Cromwell, he is the man of them all in whom one still finds human stuff. The great savage *Baresark:* he could write no euphemistic *Monarchy of Man;* did not speak, did not work with glib regularity; had no straight story to tell for himself anywhere. But he stood bare, not cased in euphemistic coat-of-mail; he grappled like a giant, face to face, heart to heart, with the naked truth of things! That, after all, is the sort of man for one. I plead guilty to valuing such a man beyond all other sorts of men. Smooth-shaven Respectabilities not a few one finds, that are not good for much. Small thanks to a man for keeping his hands clean, who would not touch the work but with gloves on!

Neither, on the whole, does this constitutional

tolerance of the Eighteenth century for the other **Liberty** happier Puritans seem to be a very great matter. **to tax** One might say, it is but a piece of Formulism and **oneself** Scepticism, like the rest. They tell us, It was a sorrowful thing to consider that the foundation of our English Liberties should have been laid by 'Superstition.' These Puritans came forward with Calvinistic incredible Creeds, Anti-Laudisms, West-minster Confessions; demanding, chiefly of all, that they should have liberty to *worship* in their own way. Liberty to *tax* themselves: that was the thing they should have demanded! It was Super-stition, Fanaticism, disgraceful Ignorance of Con-stitutional Philosophy to insist on the other thing! —Liberty to *tax* oneself? Not to pay-out money from your pocket except on reason shown? No century, I think, but a rather barren one would have fixed on that as the first right of man! I should say, on the contrary, A just man will generally have better cause than *money* in what shape soever, before deciding to revolt against his Government. Ours is a most confused world; in which a good man will be thankful to see any kind of Government maintain itself in a not in-supportable manner; and here in England, to this hour, if he is not ready to pay a great many taxes which *he* can see very small reason in, it will not go well with him, I think! He must try some other climate than this. Taxgatherer? Money? He will say: "Take my money, since you *can*, and it is so desirable to you; take it,—and take yourself away with it; and leave me alone to my work here. *I* am still here; can still work, after all the money you have taken from me!" But if they come to him, and say, "Acknowledge a Lie;

pretend to say you are worshipping God, when you are not doing it : believe not the thing that *you* find true, but the thing that I find, or pretend to find true ! "   He will answer : " No ; by God's help, no !   You may take my purse ; but I cannot have my moral Self annihilated.   The purse is any High-wayman's who might meet me with a loaded pistol : but the Self is mine and God my Maker's ; it is not yours ; and I will resist you to the death, and revolt against you, and, on the whole, front all manner of extremities, accusations and confusions, in defence of that ! "—

Really, it seems to me the one reason which could justify revolting, this of the Puritans.   It has been the soul of all just revolts among men.   Not *Hunger* alone produced even the French Revolution : no, but the feeling of the insupportable all-pervading *Falsehood* which had now embodied itself in Hunger, in universal material Scarcity and Non-entity, and thereby become *indisputably* false in the eyes of all !   We will leave the Eighteenth century with its ' liberty to tax itself.'   We will not astonish ourselves that the meaning of such men as the Puritans remained dim to it.   To men who believe in no reality at all, how shall a *real* human soul, the intensest of all realities, as it were the Voice of this world's Maker still speaking to *us*,—be intelligible ? What it cannot reduce into constitutional doctrines relative to ' taxing,' or other the like material interest, gross, palpable to the sense, such a century will needs reject as an amorphous heap of rubbish. Hampdens, Pyms, and Ship-money will be the theme of much constitutional eloquence, striving to be fervid ;—which will glitter, if not as fire does, then as *ice* does : and the irreducible Cromwell will

remain a chaotic mass of 'madness,' 'hypocrisy,' **Cromwell**
and much else.   **not a liar**

From of old, I will confess, this theory of Cromwell's falsity has been incredible to me. Nay I
cannot believe the like, of any Great Man whatever. Multitudes of Great Men figure in History
as false selfish men; but if we will consider it, they
are but *figures* for us, unintelligible shadows; we do
not see into them as men that could have existed at
all. A superficial unbelieving generation only, with
no eye but for the surfaces and semblances of things,
could form such notions of Great Men. Can a great
soul be possible without a *conscience* in it, the essence
of all *real* souls, great or small?—No, we cannot
figure Cromwell as a Falsity and Fatuity; the longer
I study him and his career, I believe this the less.
Why should we? There is no evidence of it. Is
it not strange that, after all the mountains of calumny
this man has been subject to, after being represented
as the very prince of liars, who never, or hardly ever,
spoke truth, but always some cunning counterfeit of
truth, there should not yet have been one falsehood
brought clearly home to him? A prince of liars,
and no lie spoken by him. Not one that I could
yet get sight of. It is like Pococke asking Grotius,
Where is your *proof* of Mahomet's Pigeon? No
proof!—Let us leave all these calumnious chimeras,
as chimeras ought to be left. They are not portraits of the man; they are distracted phantasms of
him, the joint product of hatred and darkness.

Looking at the man's life with our own eyes, it
seems to me, a very different hypothesis suggests
itself. What little we know of his earlier obscure
years, distorted as it has come down to us, does it

R

Crom-
well's
early life

not all betoken an earnest, affectionate, sincere kind
of man? His nervous melancholic temperament in-
dicates rather a seriousness *too* deep for him. Of
those stories of 'Spectres;' of the white Spectre in
broad daylight, predicting that he should be King of
England, we are not bound to believe much;—probably no more than of the other black Spectre, or
Devil in person, to whom the Officer *saw* him sell
himself before Worcester Fight! But the mournful, over-sensitive, hypochondriac humour of Oliver,
in his young years, is otherwise indisputably known.
The Huntingdon Physician told Sir Philip Warwick
himself, He had often been sent for at midnight;
Mr Cromwell was full of hypochondria, thought
himself near dying, and "had fancies about the
Towncross." These things are significant. Such
an excitable deep-feeling nature, in that rugged
stubborn strength of his, is not the symptom of
falsehood; it is the symptom and promise of quite
other than falsehood!

The young Oliver is sent to study Law; falls,
or is said to have fallen, for a little period, into
some of the dissipations of youth; but if so, speedily
repents, abandons all this: not much above twenty,
he is married, settled as an altogether grave and quiet
man. 'He pays-back what money he had won at
gambling,' says the story;—he does not think any
gain of that kind could be really *his*. It is very interesting, very natural, this 'conversion,' as they
well name it; this awakening of a great true soul
from the worldly slough, to see into the awful *truth*
of things;—to see that time and its shows all rested
on Eternity, and this poor Earth of ours was the
threshold either of Heaven or of Hell! Oliver's
life at St Ives or Ely, as a sober industrious Farmer,

is it not altogether as that of a true and devout man?
He has renounced the world and its ways; *its* prizes
are not the thing that can enrich him. He tills the
earth ; he reads his Bible ; daily assembles his
servants round him to worship God. He comforts
persecuted ministers, is fond of preachers ; nay can
himself preach,—exhorts his neighbours to be wise,
to redeem the time. In all this what 'hypocrisy,'
'ambition,' 'cant,' or other falsity ? The man's
hopes, I do believe, were fixed on the other Higher
World ; his aim to get well *thither*, by walking well
through his humble course in *this* world. He courts
no notice : what could notice here do for him ?
'Ever in his great Taskmaster's eye.'

It is striking, too, how he comes-out once into
public view ; he, since no other is willing to come :
in resistance to a public grievance. I mean, in that
matter of the Bedford Fens. No one else will go to
law with Authority; therefore he will. That matter
once settled, he returns back into obscurity, to his
Bible and his Plough. 'Gain influence'? His
influence is the most legitimate ; derived from
personal knowledge of him, as a just, religious,
reasonable and determined man. In this way he
has lived till past forty ; old age is now in view
of him, and the earnest portal of Death and
Eternity; it was at this point that he suddenly
became 'ambitious'! I do not interpret his
Parliamentary mission in that way !

His successes in Parliament, his successes through
the war, are honest successes of a brave man ; who
has more resolution in the heart of him, more light
in the head of him than other men. His prayers to
God ; his spoken thanks to the God of Victory,
who had preserved him safe, and carried him forward

Cromwell the regicide so far, through the furious clash of a world all set in conflict, through desperate-looking envelopments at Dunbar; through the death-hail of so many battles; mercy after mercy; to the 'crowning mercy' of Worcester Fight: all this is good and genuine for a deep-hearted Calvinistic Cromwell. Only to vain unbelieving Cavaliers, worshipping not God but their own 'lovelocks,' frivolities and formalities, living quite apart from contemplations of God, living *without* God in the world, need it seem hypocritical.

Nor will his participation in the King's death involve him in condemnation with us. It is a stern business killing of a King! But if you once go to war with him, it lies *there*; this and all else lies there. Once at war, you have made wager of battle with him: it is he to die, or else you. Reconciliation is problematic; may be possible, or, far more likely, is impossible. It is now pretty generally admitted that the Parliament, having vanquished Charles First, had no way of making any tenable arrangement with him. The large Presbyterian party, apprehensive now of the Independents, were most anxious to do so; anxious indeed as for their own existence; but it could not be. The unhappy Charles, in those final Hampton-Court negotiations, shows himself as a man fatally incapable of being dealt with. A man who, once for all, could not and would not *understand* :—whose thought did not in any measure represent to him the real fact of the matter; nay worse, whose *word* did not at all represent his thought. We may say this of him without cruelty, with deep pity rather: but it is true and undeniable. Forsaken there of all but the *name* of Kingship, he still, finding himself treated with outward respect as a King, fancied

that he might play-off party against party, and His eye
smuggle himself into his old power by deceiving for facts
both. Alas, they both *discovered* that he was
deceiving them. A man whose *word* will not
inform you at all what he means or will do, is
not a man you can bargain with. You must get
out of that man's way, or put him out of yours!
The Presbyterians, in their despair, were still for
believing Charles, though found false, unbelievable
again and again. Not so Cromwell: " For all
our fighting," says he, " we are to have a little
bit of paper?" No!—

In fact, everywhere we have to note the decisive
practical *eye* of this man; how he drives towards
the practical and practicable; has a genuine insight
into what *is* fact. Such an intellect, I maintain,
does not belong to a false man: the false man
sees false shows, plausibilities, expediences: the
true man is needed to discern even practical truth.
Cromwell's advice about the Parliament's Army,
early in the contest, How they were to dismiss
their city-tapsters, flimsy riotous persons, and choose
substantial yeomen, whose heart was in the work, to
be soldiers for them: this is advice by a man who
saw. Fact answers, if you see into Fact. Cromwell's *Ironsides* were the embodiment of this insight
of his; men fearing God; and without any other
fear. No more conclusively genuine set of fighters
ever trod the soil of England, or of any other land.

Neither will we blame greatly that word of
Cromwell's to them; which was so blamed: " If
the King should meet me in battle, I would kill
the King." Why not? These words were spoken
to men who stood as before a Higher than Kings.
They had set more than their own lives on the cast.

His success inevitable The Parliament may call it, in official language, a fighting '*for* the King;' but we, for our share, cannot understand that. To us it is no dilettante work, no sleek officiality; it is sheer rough death and earnest. They have brought it to the calling-forth of *War;* horrid internecine fight, man grappling with man in fire-eyed rage,—the *infernal* element in man called forth, to try it by that! *Do* that therefore; since that is the thing to be done.—The successes of Cromwell seem to me a very natural thing! Since he was not shot in battle, they were an inevitable thing. That such a man, with the eye to see, with the heart to dare, should advance, from post to post, from victory to victory, till the Huntingdon Farmer became, by whatever name you might call him, the acknowledged Strongest Man in England, virtually the King of England, requires no magic to explain it!—

Truly it is a sad thing for a people, as for a man, to fall into Scepticism, into dilettantism, insincerity; not to know a Sincerity when they see it. For this world, and for all worlds, what curse is so fatal? The heart lying dead, the eye cannot see. What intellect remains is merely the *vulpine* intellect. That a true *King* be sent them is of small use; they do not know him when sent. They say scornfully, Is this your King? The Hero wastes his heroic faculty in bootless contradiction from the unworthy; and can accomplish little. For himself he does accomplish a heroic life, which is much, which is all; but for the world he accomplishes comparatively nothing. The wild rude Sincerity, direct from Nature, is not glib in answering from the witness-box; in your small-debt *pie-powder* court, he is scouted as a counterfeit. The vulpine intellect 'detects' him. For being a man worth A world any thousand men, the response, your Knox, your given Cromwell gets, is an argument for two centuries, over to whether he was a man at all. God's greatest gift Quacks to this Earth is sneeringly flung away. The miraculous talisman is a paltry plated coin, not fit to pass in the shops as a common guinea.

Lamentable this! I say, this must be remedied. Till this be remedied in some measure, there is nothing remedied. 'Detect quacks'? Yes do, for Heaven's sake; but know withal the men that are to be trusted! Till we know that, what is all our knowledge; how shall we even so much as 'detect'? For the vulpine sharpness, which considers itself to be knowledge, and 'detects' in that fashion, is far mistaken. Dupes indeed are many: but, of all *dupes*, there is none so fatally situated as he who lives in undue terror of being duped. The world does exist; the world has truth in it or it would not exist! First recognise what is true, we shall *then* discern what is false ; and properly never till then.

'Know the men that are to be trusted :' alas, this is yet, in these days, very far from us. The sincere alone can recognise sincerity. Not a Hero only is needed, but a world fit for him; a world not of *Valets ;*—the Hero comes almost in vain to it otherwise! Yes, it is far from us: but it must come; thank God, it is visibly coming. Till it do come, what have we? Ballot-boxes, suffrages, French Revolutions:—if we are as Valets, and do not know the Hero when we see him, what good are all these? A heroic Cromwell comes; and for a hundred-and-fifty years he cannot have a vote from us. Why, the insincere, unbelieving world is the

Cromwell
an in-
articulate
Prophet
natural property of the Quack, and of the Father of quacks and quackeries! Misery, confusion, unveracity are alone possible there. By ballot-boxes we alter the *figure* of our Quack; but the substance of him continues. The Valet-World *has* to be governed by the Sham-Hero, by the King merely *dressed* in King-gear. It is his; he is its! In brief, one of two things: We shall either learn to know a Hero, a true Governor and Captain, somewhat better, when we see him; or else go on to be forever governed by the Unheroic;—had we ballot-boxes clattering at every street-corner, there were no remedy in these.

Poor Cromwell,—great Cromwell! The inarticulate Prophet; Prophet who could not *speak*. Rude, confused, struggling to utter himself, with his savage depth, with his wild sincerity; and he looked so strange, among the elegant Euphemisms, dainty little Falklands, didactic Chillingworths, diplomatic Clarendons! Consider him. An outer hull of chaotic confusion, visions of the Devil, nervous dreams, almost semi-madness; and yet such a clear determinate man's-energy working in the heart of that. A kind of chaotic man. The ray as of pure starlight and fire, working in such an element of boundless hypochondria, *un*formed black of darkness! And yet withal this hypochondria, what was it but the very greatness of the man? The depth and tenderness of his wild affections: the quantity of *sympathy* he had with things,—the quantity of insight he would yet get into the heart of things, the mastery he would yet get over things: this was his hypochondria. The man's misery, as man's misery always does, came of his greatness. Samuel Johnson too is that kind of man. Sorrow-

stricken, half-distracted; the wide element of His con-
mournful *black* enveloping him,—wide as the world. fusion of
It is the character of a prophetic man; a man with speech
his whole soul *seeing*, and struggling to see.

On this ground, too, I explain to myself Cromwell's reputed confusion of speech. To himself
the internal meaning was sun-clear; but the material
with which he was to clothe it in utterance was
not there. He had *lived* silent; a great unnamed
sea of Thought round him all his days; and in his
way of life little call to attempt *naming* or uttering
that. With his sharp power of vision, resolute
power of action, I doubt not he could have learned
to write Books withal, and speak fluently enough:
—he did harder things than writing of Books.
This kind of man is precisely he who is fit for
doing manfully all things you will set him on doing.
Intellect is not speaking and logicising; it is seeing
and ascertaining. Virtue, *Vir-tus*, manhood, hero-
hood, is not fair-spoken immaculate regularity; it
is first of all, what the Germans well name *it*,
Tugend (*Taugend*, *dow*-ing or *Dough*-tiness), Courage
and the Faculty to *do*. This basis of the matter
Cromwell had in him.

One understands moreover how, though he could
not speak in Parliament, he might *preach*, rhapsodic
preaching; above all, how he might be great in
extempore prayer. These are the free outpouring
utterances of what is in the heart: method is not
required in them; warmth, depth, sincerity are all
that is required. Cromwell's habit of prayer is a
notable feature of him. All his great enterprises
were commenced with prayer. In dark inextric-
able-looking difficulties, his Officers and he used to
assemble, and pray alternately, for hours, for days,

His eloquence in prayer till some definite resolution rose among them, some 'door of hope,' as they would name it, disclosed itself. Consider that. In tears, in fervent prayers, and cries to the great God, to have pity on them, to make His light shine before them. They, armed Soldiers of Christ, as they felt themselves to be; a little band of Christian Brothers, who had drawn the sword against a great black devouring world not Christian, but Mammonish, Devilish,— they cried to God in their straits, in their extreme need, not to forsake the Cause that was His. The light which now rose upon them,—how could a human soul, by any means at all, get better light? Was not the purpose so formed like to be precisely the best, wisest, the one to be followed without hesitation any more? To them it was as the shining of Heaven's own Splendour in the waste-howling darkness; the Pillar of Fire by night, that was to guide them on their desolate perilous way. *Was* it not such? Can a man's soul, to this hour, get guidance by any other method than intrinsically by that same,—devout prostration of the earnest struggling soul before the Highest, the Giver of all Light; be such *prayer* a spoken, articulate, or be it a voiceless, inarticulate one? There is no other method. 'Hypocrisy'? One begins to be weary of all that. They who call it so, have no right to speak on such matters. They never formed a purpose, what one can call a purpose. They went about balancing expediences, plausibilities; gathering votes, advices; they never were alone with the *truth* of a thing at all.—Cromwell's prayers were likely to be 'eloquent,' and much more than that. His was the heart of a man who *could* pray.

But indeed his actual Speeches, I apprehend,

were not nearly so ineloquent, incondite, as they
look. We find he was, what all speakers aim to
be, an impressive speaker, even in Parliament; one
who, from the first, had weight. With that rude
passionate voice of his, he was always understood
to *mean* something, and men wished to know what.
He disregarded eloquence, nay despised and dis-
liked it; spoke always without premeditation of the
words he was to use. The Reporters, too, in
those days seem to have been singularly candid;
and to have given the Printer precisely what they
found on their own notepaper. And withal, what
a strange proof is it of Cromwell's being the pre-
meditative ever-calculating hypocrite, acting a play
before the world, That to the last he took no more
charge of his Speeches! How came he not to
study his words a little, before flinging them out to
the public? If the words were true words, they
could be left to shift for themselves.

But with regard to Cromwell's ‘lying,’ we will
make one remark. This, I suppose, or something
like this, to have been the nature of it. All parties
found themselves deceived in him; each party
understood him to be meaning *this*, heard him even
say so, and behold he turns-out to have been meaning *that!* He was, cry they, the chief of liars.
But now, intrinsically, is not all this the inevitable
fortune, not of a false man in such times, but simply
of a superior man? Such a man must have
reticences in him. If he walk wearing his heart
upon his sleeve for daws to peck at, his journey
will not extend far! There is no use for any
man's taking-up his abode in a house built of glass.
A man always is to be himself the judge how much
of his mind he will show to other men; even to

His ‘lying’

His those he would have work along with him. There
'lying' are impertinent inquiries made: your rule is, to
leave the inquirer *un*informed on that matter; not,
if you can help it, *mis*informed; but precisely as
dark as he was! This, could one hit the right
phrase of response, is what the wise and faithful
man would aim to answer in such a case.

Cromwell, no doubt of it, spoke often in the
dialect of small subaltern parties; uttered to them
a *part* of his mind. Each little party thought him
all its own. Hence their rage, one and all, to find
him not of their party, but of his own party!
Was it his blame? At all seasons of his history
he must have felt, among such people, how, if he
explained to them the deeper insight he had, they
must either have shuddered aghast at it, or believing
it, their own little compact hypothesis must have
gone wholly to wreck. They could not have
worked in his province any more; nay perhaps they
could not now have worked in their own province.
It is the inevitable position of a great man among
small men. Small men, most active, useful, are to
be seen everywhere, whose whole activity depends
on some conviction which to you is palpably a
limited one; imperfect, what we call an *error*.
But would it be a kindness always, is it a duty
always or often, to disturb them in that? Many a
man, doing loud work in the world, stands only
on some thin traditionality, conventionality; to him
indubitable, to you incredible: break that beneath
him, he sinks to endless depths! "I might have
my hand full of truth," said Fontenelle, "and
open only my little finger."

And if this be the fact even in matters of doctrine,
how much more in all departments of practice! He

that cannot withal *keep his mind to himself* cannot **His** practise any considerable thing whatever. And we **'ambi-** call it 'dissimulation,' all this? What would you **tion'** think of calling the general of an army a dissembler because he did not tell every corporal and private soldier, who pleased to put the question, what his thoughts were about everything? — Cromwell, I should rather say, managed all this in a manner we must admire for its perfection. An endless vortex of such questioning 'corporals' rolled confusedly round him through his whole course; whom he did answer. It must have been as a great true-seeing man that he managed this too. Not one proved falsehood, as I said; not one! Of what man that ever wound himself through such a coil of things will you say so much?—

But in fact there are two errors, widely prevalent, which pervert to the very basis our judgments formed about such men as Cromwell; about their 'ambition,' 'falsity,' and such-like. The first is what I might call substituting the *goal* of their career for the course and starting point of it. The vulgar Historian of a Cromwell fancies that he had determined on being Protector of England, at the time when he was ploughing the marsh lands of Cambridgeshire. His career lay all mapped-out: a program of the whole drama; which he then step by step dramatically unfolded, with all manner of cunning, deceptive dramaturgy, as he went on,— the hollow, scheming Ὑποκριτής, or Play-actor that he was! This is a radical perversion; all but universal in such cases. And think for an instant how different the fact is! How much does one of *us* foresee of his own life? Short way ahead of

His 'ambi- tion' us it is all dim ; an *un*wound skein of possibilities, of apprehensions, attemptabilities, vague - looming hopes. This Cromwell had *not* his life lying all in that fashion of Program, which he needed then, with that unfathomable cunning of his, only to enact dramatically, scene after scene ! Not so. We see it so ; but to him it was in no measure so. What absurdities would fall-away of themselves, were this one undeniable fact kept honestly in view by History ! Historians indeed will tell you that they do keep it in view ;—but look whether such is practically the fact ! Vulgar History, as in this Cromwell's case, omits it altogether ; even the best kinds of History only remember it now and then. To remember it duly with rigorous perfection, as in the fact it *stood*, requires indeed a rare faculty; rare, nay impossible. A very Shakspeare for faculty ; or more than Shakspeare ; who could *enact* a brother-man's biography, see with the brother-man's eyes at all points of his course what things *he* saw ; in short, *know* his course and him, as few 'Historians' are like to do. Half or more of all the thick-plied perversions which distort our image of Cromwell, will disappear, if we honestly so much as try to represent them so ; in sequence, as they *were ;* not in the lump, as they are thrown-down before us.

But a second error, which I think the generality commit, refers to this same 'ambition' itself. We exaggerate the ambition of Great Men ; we mistake what the nature of it is. Great Men are not ambitious in that sense ; he is a small poor man that is ambitious so. Examine the man who lives in misery because he does not shine above other men ; who goes about producing himself, pruriently anxious

about his gifts and claims; struggling to force every- **Great**
body, as it were begging everybody for God's sake, **Men not**
to acknowledge him a great man, and set him over **ambitious**
the heads of men! Such a creature is among the
wretchedest sights seen under this sun. A *great*
man? A poor morbid prurient empty man; fitter
for the ward of a hospital, than for a throne among
men. I advise you to keep-out of his way. He
cannot walk on quiet paths; unless you will look
at him, wonder at him, write paragraphs about him,
he cannot live. It is the *emptiness* of the man, not
his greatness. Because there is nothing in himself,
he hungers and thirsts that you would find something in him. In good truth, I believe no great
man, not so much as a genuine man who had health
and real substance in him of whatever magnitude,
was ever much tormented in this way.

Your Cromwell, what good could it do him to
be 'noticed' by noisy crowds of people? God
his Maker already noticed him. He, Cromwell,
was already there; no notice would make *him* other
than he already was. Till his hair was grown gray;
and Life from the downhill slope was all seen to be
limited, not infinite but finite, and all a measurable
matter *how* it went,—he had been content to plough
the ground, and read his Bible. He in his old days
could not support it any longer, without selling himself to Falsehood, that he might ride in gilt carriages
to Whitehall, and have clerks with bundles of papers
haunting him, "Decide this, decide that," which in
utmost sorrow of heart no man can perfectly decide!
What could gilt carriages do for this man? From
of old, was there not in his life a weight of meaning, a terror and a splendour as of Heaven itself?
His existence there as man set him beyond the need

The 'Empire of Silence' of gilding. Death, Judgment and Eternity: these already lay as the background of whatsoever he thought or did. All his life lay begirt as in a sea of nameless Thoughts, which no speech of a mortal could name. God's Word, as the Puritan prophets of that time had read it : this was great, and all else was little to him. To call such a man 'ambitious,' to figure him as the prurient windbag described above, seems to me the poorest solecism. Such a man will say : " Keep your gilt carriages and huzzaing mobs, keep your red-tape clerks, your influentialities, your important businesses. Leave me alone, leave me alone; there is *too much of life* in me already ! " Old Samuel Johnson, the greatest soul in England in his day, was not ambitious. 'Corsica Boswell' flaunted at public shows with printed ribbons round his hat; but the great old Samuel stayed at home. The world-wide soul wrapt-up in its thoughts, in its sorrows ;—what could paradings, and ribbons in the hat, do for it ?

Ah yes, I will say again : The great *silent* men ! Looking round on the noisy inanity of the world, words with little meaning, actions with little worth, one loves to reflect on the great Empire of *Silence*. The noble silent men, scattered here and there, each in his department ; silently thinking, silently working; whom no Morning Newspaper makes mention of ! They are the salt of the Earth. A country that has none or few of these is in a bad way. Like a forest which had no *roots* ; which had all turned into leaves and boughs ;—which must soon wither and be no forest. Woe for us if we had nothing but what we can *show*, or speak. Silence, the great Empire of Silence : higher than the stars ; deeper than the Kingdoms of Death ! It alone is great ;

all else is small.—I hope we English will long **Two** maintain our *grand talent pour le silence.* Let others **kinds of** that cannot do without standing on barrel-heads, to **ambition** spout, and be seen of all the market-place, cultivate speech exclusively,—become a most green forest without roots ! Solomon says, There is a time to speak ; but also a time to keep silence. Of some great silent Samuel, not urged to writing, as old Samuel Johnson says he was, by *want of money*, and nothing other, one might ask, " Why do not you too get up and speak ; promulgate your system, found your sect ? " " Truly," he will answer, " I am *continent* of my thought hitherto ; happily I have yet had the ability to keep it in me, no compulsion strong enough to speak it. My ' system ' is not for promulgation first of all ; it is for serving myself to live by. That is the great purpose of it to me. And then the ' honour ' ? Alas, yes ;—but as Cato said of the statue : So many statues in that Forum of yours, may it not be better if they ask, Where is Cato's statue ? "———

But, now, by way of counterpoise to this of Silence, let me say that there are two kinds of ambition ; one wholly blamable, the other laudable and inevitable. Nature has provided that the great silent Samuel shall not be silent too long. The selfish wish to shine over others, let it be accounted altogether poor and miserable. ' Seekest thou great things, seek them not : ' this is most true. And yet, I say, there is an irrepressible tendency in every man to develop himself according to the magnitude which Nature has made him of ; to speak-out, to act-out, what Nature has laid in him. This is proper, fit, inevitable ; nay it is a duty, and even the summary of duties for a man. The meaning of life

True ambition here on earth might be defined as consisting in this : To unfold your *self*, to work what thing you have the faculty for. It is a necessity for the human being, the first law of our existence. Coleridge beautifully remarks that the infant learns to *speak* by this necessity it feels.—We will say therefore : To decide about ambition, whether it is bad or not, you have two things to take into view. Not the coveting of the place alone, but the fitness of the man for the place withal : that is the question. Perhaps the place was *his ;* perhaps he had a natural right, and even obligation, to seek the place ! Mirabeau's ambition to be Prime Minister, how shall we blame it, if he were 'the only man in France that could have done any good there'? Hopefuler perhaps had he not so clearly *felt* how much good he could do ! But a poor Necker, who could do no good, and had even felt that he could do none, yet sitting broken-hearted because they had flung him out, and he was now quit of it, well might Gibbon mourn over him.—Nature, I say, has provided amply that the silent great man shall strive to speak withal ; *too* amply, rather !

Fancy, for example, you had revealed to the brave old Samuel Johnson, in his shrouded-up existence, that it was possible for him to do priceless divine work for his country and the whole world. That the perfect Heavenly Law might be made law on this earth ; that the prayer he prayed daily, 'Thy kingdom come,' was at length to be fulfilled ! If you had convinced his judgment of this ; that it was possible, practicable ; that he the mournful silent Samuel was called to take a part in it ! Would not the whole soul of the man have flamed up into a divine clearness, into noble utterance and determination to act; casting all sorrows **Crom-** and misgivings under his feet, counting all affliction **well's** and contradiction small,—the whole dark element **mission** of his existence blazing into articulate radiance of light and lightning? It were a true ambition this! And think now how it actually was with Cromwell. From of old, the sufferings of God's Church, true zealous preachers of the truth flung into dungeons, whipt, set on pillories, their ears cropt off, God's Gospel-cause trodden under foot of the unworthy: all this had lain heavy on his soul. Long years he had looked upon it, in silence, in prayer; seeing no remedy on Earth; trusting well that a remedy in Heaven's goodness would come,—that such a course was false, unjust, and could not last forever. And now behold the dawn of it; after twelve years silent waiting, all England stirs itself; there is to be once more a Parliament, the Right will get a voice for itself: inexpressible well-grounded hope has come again into the Earth. Was not such a Parliament worth being a member of? Cromwell threw down his ploughs and hastened thither.

He spoke there,—rugged bursts of earnestness, of a self-seen truth, where we get a glimpse of them. He worked there; he fought and strove, like a strong true giant of a man, through cannon-tumult and all else,—on and on, till the Cause *triumphed*, its once so formidable enemies all swept from before it, and the dawn of hope had become clear light of victory and certainty. That *he* stood there as the strongest soul of England, the undisputed Hero of all England,—what of this? It was possible that the law of Christ's Gospel could now establish itself in the world! The Theocracy which John Knox in his pulpit might dream of as

Crom-
well's
mission

a 'devout imagination,' this practical man, ex-
perienced in the whole chaos of most rough practice,
dared to consider as capable of being *realised.*
Those that were highest in Christ's Church, the
devoutest wisest men, were to rule the land: in
some considerable degree, it might be so and should
be so. Was it not *true*, God's truth? And if
true, was it not then the very thing to do? The
strongest practical intellect in England dared to
answer, Yes! This I call a noble true purpose;
is it not, in its own dialect, the noblest that could
enter into the heart of Statesman or man? For
a Knox to take it up was something; but for a
Cromwell, with his great sound sense and experience
of what our world *was*,—History, I think, shows
it only this once in such a degree. I account it
the culminating point of Protestantism; the most
heroic phasis that 'Faith in the Bible' was appointed to exhibit here below. Fancy it: that
it were made manifest to one of us, how we could
make the Right supremely victorious over Wrong,
and all that we had longed and prayed for, as the
highest good to England and all lands, an attainable
fact!

Well, I must say, the *vulpine* intellect, with its
knowingness, its alertness and expertness in 'detecting hypocrites,' seems to me a rather sorry
business. We have had one such Statesman in
England; one man, that I can get sight of, who
ever had in the heart of him any such purpose at
all. One man, in the course of fifteen hundred
years; and this was his welcome. He had adherents by the hundred or the ten; opponents by
the million. Had England rallied all round him,
—why, then, England might have been a *Christian*

land! As it is, vulpine knowingness sits yet at its hopeless problem, 'Given a world of Knaves, to educe an Honesty from their united action;'— how cumbrous a problem, you may see in Chancery Law-Courts, and some other places! Till at length, by Heaven's just anger, but also by Heaven's great grace, the matter begins to stagnate; and this problem is becoming to all men a *palpably* hopeless one.—

'Fanatic-Hypo-crite' theory of Cromwell

But with regard to Cromwell and his purposes: Hume and a multitude following him, come upon me here with an admission that Cromwell *was* sincere at first; a sincere 'Fanatic' at first, but gradually became a 'Hypocrite' as things opened round him. This of the Fanatic-Hypocrite is Hume's theory of it; extensively applied since,— to Mahomet and many others. Think of it seriously, you will find something in it; not much, not all, very far from all. Sincere hero hearts do not sink in this miserable manner. The Sun flings forth impurities, gets balefully incrusted with spots; but it does not quench itself, and become no Sun at all, but a mass of Darkness! I will venture to say that such never befell a great, deep Cromwell; I think, never. Nature's own lion-hearted Son! Antæus-like, his strength is got by *touching the Earth*, his Mother; lift him up from the Earth, lift him up into Hypocrisy, Inanity, his strength is gone. We will not assert that Cromwell was an immaculate man; that he fell into no faults, no insincerities among the rest. He was no dilettante professor of 'perfections,' 'immaculate conducts.' He was a rugged Orson, rending his rough way through actual true *work*,—doubtless

Cromwell no hypocrite with many a *fall* therein.   Insincerities, faults, very many faults daily and hourly : it was too well known to him ; known to God and him !   The Sun was dimmed many a time ; but the Sun had not himself grown a Dimness.   Cromwell's last words, as he lay waiting for death, are those of a Christian heroic man.   Broken prayers to God, that He would judge him and this Cause, He since man could not, in justice yet in pity.   They are most touching words.   He breathed out his wild great soul, its toils and sins all ended now, into the presence of his Maker, in this manner.

I, for one, will not call the man a Hypocrite ! Hypocrite, mummer, the life of him a mere theatricality ; empty barren quack, hungry for the shouts of mobs ?   The man had made obscurity do very well for him till his head was gray ; and now he *was*, there as he stood recognised unblamed, the virtual King of England.   Cannot a man do without King's Coaches and Cloaks ?   Is it such a blessedness to have clerks forever pestering you with bundles of papers in red tape ?   A simple Diocletian prefers planting of cabbages ; a George Washington, no very immeasurable man, does the like.   One would say, it is what any genuine man could do ; and would do.   The instant his real work were out in the matter of Kingship,—away with it !

Let us remark, meanwhile, how indispensable everywhere a *King* is, in all movements of men. It is strikingly shown, in this very War, what becomes of men when they cannot find a Chief Man, and their enemies can.   The Scotch Nation was all but unanimous in Puritanism ; zealous and of one mind about it, as in this English end of the

Island was far from being the case. But there was **A king** no great Cromwell among them; poor tremulous, **indis-** hesitating, diplomatic Argyles and suchlike; none **pensable** of them had a heart true enough for the truth, or durst commit himself to the truth. They had no leader; and the scattered Cavalier party in that country had one: Montrose, the noblest of all the Cavaliers; an accomplished, gallant-hearted, splendid man; what one may call the Hero-Cavalier. Well, look at it; on the one hand subjects without a King; on the other a King without subjects! The subjects without King can do nothing; the subjectless King can do something. This Montrose, with a handful of Irish or Highland savages, few of them so much as guns in their hands, dashes at the drilled Puritan armies like a wild whirlwind; sweeps them, time after time, some five times over, from the field before him. He was at one period, for a short while, master of all Scotland. One man; but he was a man: a million zealous men, but *without* the one; they against him were powerless! Perhaps of all the persons in that Puritan struggle, from first to last, the single indispensable one was verily Cromwell. To see and dare, and decide; to be a fixed pillar in the welter of uncertainty;—a King among them, whether they called him so or not.

Precisely here, however, lies the rub for Cromwell. His other proceedings have all found advocates, and stand generally justified; but this dismissal of the Rump Parliament and assumption of the Protectorship, is what no one can pardon him. He had fairly grown to be King in England; Chief Man of the victorious party in England: but

Cromwell and the 'Rump' Parliament

it seems he could not do without the King's Cloak, and sold himself to perdition in order to get it. Let us see a little how this was.

England, Scotland, Ireland, all lying now subdued at the feet of the Puritan Parliament, the practical question arose, What was to be done with it? How will you govern these Nations, which Providence in a wondrous way has given-up to your disposal? Clearly those hundred surviving members of the Long Parliament, who sit there as supreme authority, cannot continue for ever to sit. What *is* to be done?—It was a question which theoretical constitution-builders may find easy to answer; but to Cromwell, looking there into the real practical facts of it, there could be none more complicated. He asked of the Parliament, What it was they would decide upon? It was for the Parliament to say. Yet the Soldiers too, however contrary to Formula, they who had purchased this victory with their blood, it seemed to them that they also should have something to say in it! We will not " For all our fighting have nothing but a little piece of paper." We understand that the Law of God's Gospel, to which He through us has given the victory, shall establish itself, or try to establish itself, in this land!

For three years, Cromwell says, this question had been sounded in the ears of the Parliament. They could make no answer; nothing but talk, talk. Perhaps it lies in the nature of parliamentary bodies; perhaps no Parliament could in such case make any answer but even that of talk, talk! Nevertheless the question must and shall be answered. You sixty men there, becoming fast odious, even despicable, to the whole nation, whom the nation already calls Rump Parliament, *you* cannot continue to sit there: who or what then is to follow? 'Free Parliament,' right of Election, Constitutional Formulas of one sort or the other,— the thing is a hungry Fact coming on us, which we must answer or be devoured by it! And who are you that prate of Constitutional Formulas, rights of Parliament? You have had to kill your King, to make Pride's Purges, to expel and banish by the law of the stronger whosoever would not let your Cause prosper: there are but fifty or three-score of you left there, debating in these days. Tell us what we shall do; not in the way of Formula, but of practicable Fact!

Cromwell and the 'Rump' Parliament

How they did finally answer, remains obscure to this day. The diligent Godwin himself admits that he cannot make it out. The likeliest is, that this poor Parliament still would not, and indeed could not dissolve and disperse; that when it came to the point of actually dispersing, they again, for the tenth or twentieth time, adjourned it,—and Cromwell's patience failed him. But we will take the favourablest hypothesis ever started for the Parliament; the favourablest, though I believe it is not the true one, but too favourable.

According to this version: At the uttermost crisis, when Cromwell and his Officers were met on the one hand, and the fifty or sixty Rump Members on the other, it was suddenly told Cromwell that the Rump in its despair *was* answering in a very singular way; that in their splenetic envious despair, to keep-out the army at least, these men were hurrying through the House a kind of Reform Bill,—Parliament to be chosen by the whole of England; equable electoral division into districts;

Dissolu-
tion
of the
'Rump'
Parlia-
ment
free suffrage, and the rest of it!   A very questionable, or indeed for *them* an unquestionable thing.
Reform Bill, free suffrage of Englishmen?   Why,
the Royalists themselves, silenced indeed but not
exterminated, perhaps out*number* us;   the great
numerical majority of England was always indifferent to our Cause, merely looked at it and submitted
to it.   It is in weight and force, not by counting of
heads, that we are the majority!   And now with
your Formulas and Reform Bills, the whole matter,
sorely won by our swords, shall again launch itself
to sea; become a mere hope, and likelihood, *small*
even as a likelihood?   And it is not a likelihood;
it is a certainty, which we have won, by God's
strength and our own right hands, and do now hold
here.   Cromwell walked down to these refractory
Members; interrupted them in that rapid speed of
their Reform Bill;—ordered them to begone, and
talk there no more.—Can we not forgive him?
Can we not understand him?   John Milton, who
looked on it all near at hand, could applaud him.
The Reality had swept the Formulas away before
it.   I fancy, most men who were realities in
England might see into the necessity of that.

The strong daring man, therefore, has set all
manner of Formulas and logical superficialities
against him; has dared appeal to the genuine fact
of this England, Whether it will support him or
not?   It is curious to see how he struggles to
govern in some constitutional way; find some
Parliament to support him; but cannot.   His first
Parliament, the one they call Barebones's Parliament, is, so to speak, a *Convocation of the Notables.*
From all quarters of England the leading Ministers
and chief Puritan Officials nominate the men most

distinguished by religious reputation, influence and
attachment to the true Cause: these are assembled
to shape-out a plan. They sanctioned what was
past; shaped as they could what was to come.
They were scornfully called *Barebones's Parliament*,
the man's name, it seems, was not *Barebones*, but
Barbone,—a good enough man. Nor was it a jest,
their work; it was a most serious reality,—a trial
on the part of these Puritan Notables how far the
Law of Christ could become the Law of this
England. There were men of sense among them,
men of some quality; men of deep piety I suppose
the most of them were. They failed, it seems, and
broke down, endeavouring to reform the Court of
Chancery! They dissolved themselves, as incom-
petent; delivered-up their power again into the
hands of the Lord-General Cromwell, to do with
it what he liked and could.

The 'Bare-bones' Parlia-ment

What *will* he do with it? The Lord-General
Cromwell, 'Commander-in Chief of all the Forces
raised and to be raised;' he hereby sees himself, at
this unexampled juncture, as it were the one available
Authority left in England, nothing between England
and utter Anarchy but him alone. Such is the undeniable Fact of his position and England's, there
and then. What will he do with it? After de-
liberation, he decides that he will *accept* it; will
formally, with public solemnity, say and vow before
God and men, "Yes, the Fact is so, and I will do
the best I can with it!" Protectorship, Instrument of Government,—these are the external forms
of the thing; worked-out and sanctioned as they
could in the circumstances be, by the Judges, by the
leading Official people, 'Council of Officers and
Persons of interest in the Nation:' and as for the

thing itself, undeniably enough, at the pass matters
had now come to, there *was* no alternative but
Anarchy or that. Puritan England might accept it
or not; but Puritan England was, in real truth,
saved from suicide thereby!—I believe the Puritan
People did, in an inarticulate, grumbling, yet on the
whole grateful and real way, accept this anomalous
act of Oliver's; at least, he and they together made
it good, and always better to the last. But in their
Parliamentary *articulate* way, they had their difficulties, and never knew fully what to say to it!—

Oliver's second Parliament, properly his *first*
regular Parliament, chosen by the rule laid-down in
the Instrument of Government, did assemble, and
worked;—but got, before long, into bottomless
questions as to the Protector's *right*, as to 'usurpa-
tion,' and so forth; and had at the earliest legal day
to be dismissed. Cromwell's concluding Speech
to these men is a remarkable one. So likewise
to his third Parliament, in similar rebuke for their
pedantries and obstinacies. Most rude, chaotic,
all these Speeches are; but most earnest-looking.
You would say, it was a sincere helpless man; not
used to *speak* the great inorganic thought of him,
but to act it rather! A helplessness of utterance,
in such bursting fulness of meaning. He talks much
about 'births of Providence:' All these changes,
so many victories and events, were not forethoughts,
and theatrical contrivances of men, of *me* or of
men; it is blind blasphemers that will persist in
calling them so! He insists with a heavy sulphur-
ous wrathful emphasis on this. As he well might.
As if a Cromwell in that dark huge game he had
been playing, the world wholly thrown into chaos
round him, had *foreseen* it all, and played it all off

like a precontrived puppetshow by wood and wire! His speech to his third Parliament
These things were foreseen by no man, he says; no
man could tell what a day would bring forth: they
were 'births of Providence,' God's finger guided us
on, and we came at last to clear height of victory,
God's Cause triumphant in these Nations; and you
as a Parliament could assemble together, and say in
what manner all this could be *organised*, reduced
into rational feasibility among the affairs of men.
You were to help with your wise counsel in doing
that. "You have had such an opportunity as no
Parliament in England ever had." Christ's Law,
the Right and True, was to be in some measure
made the Law of this land. In place of that, you
have got into your idle pedantries, constitutionalities,
bottomless cavillings and questionings about written
laws for *my* coming here;—and would send the
whole matter into Chaos again, because I have no
Notary's parchment, but only God's voice from the
battle-whirlwind, for being President among you!
That opportunity is gone; and we know not when
it will return. You have had your constitutional
Logic; and Mammon's Law, not Christ's Law,
rules yet in this land. "God be judge between you
and me!" These are his final words to them:
Take you your constitution-formulas in your hand;
and I my̆ *in*formal struggles, purposes, realities and
acts; and "God be judge between you and me!"—

We said above what shapeless, involved chaotic
things the printed Speeches of Cromwell are. *Wil-
fully* ambiguous, unintelligible, say the most: a hypocrite shrouding himself in confused Jesuitic jargon!
To me they do not seem so. I will say rather,
they afforded the first glimpses I could ever get into
the reality of this Cromwell, nay into the possibility

The way of Despotism of him. Try to believe that he means something, search lovingly what that may be : you will find a real *speech* lying imprisoned in these broken rude tortuous utterances; a meaning in the great heart of this inarticulate man ! You will, for the first time, begin to see that he was a man ; not an enigmatic chimera, unintelligible to you, incredible to you. The Histories and Biographies written of this Cromwell, written in shallow sceptical generations that could not know or conceive of a deep believing man, are far more *obscure* than Cromwell's Speeches. You look through them only into the infinite vague of Black and the Inane. 'Heats and Jealousies,' says Lord Clarendon himself : 'heats and jealousies,' mere crabbed whims, theories and crochets; these induced slow sober quiet Englishmen to lay down their ploughs and work; and fly into red fury of confused war against the best-conditioned of Kings ! *Try* if you can find that true. Scepticism writing about Belief may have great gifts ; but it is really *ultra vires* there. It is Blindness laying-down the Laws of Optics.—

Cromwell's third Parliament split on the same rock as his second. Ever the constitutional Formula : How came *you* there? Show us some Notary parchment ! Blind pedants : — " Why, surely the same power which makes you a Parliament, that, and something more, made me a Protector ! " If my Protectorship is nothing, what in the name of wonder is your Parliamenteership, a reflex and creation of that ?—

Parliaments having failed, there remained nothing but the way of Despotism. Military Dictators, each with his district, to *coerce* the Royalists and other gainsayers, to govern them, if not by act of

Parliament, then by the sword. Formula shall *not* **Cromwell** carry it, while the Reality is here! I will go on, **could not** protecting oppressed Protestants abroad, appointing **retire** just judges, wise managers, at home, cherishing true Gospel ministers; doing the best I can to make England a Christian England, greater than old Rome, the Queen of Protestant Christianity; I, since you will not help me; I while God leaves me life!—Why did he not give it up; retire into obscurity again, since the Law would not acknowledge him? cry several. That is where they mistake. For him there was no giving of it up! Prime Ministers have governed countries, Pitt, Pombal, Choiseul; and their word was a law while it held: but this Prime Minister was one that *could not get resigned.* Let him once resign, Charles Stuart and the Cavaliers waited to kill him; to kill the Cause *and* him. Once embarked, there is no retreat, no return. This Prime Minister could *retire* nowhither except into his tomb.

One is sorry for Cromwell in his old days. His complaint is incessant of the heavy burden Providence has laid on him. Heavy; which he must bear till death. Old Colonel Hutchinson, as his wife relates it, Hutchinson, his old battle-mate, coming to see him on some indispensable business, much against his will,—Cromwell 'follows him to the door,' in a most fraternal, domestic, conciliatory style; begs that he would be reconciled to him, his old brother in arms; says how much it grieves him to be misunderstood, deserted by true fellow-soldiers, dear to him from of old: the rigorous Hutchinson, cased in his republican formula, sullenly goes his way.—And the man's head now white; his strong arm growing weary with its long work! I think

The third act of Protestantism always too of his poor Mother, now very old, living in that Palace of his; a right brave woman: as indeed they lived all an honest God-fearing Household there: if she heard a shot go off, she thought it was her son killed. He had to come to her at least once a day, that she might see with her own eyes that he was yet living. The poor old Mother! ——What had this man gained; what had he gained? He had a life of sore strife and toil, to his last day. Fame, ambition, place in History? His dead body was hung in chains; his 'place in History,'—place in History forsooth!—has been a place of ignominy, accusation, blackness and disgrace; and here, this day, who knows if it is not rash in me to be among the first that ever ventured to pronounce him not a knave and a liar, but a genuinely honest man! Peace to him. Did he not, in spite of all, accomplish much for us? *We* walk smoothly over his great rough heroic life; step-over his body sunk in the ditch there. We need not *spurn* it, as we step on it!—Let the Hero rest. It was not to *men's* judgment that he appealed; nor have men judged him very well.

Precisely a century and a year after this of Puritanism had got itself hushed-up into decent composure, and its results made smooth in 1688, there broke-out a far deeper explosion, much more difficult to hush-up, known to all mortals, and like to be long known, by the name of French Revolution. It is properly the third and final act of Protestantism; the explosive confused return of Mankind to Reality and Fact, now that they were perishing of Semblance and Sham. We call our English Puritanism the second act: "Well then, the Bible is true; let us go by the Bible!" "In Napoleon Church," said Luther; "In Church and State," and said Cromwell, "let us go by what actually *is* Cromwell God's Truth." Men have to return to reality; they cannot live on semblance. The French Revolution, or third act, we may well call the final one; for lower than that savage *Sansculottism* men cannot go. They stand there on the nakedest haggard Fact, undeniable in all seasons and circumstances; and may and must begin again confidently to build-up from that. The French explosion, like the English one, got its King,—who had no Notary parchment to show for himself. We have still to glance for a moment at Napoleon, our second modern King.

Napoleon does by no means seem to me so great a man as Cromwell. His enormous victories which reached over all Europe, while Cromwell abode mainly in our little England, are but as the high *stilts* on which the man is seen standing; the stature of the man is not altered thereby. I find in him no such *sincerity* as in Cromwell; only a far inferior sort. No silent walking, through long years, with the Awful Unnamable of this Universe; 'walking with God,' as he called it; and faith and strength in that alone: *latent* thought and valour, content to lie latent, then burst out as in blaze of Heaven's lightning! Napoleon lived in an age when God was no longer believed; the meaning of all Silence, Latency, was thought to be Nonentity: he had to begin not out of the Puritan Bible, but out of poor Sceptical *Encyclopédies*. This was the length the man carried it. Meritorious to get so far. His compact, prompt, everyway articulate character is in itself perhaps small, compared with our great chaotic inarticulate Cromwell's. Instead of 'dumb Prophet struggling to speak,' we have a portentous mixture of the Quack withal! Hume's notion of the Fanatic-Hypocrite, with such truth as it has, will apply much better to Napoleon than it did to Cromwell, to Mahomet or the like,—where indeed taken strictly it has hardly any truth at all. An element of blamable ambition shows itself, from the first, in this man; gets the victory over him at last, and involves him and his work in ruin.

'False as a bulletin' became a proverb in Napoleon's time. He makes what excuse he could for it: that it was necessary to mislead the enemy, to keep up his own men's courage, and so forth. On the whole, there are no excuses. A man in no case has liberty to tell lies. It had been, in the long-run, *better* for Napoleon too if he had not told any. In fact, if a man have any purpose reaching beyond the hour and day, meant to be found extant *next* day, what good can it ever be to promulgate lies? The lies are found-out; ruinous penalty is exacted for them. No man will believe the liar next time even when he speaks truth, when it is of the last importance that he be believed. The old cry of wolf!—A Lie is *no*-thing; you cannot of nothing make something; you make *nothing* at last, and lose your labour into the bargain.

Yet Napoleon *had* a sincerity; we are to distinguish between what is superficial and what is fundamental in insincerity. Across these outer manœuverings and quackeries of his, which were many and most blamable, let us discern withal that the man had a certain instinctive ineradicable feeling for reality; and did base himself upon fact, so long as he had any basis. He has an instinct of Nature

better than his culture was.   His *savans*, Bourrienne 'Who
tells us, in that voyage to Egypt were one evening made all
busily occupied arguing that there could be no God. that?'
They had proved it, to their satisfaction, by all
manner of logic.   Napoleon looking up into the
stars, answers, "Very ingenious, Messieurs: but
who made all that?"   The Atheistic logic runs-
off from him like water; the great Fact stares him
in the face: "Who made all that?"   So too in
Practice: he, as every man that can be great, or
have victory in this world, sees, through all entangle-
ments, the practical heart of the matter; drives
straight towards that.   When the steward of his
Tuileries Palace was exhibiting the new upholstery,
with praises, and demonstration how glorious it was,
and how cheap withal, Napoleon, making little
answer, asked for a pair of scissors, clipt one of
the gold tassels from a window-curtain, put it in
his pocket, and walked on.   Some days afterwards,
he produced it at the right moment, to the horror
of his upholstery functionary; it was not gold but
tinsel!   In Saint Helena, it is notable how he still,
to his last days, insists on the practical, the real.
"Why talk and complain; above all, why quarrel
with one another?   There is no *result* in it;
it comes to nothing that one can *do*.   Say nothing,
if one can do nothing!"   He speaks often so,
to his poor discontented followers; he is like
a piece of silent strength in the middle of their
morbid querulousness there.

And accordingly was there not what we can call
a *faith* in him, genuine so far as it went?   That
this new enormous Democracy asserting itself here
in the French Revolution is an insuppressible Fact,
which the whole world, with its old forces and

A Demo-
crat
hating
anarchy
institutions cannot put down; this was a true insight of his, and took his conscience and enthusiasm along with it,—a *faith*. And did he not interpret the dim purport of it well? '*La carrière ouverte aux talens*, The implements to him who can handle them:' this actually is the truth, and even the whole truth; it includes whatever the French Revolution, or any Revolution, could mean. Napoleon, in his first period, was a true Democrat. And yet by the nature of him, fostered too by his military trade, he knew that Democracy, if it were a true thing at all, could not be an anarchy: the man had a heart-hatred for anarchy. On that Twentieth of June (1792), Bourrienne and he sat in a coffee-house, as the mob rolled by: Napoleon expresses the deepest contempt for persons in authority that they do not restrain this rabble. On the Tenth of August he wonders why there is no man to command these poor Swiss; they would conquer if there were. Such a faith in Democracy, yet hatred of Anarchy, it is that carries Napoleon through all his great work. Through his brilliant Italian Campaigns, onwards to the Peace of Leoben, one would say, his inspiration is: 'Triumph to the 'French Revolution; assertion of it against these 'Austrian Simulacra that pretend to call it a Simu-'lacrum!' Withal, however, he feels, and has a right to feel, how necessary a strong Authority is; how the Revolution cannot prosper or last without such. To bridle-in that great devouring, self-devouring French Revolution; to *tame* it, so that its intrinsic purpose can be made good, that it may become *organic*, and be able to live among other organisms and *formed* things, not as a wasting destruction alone: is not this still what he partly

aimed at, as the true purport of his life; nay what The
he actually managed to do? Through Wagrams, Char-
Austerlitzes; triumph after triumph,—he triumphed latan
so far. There was an eye to see in this man, element
a soul to dare and do. He rose naturally to be the
King. All men saw that he *was* such. The
common soldiers used to say on the march:
" These babbling *Avocats*, up at Paris; all talk
and no work! What wonder it runs all wrong?
We shall have to go and put our *Petit Caporal*
there!" They went, and put him there; they
and France at large. Chief-consulship, Emperor-
ship, victory over Europe;—till the poor Lieutenant
of *La Fère*, not unnaturally, might seem to himself
the greatest of all men that had been in the world
for some ages.

But at this point, I think, the fatal charlatan-
element got the upper hand. He apostatised from
his old Faith in Facts: took to believing in
Semblances; strove to connect himself with
Austrian Dynasties, Popedoms, with the old false
Feudalities which he once saw clearly to be false;—
considered that *he* would found " his Dynasty "
and so forth; that the enormous French Revolution meant only that! The man was 'given-up to
strong delusion, that he should believe a lie;'
a fearful but most sure thing. He did not know
true from false now when he looked at them,—the
fearfulest penalty a man pays for yielding to untruth
of heart. *Self* and false ambition had now become
his god: *self*-deception once yielded to, *all* other
deceptions follow naturally more and more. What a
paltry patch-work of theatrical paper-mantles, tinsel
and mummery, had this man wrapt his own great
reality in, thinking to make it more real thereby!

A house His hollow Pope's-*Concordat*, pretending to be a
built upon re-establishment of Catholicism, felt by himself
cloud to be the method of extirpating it, "*la vaccine de la
religion:*" his ceremonial Coronations, consecra-
tions by the old Italian Chimera in Notre-Dame,—
"wanting nothing to complete the pomp of it,"
as Augereau said, "nothing but the half-million
of men who had died to put an end to all that"!
Cromwell's Inauguration was by the Sword and
Bible; what we must call a genuinely *true* one.
Sword and Bible were borne before him, without
any chimera : were not these the *real* emblems
of Puritanism; its true decoration and insignia?   It
had used them both in a very real manner, and
pretended to stand by them now!   But this poor
Napoleon mistook: he believed too much in the
Dupeability of men; saw no fact deeper in men
than Hunger and this!   He was mistaken.   Like
a man that should build upon cloud; his house
and he fall down in confused wreck, and depart
out of the world.

Alas, in all of us this charlatan-element exists;
and *might* be developed, were the temptation strong
enough.   'Lead us not into temptation'!   But it
is fatal, I say, that it *be* developed.   The thing into
which it enters as a cognisable ingredient is doomed
to be altogether transitory; and, however huge it
may *look*, is in itself small.   Napoleon's working,
accordingly, what was it with all the noise it made?
A flash as of gunpowder wide-spread; a blazing-up
as of dry heath.   For an hour the whole Universe
seems wrapt in smoke and flame; but only for an
hour.   It goes out: the Universe with its old
mountains and streams, its stars above and kind soil
beneath, is still there.

The Duke of Weimar told his friends always, 'La carrière ouverte aux talens' To be of courage; this Napoleonism was *unjust*, a falsehood, and could not last. It is true doctrine. The heavier this Napoleon trampled on the world, holding it tyrannously down, the fiercer would the world's recoil against him be, one day. Injustice pays itself with frightful compound-interest. I am not sure but he had better have lost his best park of artillery, or had his best regiment drowned in the sea, than shot that poor German Bookseller, Palm! It was a palpable tyrannous murderous injustice, which no man, let him paint an inch thick, could make-out to be other. It burnt deep into the hearts of men, it and the like of it; suppressed fire flashed in the eyes of men, as they thought of it,— waiting their day! Which day *came :* Germany rose round him.—What Napoleon *did* will in the long-run amount to what he did *justly ;* what Nature with her laws will sanction. To what of reality was in him; to that and nothing more. The rest was all smoke and waste. *La carrière ouverte aux talens :* that great true Message, which has yet to articulate and fulfil itself everywhere, he left in a most inarticulate state. He was a great *ébauche*, a rude-draught never completed; as indeed what great man is other? Left in *too* rude a state, alas!

His notions of the world, as he expresses them there at St Helena, are almost tragical to consider. He seems to feel the most unaffected surprise that it has all gone so; that he is flung-out on the rock here, and the World is still moving on its axis. France is great, and all-great; and at bottom, he is France. England itself, he says, is by Nature only an appendage of France; "another Isle of Oleron to France." So it was *by Nature*, by

Our last Great Man Napoleon-Nature; and yet look how in fact,— HERE AM I! He cannot understand it: inconceivable that the reality has not corresponded to his program of it; that France was not all-great, that he was not France. 'Strong delusion,' that he should believe the thing to be which *is* not! The compact, clear-seeing, decisive Italian nature of him, strong, genuine, which he once had, has enveloped itself, half-dissolved itself, in a turbid atmosphere of French fanfaronade. The world was not disposed to be trodden-down underfoot; to be bound into masses, and built together, as *he* liked, for a pedestal to France and him: the world had quite other purposes in view! Napoleon's astonishment is extreme. But alas, what help now? He had gone that way of his; and Nature also had gone her way. Having once parted with Reality, he tumbles helpless in Vacuity; no rescue for him. He had to sink there, mournfully as man seldom did; and break his great heart, and die,—this poor Napoleon: a great implement too soon wasted, till it was useless: our last Great Man!

Our last, in a double sense. For here finally these wide roamings of ours through so many times and places, in search and study of Heroes, are to terminate. I am sorry for it: there was pleasure for me in this business, if also much pain. It is a great subject, and a most grave and wide one, this which, not to be too grave about it, I have named *Hero-worship*. It enters deeply, as I think, into the secret of Mankind's ways and vitalest interests in this world, and is well worth explaining at present. With six months, instead of six days, we might have done better. I promised to break-ground on it; I know not whether I have even **Closing** managed to do that. I have had to tear it up in **words** the rudest manner in order to get into it at all. Often enough, with these abrupt utterances thrown-out isolated, unexplained, has your tolerance been put to the trial. Tolerance, patient candour, all-hoping favour and kindness, which I will not speak of at present. The accomplished and distinguished, the beautiful, the wise, something of what is best in England, have listened patiently to my rude words. With many feelings, I heartily thank you all; and say, Good be with you all!